BULLEID'S PACIFICS

BULLEID'S PACIFICS

by

D. W. Winkworth

London
George Allen & Unwin Ltd
Ruskin House   Museum Street

To
The Footplatemen of the Southern
who drove and fired
the Bulleid Pacifics

First published 1974

ISBN 0 04 625005 0

The author's profits accruing from the sale of this book are being donated to the Southern Railwaymen's Home for Children and the Southern Railway Home for Old People at Woking.

Printed in Great Britain
in 11 point Plantin type
by William Clowes & Sons, Limited
London, Beccles and Colchester

Contents

Illustrations

PROEM

Of Mr Bulleid's Pacific-type locomotives it has been said that 'you either hate or love 'em'. It is to be hoped that these extremes have been avoided in the present volume, although a sympathetic approach to the subject can scarcely be denied. Despite this, the warts have not been overlooked nor explained away.

The principal aim has been to collect and present the performance records of the four varieties of locomotive to allow the student of performance to have data available to make his own assessment of the general capacity of the design and the relative capabilities of the variations. It has not been deemed necessary to recapitulate, save in broad terms, the technical *minutiae* of the design because the volume is not primarily directed to the engineer reader.

Space limitation has been the factor which has caused some proposed chapters (about liveries and tenders, for example) to be omitted. These would ideally be catered for by booklets which, might it be suggested, the preservation societies most closely associated with the classes could prepare and publish from within their own ranks? It is in no small measure thanks to these societies that this design of the steam locomotive, combining in its original state enough unusual features for it to be termed unorthodox, will go down into history not unnoticed nor yet unlamented.

Acknowledgements

No single author could hope to cover the performance of 140 steam locomotives over the length and breadth of a system as large as the old Southern Railway by his own efforts and any work such as this has to lean very heavily on data submitted by correspondents. Without such correspondents the volume would be much reduced in value and it is to the recorders who are named in each log that the author is indebted.

However, the amount of records that has been chosen represents, in some cases, a fraction of the material available and some recorders may see no more than five per cent of that made available actually in print. Some correspondents, indeed, may fail to find any reference at all to their logs, although they may be assured their data was not overlooked.

In addition to the recorders named in the performance table details, the author wishes to express his grateful thanks to the following persons who have, in one way or another, assisted in providing information: Messrs D. Bradley; L. Elsey; J. N. Faulkner; A. H. Holden; J. Lulham; G. O. P. Pearce; K. Rogers; R. Russell and E. S. Youldon.

The editor of the *Railway Magazine* has kindly permitted reproduction of the diagrams of the rebuilt locomotives included in Chapter 1. Photographs attributed to Rev. A. C. Cawston are from the D. Cobbe Collection.

Additionally a special word of gratitude is due to Group Captain J. N. C. Law for contributing Chapter 13; to G. F. Bloxam for help in many ways, particularly in regard to the selection of illustrations; and to B. I. Fletcher for livery and case history details. A final expression of thanks is due to S. C. Nash who has continually encouraged when problems arose and very willingly took upon himself the burden of reading through the whole text and made suggestions for corrections and improvements.

In a work of this type, with so much tabulation, it is inevitable that some errors of commission—to say nothing of those of omission—will have slipped through and for these the author absolves all contributors and craves the indulgence of the reader.

It would be esteemed a favour if the author could be notified (through the publisher) of any such shortcomings and, in particular, of any additional relevant information. Such material should, if possible, be backed with documentary or photographic evidence. Three examples may illustrate this point: first, notwithstanding published reports at the time, No. 21C8 was not named on 1 November 1942 (a Sunday) but on the day following; second, despite a caption to a photograph in a popular railway journal purporting to show No. 34105 *Swanage* with a shield, that engine never carried one (the photograph would appear to be of No. 34015 which did bear a shield); finally, in 'proving' that a certain locomotive attained 100 m.p.h. (such as No. 35023 at Porton in Table 97) it is desirable that evidence additional to that printed for point-to-point times be given, if possible for a series of quarter-mile lengths.

Chapter 1

DESIGN AND
MECHANICAL FEATURES

Oliver Vaughan Snell Bulleid became Chief Mechanical
Engineer of the Southern Railway in the autumn of 1937, when
the emphasis for future traction requirements was on electricity,
particularly in the form of multiple units. Bulleid came to the
Southern very much as a new broom from the London and
North Eastern Railway, with its Gresley traditions, and also
with the realisation that he had but a limited time to make his
mark.

A CME who had yet to design his first locomotive at the age
of fifty-five would not, in retrospect, seem to be a very exciting
choice for the SR although probably perfectly adequate in view
of the policy of the company. Little did anybody then consider
that, under Bulleid's guidance, the Southern would come to
possess more Pacific-type locomotives than the LMSR, yet such
was to be the case.

With retirement in view and his *Schools* class marking the
peak of his career the outgoing CME, Maunsell, had been content to let steam traction take a secondary role to Southern
Electric, especially in view of the management's passion for that
type of traction. True, he had tinkered about with modifications
for the *Lord Nelson* class and had a design prepared for a
Pacific-type locomotive, but there was little or no drive behind
it all.

As an import, Bulleid was entirely unfettered by any allegi-
ance to the Southern tradition—or torpidity. Urgency invaded
the CME's chair, with tours of inspection, reports and new
proposals following fast one upon another. One or two immediate improvements were made and were quickly reflected in
the performance columns of the *Railway Magazine*. First of all,
Bulleid obtained better grades of coal for his enginemen and,
secondly, he backed them and encouraged them to run, reversing

the negative attitude which had descended with the previous
regime. Then he turned his attention to the *Lord Nelson* class
and effected an improvement by the fitting of Lemaitre multiple-jet exhausts, carried out from June 1938 until the last of
the class was so equipped in December 1939. In 1939 this class
also started to receive new cylinders with 10 in valve travel and
improved steam passages, a process which dragged on over a
considerable number of years (even into BR days after Bulleid
had gone) and never was carried out completely, with locomotives going for scrap in the old condition. Some writers have
seized upon the cylinder change as being the way Bulleid improved the class, an odd explanation in view of the foregoing
and also because cylinder design was not a particularly strong
point with Bulleid. Rather it was the Lemaitre exhaust which
transformed the class. Half the *Schools* class were likewise
fitted and a few of the N15 class 4-6-0s also received the treatment before the war stopped further work in that direction: the
Q class was similarly treated later.

If any one steam locomotive could have been said to affect
Bulleid's work strongly it was probably the LNER 2-8-2 *Cock o'
the North*, designed for heavy loading conditions on the
awkwardly graded and curving line between Edinburgh and
Aberdeen and yet able to return a good performance on the
faster main line out of London. Bulleid set himself the task to
produce a machine capable of running at 60 m.p.h. start-to-
stop on 600-ton boat trains from Victoria to Dover. Both
routes to Dover had awkward lengths: the common route out to
Bickley had sharp climbs to Grosvenor bridge, to Penge tunnel
and from Beckenham Junction to Bickley. Beyond Bickley the
North Downs had to be cleared either at Knockholt or before
the Medway crossing. After Knockholt the down trains had a
good run, although in the opposite direction the climbing was of
a heavy nature from Tonbridge to Knockholt. On the other
route there was not a lot of room for fast running but plenty of
hill-climbing to be done, especially inwards up Sole Street
bank. The route configuration, therefore, had more in common
with the East Coast route north of Edinburgh than that south of
Newcastle, and this could be a factor in Bulleid first examining
the 4-8-2 and 2-8-2 wheel arrangements as a solution. Had it
not been for obstruction from the civil engineering department

he would probably have chosen the 2–8–2 design. As it was he had to settle for the more conventional 4–6–2 arrangement and, moreover, had to keep the weight within definite bounds for that type.

The answer which was produced owed nothing to established Southern practice, and it was obvious that Bulleid was not content to be a nominal designer but rather a very active one. Despite the war conditions upsetting some intentions, Bulleid had the satisfaction of seeing his brain child named *Channel Packet* and in steam early in 1941. Certainly nothing like it had run on the Southern before nor, in many respects, in the United Kingdom as a whole. It was as if all the designer's ideas formed over a period of thirty or so years had been poured into the design in the knowledge that this might be the sole opportunity to use them; not just one innovation, nor two, but several, which a more conservative engineer would have introduced and tested over a period of years. But Bulleid was in at the deep end —and going strongly! Time had never been his ally and, seemingly sensing this, Bulleid could afford none to experiment. Basically he designed three types of steam locomotive—the Pacifics, the orthodox and ugly Q1 0–6–0 and the bogie-type *Leader*—and events certainly proved he had no reserves of time to test out proposals at leisure in any of these designs.

The result then was a 4–6–2 having three cylinders with a chain-driven three-throw crank shaft operating valve gears for each of those cylinders and an oil-bath enclosing the inside motion and valve gears. Boiler pressure was 280 lb per sq in and the engine was encased above the wheels, the casing not continuing across the front of the smokebox.

These few and important special features would have been sufficient for most locomotive engineers to contend with in a new design, but not for Bulleid. Working from the rail upwards, the points of the design may be enumerated in greater detail. The wheels were 3 ft 1 in diameter for the leading bogie, 6 ft 2 in diameter for the coupled wheels and 3 ft 7 in for the trailing axle (comparative figures for *Cock o' the North* were strikingly similar, being 3 ft 2 in, 6 ft 2 in and 3 ft 8 in respectively), all of which were of the Bulleid–Firth–Brown type, not dissimilar in appearance to the 'Boxpok' wheels introduced in North America. In the B–F–B type the usual spokes were dispensed with in favour of bridging pieces radiating from a corrugated centre plate to give support to the tyre. The advantages claimed, with justification, for this type of wheel included 10 per cent reduction in weight, the ability to dispense with the usual Gibson retaining ring, no loose tyres and better distribution of stresses. No reciprocating balance weights were incorporated in the driving wheels, so saving hammer-blow on the track, but balance weights were inserted in the wheel rims in respect of rotating weights. The trailing truck had 'delta' type framing combining pendulum and pivotal principles. Braking was on the driving wheels by means of another innovation—clasp-type brakes with the brake pull rods in pairs either side of the wheels and the brake blocks (two to each wheel) set at a 'ten minutes to four o'clock' position. Steam sanding was employed to the centre coupled wheels only.

The three cylinders (the inside one being inclined and placed above the second axle of the leading bogie) were of 18 in diameter and 24 in stroke, being separately fabricated. The valves were of 11 in diameter, having a maximum travel of $6\frac{1}{4}$ in, those of the two outside cylinders being driven indirectly by a rocking shaft from the valve gear which passed into the exhaust chamber of the steamchest, thus involving outside admission. The steam-chests were placed on the same vertical centre line as the cylinders. The stroke therefore was short and the valve dia-meter large. Piston area was 764 sq in and cylinder volume 18,335 cu in. The exhausts from the cylinders were led to the Lemaitre blastpipe arrangement having five orifices each of $2\frac{5}{8}$ in diameter (total cross-sectional area of 27 sq in) placed over the middle cylinder, and discharged through a large dia-meter chimney (2 ft 5 in at top, 2 ft 1 in at choke).

The drive from all three cylinders was taken onto the middle coupled axle. The middle connecting-rod, crosshead, slide-bar and crank-pin together with the patent chain-driven radial gear and three sets of motion were encased in a 40-gallon capacity oil-bath enclosure which included reversible gear pumps, chain driven from the valve crankshaft, to lift oil from the sump and distribute it, through pipes, over the moving parts. This was in an endeavour—not entirely successful—to ensure trouble-free maintenance of inaccessible parts. Unfortunately, but not en-tirely unexpectedly, the oil-baths leaked at first and the escaping oil was thrown upon and soaked up by the spun-glass boiler lagging, which would sometimes catch fire.

The chain-driven radial gear was not the first choice for valve gear. Originally it was intended to employ a propeller shaft with gears, but because of war conditions the gears could not be fabricated and so recourse had to be made (there not being room to accommodate the conventional Walschaerts' gear) to a chain-driven valve gear.

This radial type valve motion was driven by means of cranks, or eccentrics, on a secondary shaft mounted within and on bearings supported from the frames, rather than by cranks on the driving axle. This secondary shaft was driven by a sprocket and chain from a countershaft mounted on the frames at a higher elevation and level with the driving axle. From the secondary shaft three cranks (or eccentrics) were arranged to give the sequence of valve events to the respective cylinders. The radius (or expansion) links were mounted above the secondary shaft and rocked by eccentric rods connected with the eccentrics on the shaft. The eccentric rods were in an almost vertical position. Combination levers, vertically arranged, were pivoted onto the rear ends of short rods which were, in turn, connected with the valve rods. Radius rods were pivoted to the upper ends of their respective combination levers, each radius rod extending rearward beyond its expansion link to connect with the reversing mechanism. The lower end of each combination lever was connected by a horizontal union link with a pivot of the big end of the respective vertical eccentric rods.

Each piston valve comprised two pistons connected by two spaced webs and operated within the cylinder. A horizontal link connected at one end with a pivot mounted between the webs near to the piston head and, at the other end, with the upper end of an arm secured to a transverse rock shaft. A depending arm was secured to the rock shaft and connected to the valve rod. This gave a $3:8$ ratio.

To supply steam *Channel Packet* was provided with a boiler of welded construction having a barrel length of 16 ft $9\frac{5}{8}$ in tapering from 6 ft $3\frac{1}{2}$ in to 5 ft $9\frac{3}{4}$ in (outside diameters), 124 small ($2\frac{1}{4}$ in diameter) and 40 large ($5\frac{1}{4}$ in diameter) tubes, 40 superheater elements ($1\frac{1}{2}$ in diameter) giving a total combined heating surface of 3,273 sq ft. The boiler pressure was of the unusually high figure of 280 lb per sq in. The wide firebox, of steel construction, had a grate area of 48½ sq ft and had two Nicholson thermic syphons to assist in water circulation. Three safety valves of the Ross pop type were fitted on the front ring of the boiler barrel, being so placed to avoid lifting steam over the thermic syphons. Spun–glass was used for lagging the boiler. The smokebox was not of the usual cylindrical form but of irregular shape. A triple ashpan, each section with a self-cleaning hopper, was fitted.

Inside the cab, which rode extremely smoothly on the excellently designed trailing truck, the improvements were as radical. The driver's controls were fitted within easy reach of his seat on the left-hand side, and on the fireman's side all the injectors were placed. The firebox doors could be opened by the fireman actuating a pedal with his foot (this in turn operated a small steam cylinder to move the doors), and this feature came to be exploited no more deftly than by firemen from Exmouth Junction shed. The steam-operated reverse in the form of a lever in a quadrant frame (arranged for 70 per cent maximum cut-off) was placed parallel to the cab sidesheets, while the regulator was of the 'pull-out' type which the driver pulled up and towards him. A steam-chest pressure gauge was fitted, and this and other gauges were illuminated by various means (including ultra-violet rays) which avoided the use of distracting light. Inspection lights and headcode lamps were electrically lit by means of a steam turbo-generator, and later construction even included a lamp at the rear of the tender to give light when coupling to or uncoupling from a train in the dark. The cab, in conjunction with the tender, gave overall protection to the crew, so much so that at times coal dust tended to get trapped in the confined air space and make life tiresome. Generally it could be said that these cabs were the best planned of any of their time, although the forward vision left something to be desired.

The whole of the engine from the wheels up was swathed in a casing, independent of the boiler, described by the designer as 'air-smoothing', to allow cleaning through carriage-washing plants. Flat at the top, it even had a pivoted cover to slide over the chimney! To match the many innovations within the machine Mr Bulleid introduced a new numbering system— 21C1—of which the letter C (slightly larger than the numerals) indicated three coupled axles, the preceding figures indicating bogie and trailing axles respectively and the final numeral the individual machine number. At least it had the virtue of starting the class enumeration at 1 instead of 0 as had been so often the case in the past, although oddly the 'artist's impression' issued by the SR had 21C0. Even the nameplates were of distinctive type, to say nothing of the fixture on the smokebox door, the numberplates and the company's nameplates on the tender. The tender was carried on three axles and had a pleasing flush side to set the profile of the coaching stock to follow. Coal capacity was 5 tons, water gallonage being 5000. Water pick-up apparatus was eschewed.

Weight in working order was $142\frac{1}{2}$ tons of which the locomotive accounted for $92\frac{1}{2}$ tons and had 63 tons available for adhesion. Length of engine and tender over buffers was 69 ft $7\frac{3}{4}$ in.

This, briefly, was the engine that had a plate fixed in the cab to commemorate its naming at Eastleigh on 10 March 1941. No. 21C2, following shortly afterwards, was virtually the same. Then came a long period of running-in when various defects became apparent. No. 21C1 had run but a small mileage before the front numberplate was moved down from the sloping plating over the buffer beam to the vertical, two footholds were made in the sloping plating and the three lamps and lampirons transferred to that position and steps added to the off-side front buffer. These alterations appear to have been done early enough for the second engine to emerge in the revised form.

Both engines were found to be in excess of the estimated weight and immediate steps had to be taken to reduce it, not only in the two locomotives so far constructed but in following members of the class. Cast numberplates for No. 21C3 had already been manufactured but, in view of this necessity, remained in Eastleigh works for about twenty years without being fixed, it having been decided to revert to the normal method of displaying numerals. Holes were bored in the main frames of Nos. 21C1–5 and thereafter lighter frames were designed. Nos. 21C3–10 had the sheet casing to the locomotive—including the cab—made of 'Limpet' board (a light asbestos composition fibre substance) instead of metal, and these engines, in their original form, were easily distinguishable by reason of a horizontal rib midway down the casing introduced in this connection. The chimney cover was dispensed with and the top part of the casing in front of and around the chimney cut away, which also assisted in lifting the exhaust. Although it has been stated that the wheel splashers under the casing were not fitted it is known that at least one member of the 21C3–10 batch was so equipped.

Dispersal of the exhaust was a problem, but it was not so immediate as to warrant any alteration before the remaining eight engines of the first order were placed in traffic. After a period of experimentation, an arrangement was alighted upon which gave the most help in lifting the exhaust; this consisted of short smoke deflectors extending, for the upper part of the casing, from the front end of the locomotive to a point level with the rear of the outside cylinder casing and a hood, or inverted scoop, fixed to the horizontal part of the casing ahead of the chimney. This became the standard fitting early in 1943.

Meanwhile breakages to the rocker shaft arms to the cylinders had occurred and remedial action, in the form of a balance pipe between the ends of each steamchest and additional bearings to support the rocker shafts, was undertaken.

Trouble also came in the form of cracks in boiler plates owing to excessive contraction, and to avoid this twelve hours had to be allowed to elapse after an engine came on shed before boilers could be washed out. Similarly cracks in the all-welded steel firebox plates were hastened by cooling-off too quickly.

All these modifications were incorporated in the second batch of ten *Merchant Navy* engines, Nos. 21C11–20. The weight of this series went up to 84 tons 14 cwt empty and, in working order, $94\frac{3}{4}$ tons compared with the revised figure of 84 tons 9 cwt empty for the first ten. The overall height was reduced $1\frac{3}{4}$ in, but it was the unseen differences that were more important: the valves were redesigned to give better operation of the reverser, after a proposal to install a hand reverser instead of the steam type had to be dropped owing to space limitations; the boiler form was altered by putting the taper on the underside at the back, rather than on top at the front as previously, thus reducing water capacity—and weight!—but not the heating surface. Also sanding was introduced on the leading and rear coupled wheels, and to cater for this additional sandboxes were required, their presence being betrayed by additional sliders, instead of the one in the casing each side of the locomotive.

The cab and tender also were altered. The cab side sheets were turned inwards at the rear for a foot on either side and glazed in the upper portion. The tenders were so arranged to give a narrow viewing space between the side sheets and the coal bunker for stowing fire-irons and, with the protection of a window, a look-out for tender-first running. Too often, however, coal would find its way into this canyon and nullify its intended use.

In the same month (June 1945) as the last members of the second batch of *Merchant Navy* class were put into service the first of the new *West Country* class also were placed in traffic. These were a scaled down version of the 21C11-20 batch, designed to have the same route availability as the N class 2-6-0s and to be able to work between Tonbridge and Bo-Peep Junction on the Hastings via Battle route, which included the narrow Mountfield tunnel.

The scaling down is best appreciated by comparing the principal dimensions and details thus:

	West Country class	*Merchant Navy* class
Cylinders	(3) 16⅝ in × 24 in	(3) 18 in × 24 in
Valves		
Diameter	10 in	11 in
Travel	6¼ in	6¼ in
Coupled wheel diameter	6 ft 2 in	6 ft 2 in
Boiler		
Maximum diameter	6 ft 3½ in	6 ft 3½ in
Distance between tube-plates	17 ft	17 ft
Tubes	(112) 2¼ in	(124) 2¼ in
Flues	(32) 5¼ in	(40) 5¼ in
Heating surface		
Total evaporative	2,122 sq ft	2,451 sq ft
Superheater	545 sq ft	822 sq ft
Combined total	2,667 sq ft	3,273 sq ft
Grate area	38¼ sq ft	48½ sq ft
Length (engine and tender)	67 ft 4¾ in	69 ft 7¾ in
Tender water capacity	4,500 gals	5,000 gals
Weight empty	77 tons	84 tons 14 cwt
Weight in working order		
Adhesion	56¼ tons	63 tons
Total engine	86 tons	94¾ tons

The length was reduced chiefly by reason of a shorter firebox and smaller cab; the boiler pressure was the same high figure of 280 lb per sq in, but the trailing truck wheel diameter was reduced to 37 in. Welding was employed extensively in the fabrication of the locomotive and tender as a deliberate policy to keep the weight down, whereas with the larger class it had been used mainly for convenience. Confidence in the performance of the class was high enough to make public the intention to build seventy of the 'lightweights' as they were to be known, and this confidence was shown not to have been misplaced when the first units went into traffic. Although designated mixed-traffic locomotives they went straight on to passenger duties with assurance.

An early modification involved repositioning the pair of lamp irons from the inside face of the smoke deflector sheets to the smokebox door (but not the accompanying electric lamp indicators) because the forward vision was impaired when a circular route indicator disc was placed on either of these irons. At least seventeen of the class were turned out before this modification, made near the end of 1945, became standard for further production; existing locomotives, including the larger *Merchant Navy* class, were quickly altered in the spring of 1946. Trouble with smoke drifting down to obscure the driver's vision persisted and efforts to overcome it resulted in the smoke deflectors being lengthened backwards to a point level with the leading edge of the first coupled wheel of the locomotive. This alteration was made to all Pacifics entering works as from a date late in 1946 and to new construction commencing with No. 21C158 in April 1947. It was followed by amending the front of the cabs to a wedge shape, giving a greater area and making less difficult the task of keeping the glass clean. New construction having this modification started with No. 21C164 in June 1947, and two months later it was applied to the existing classes of both types, all members of which were so treated.

A rather more radical alteration was the conversion, in July 1947, of a *West Country* engine to burn oil fuel instead of coal. As a subject for conversion it was not the best choice because wide fireboxes are less well suited than a long narrow grate for this mode of firing. At first one burner was fitted, although eventually resort had to be made to two, reflecting the disadvant-

1. The second engine of the class, No. 21C2, in unlined malachite green livery and with nameplates covered comes off the turntable at Bournemouth shed after a trial run on 7 June 1941. 2. No. 21C8 *Orient Line*, of the batch having a longitudinal mid-rib on the casing, in wartime black livery at Waterloo on 2 November 1942 after the official naming ceremony. One of the figures on the platform ramp appears to be Mr O. V. Bulleid. Note large cut-away area around chimney. 3. Penultimate member of the class, No. 35029, at Stewarts Lane shed on 10 June 1950 in lined malachite green livery with unlettered tender and covered nameplate. Built with modified cab and standard smoke deflecting front end.

4. No. 21C8 *Orient Line*, passing Surbiton with the 12.50 p.m. Waterloo–West of England train, still in black livery but with modified smoke deflecting arrangement.

5. Breasting the summit at Semley with an up train in August 1948, No. 21C2 *Union Castle* had received the standard smoke deflecting arrangement, was restored to full malachite green livery, had the lamp-irons transferred from the side wings to the smokebox door and was fitted with a batten high up on each of the side wings to take *Devon Belle* boards.

6. No. 35019 *French Line C.G.T.* in malachite green livery approaching Salisbury with the down *Devon Belle*. Cab modified and smoke deflector wings lengthened; renumbered but still retaining Southern lettered tender and roundel on smokebox door, which door also carried repositioned lamp-irons.

7. No. 35020 *Bibby Line* at Waterloo on 18 May 1948. Cab modified and very long smoke deflector wings fitted (unique for the class) and renumbered although retaining smokebox roundel. Fitted with LMSR tender (in black livery) for Locomotive Interchange purposes.

8. The 'Classic Way to the Continent'. A magnificent *ensemble*—chocolate and cream Pullmans and blue liveried No. 35027 *Port Line*—forming the elegant down *Golden Arrow* in June 1951.

age of the locomotive's wide firebox. Another of the class was also converted to oil-firing before the scheme had to be abandoned, not due to lack of technical success, but to governmental decree. The conversion had also been made at the behest of the government and turned out to be an expensive exercise, although useful research in this direction continued (with No. 21C136) before re-conversion of both locomotives was completed.

The year 1948, with the dawn of nationalisation, brought several changes, apart from renumbering. First of all there was a further lengthening of the smoke deflectors (to a point nearly level with the rear edge of the leading coupled wheel) to the three *West Country* engines and one *Merchant Navy* (No. 35020) selected for the Interchange Trials, a modification which remained with No. 34006 to the time of withdrawal and with the others until rebuilding, but was never extended to any other members of either class. Another batch of light 4–6–2s was started (with No. 34071) and this lot had cabs 9 ft wide and were fitted with 5,500-gallon tenders. Later in the year the last batch of *Merchant Navy* locomotives started to come out of Eastleigh with the added refinement, in addition to modified cabs and longer smoke deflectors (i.e. standard, as opposed to very long on No. 35020), of the TIA (Trâitement Intégrale Armand) type water-treatment system which had been applied to the smaller engines the previous year and became standard equipment for the classes. This final lot of *Merchant Navy* engines was eventually fitted with tenders of 6,000 gallon capacity. Water filling points in the tenders were not fitted (these were abandoned also for the earlier two batches).

Meanwhile No. 35005 had been the subject of an experiment in mechanical coal-firing, being fitted with a Berkley mechanical stoker, of a design imported from North America. The stoker consisted of a coal crusher and conveying screws to deliver coal from the tender to a distributor plate fitted in the firehole door. These screws were driven by a small steam engine on the tender and the rate of delivery of coal was regulated by altering the speed of this engine. From the distributor plate the coal was discharged by a range of steam jets; these jets could be manipulated by varying the steam pressure which in turn governed the amount of coal fed into the various parts of the grate. The trials were prolonged and proved very satisfactory from the performance viewpoint. The main difficulty was that the coal had to be graded to less than 6 in cubes and, strange as it may seem twenty-five years later, the coal used at that time contained a high proportion of large lumps. It would have meant that the existing coaling plants would have to have been adapted either to screen the coal or to reduce it to the special requirements, and it was upon this stumbling block that the proposal failed.

Bulleid left British Railways at the end of September 1949 and with him went the impetus for improving the Pacifics in the original form. Thereafter there was nothing more to note other than minor alterations, the adoption of BR standard designs for some components and a general 'fiddling around' with small details. Immediately after his farewell took place, newly-constructed No. 34093 came out with circular flaps hinged at the bottom over the sand-box filler chutes instead of the sliders fitted previously. Being hinged at the bottom meant that to remain closed a couple of screws at the top had to be rotated, a chore which more often than not failed to be carried out. Consequently the flaps dropped down and soon broke off: to remedy this the flaps were refixed with the hinges at the top, but eventually Nos. 34093–34110 were fitted with the standard slides. Sand caused trouble by working on to the slidebars, and it was to avoid this that covers were fitted over the slidebars. As a remedy it failed and the covers, together with the sanding gear to the leading coupled wheels, were removed.

Although the Locomotive Interchanges had taken place early in 1948 investigations into the *Merchant Navy* class by BR continued, and in this connection one engine was fitted in 1951 with a single blastpipe and another with a boiler without thermic syphons. In mid-1952 the sides of the tenders were cut down to allow the bags of the water columns to swing across the tender with less obstruction, and this modification became standard, although the rate of carrying it out was rather slow. Reduction in boiler pressure from 280 to 250 lb per sq in was commenced in March 1954, permitting a standard grade of steel to be used for firebox stays instead of a special grade difficult to obtain. A side effect of this reduction was the better functioning of the injectors.

Then, nearly eight years after the Locomotive Interchanges,

in February 1956, there emerged from Eastleigh works the first of the modified, or rebuilt, Pacifics—No. 35018. Thereafter locomotives arriving at Eastleigh were taken at random for rebuilding as works capacity allowed, no other works being involved in the conversions, except for providing assistance in the preparation of the details and in fabricating some new components.

The main alterations were the removal of the steam reverser, the substitution of three sets of Walschaerts' valve gear for the Bulleid chain-driven gear and the de-frocking of the locomotive by the removal of the 'air-smoothing' casing. The cylinder arrangements remained unchanged in principle although a new inside cylinder had to be cast having inside admission and the steam–chest offset to one side. A steel casting, having cast-iron liners to both the cylinder barrel and steam-chests was introduced. To avoid the expense of making new outside cylinders the existing ones, with outside admission, were retained. This required the use of a high-pressure gland for the valve spindle as well as special measures to translate the actuation from the plane of the valve gear to the steam–chest centre line.

The oil-bath enclosed valve gear was replaced by three separate sets of Walschaerts' valve gear. The outside valve gears (for outside admission) transmitted the motion to the valve spindle from the top of the combination lever by means of a suspension link to the valve spindle crosshead. This did away with the normal requirement of valve spindle crosshead guides. Some difficulty was encountered with this at first. The inside valve gear was driven by an eccentric mounted on the right-hand crank web of the driving (middle) axle. The wheels on this axle had small segmental counterbalance weights introduced externally.

Screw reversing gear replaced the original steam-operated reverser. The new arrangement was of LMSR origin and employed a cut-off indicator of the drum type and a single shaft for all three gears. Maximum cut-off was increased from 70 per cent to 75 per cent. The smokebox was altered to the normal cylindrical shape although the elliptical shape of the smokebox door was retained. Some alterations were made to the superheater and the diameter of the chimney at the choke was reduced by $1\frac{1}{2}$ in to 1 ft $11\frac{1}{2}$ in.

The engine acquired the orthodox appearance of a steam locomotive by the introduction of boiler clothing plates mounted on crinolines, the spun-glass mattresses being retained. Foot-plating—high without splashers, not unlike the BR standard style—was fitted as well as smoke deflectors which helped to cloak the high step up from buffer beam. This plating did not drop at the rear and gave the cab a mean look on elevation.

A rocking grate with twelve rocking sections was fitted, having an air space of 37·3 per cent. A new ashpan, with four bottom doors, was also fitted and six damper doors (three for running in each direction). The steam-operated gear for foot-actuated opening of the firehole door was removed and a de-flector plate fitted to the firehole. Sanding gear was fitted for forward running for the first two coupled axles and rearward running for the centre coupled axle, the sanding gear on the tender being removed. These alterations had the cumulative effect of increasing the weight of the engines.

The smaller *West Country* class was treated on almost identi-cal lines, beginning with No. 34005 in the summer of 1957. There were ten, rather than twelve, sections to the rocking grate but otherwise the changes made were virtually the same, although made to different dimensions for the smaller loco-motives.

DIMENSIONS ETC. ALTERED IN REBUILDING

	Merchant Navy class		West Country class	
	Original	Rebuilt	Original	Rebuilt
Superheat heating surface	822 sq ft	612 sq ft	515 sq ft	488 sq ft
Weight in working order (locomotive)	94 tons 15 cwt	97 tons 18 cwt	86 tons	90 tons 1 cwt
Weight empty (locomotive)	84 tons 14 cwt	88 tons 5 cwt	77 tons	81 tons 1 cwt
Adhesion weight	63 tons	64 tons 18 cwt	56 tons 5 cwt	61 tons 6 cwt
Adhesion factor	3·76	4·34	4·06	4·72

After this rebuilding, which, from an engineering point of view, produced a less complicated (and therefore better) machine, minor modifications continued to be made to both classes. Of most significance was that to reduce spark throwing: as late as February 1964 rebuild No. 34101 was fitted with spark arrestor gear and thereupon quickly gained a reputation as a poor steamer. It was in this connection also that No. 34064, an unmodified engine, had been fitted in 1962 with a combined Giesl exhaust ejector and spark arrestor in an attempt to offset the loss of efficiency due to the spark arrestor equipment rather than to test the Giesl ejector in its own right.

February 1964 was the month in which No. 35013 was considered for scrap but was reprieved: even so the first withdrawals came when two members of the class were condemned later that month, by which time further technical developments had been halted.

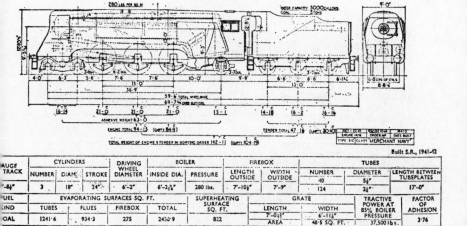

GAUGE TRACK	CYLINDERS			DRIVING WHEEL DIAMETER	BOILER			FIREBOX		TUBES		
	NUMBER	DIAM.	STROKE		INSIDE DIA.	PRESSURE	LENGTH OUTSIDE	WIDTH OUTSIDE	NUMBER	DIAMETER	LENGTH BETWEEN TUBEPLATES
4'-8½"	3	18"	24"	6'-2"	6'-2⅜"	280 lbs.	7'-10½"	7'-9"	40 124	5¼" 2¼"	17'-0"

FUEL KIND COAL	EVAPORATING SURFACES SQ. FT.				SUPERHEATING SURFACE SQ. FT.	GRATE		TRACTIVE POWER AT 85% BOILER PRESSURE	FACTOR OF ADHESION
	TUBES	FLUES	FIREBOX	TOTAL		LENGTH WIDTH	AREA		
	1241·6	934·3	275	2450·9	822	7'-0⅛" 6'-11½"	48·5 SQ. FT.	37,500 lbs.	3·76

TENDER CAPACITY :—WATER, 5,000 GALLONS ; COAL, 5 TONS.

Designed by O. V. BULLEID, Chief Mech. Eng.

Fig. 1. *Merchant Navy* class

SOUTHERN RAILWAY

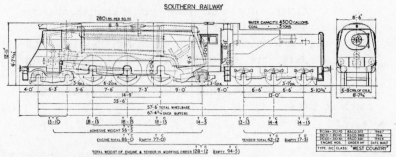

FITTED WITH THE BULLEID PATENT VALVE GEAR   Built S.R., 1945-4

GAUGE OF TRACK	CYLINDERS			DRIVING WHEEL DIAMETER	BOILER		FIREBOX		TUBES		LENGTH BETWEEN TUBEPLATES
	NUMBER	DIAM.	STROKE		INSIDE DIA.	PRESSURE	LENGTH OUTSIDE	WIDTH OUTSIDE	NUMBER 32	DIAMETER 5¼"	
4'-8½"	3	16½"	24"	6'-2"	6'-2¾"	280 lbs.	6'-6½"	7'-9"	112	2¼"	17'-0"

FUEL	EVAPORATING SURFACES SQ. FT.				SUPERHEATING SURFACE SQ. FT.	GRATE		TRACTIVE POWER AT 85% BOILER PRESSURE	FACTOR OF ADHESION
KIND	TUBES	FLUES	FIREBOX	TOTAL		LENGTH 5'-6½"	WIDTH 6'-11½"	31,000 lbs.	4·06
COAL	1121	748	253	2122	545	AREA 38·25 SQ. FT.			

SIX WHEELED TENDER CAPACITY :—WATER, 4,500 GALLONS; COAL, 5 TONS.   Designed by O. V. BULLEID, Chief Mech. Eng.

Fig. 2. *West Country* class

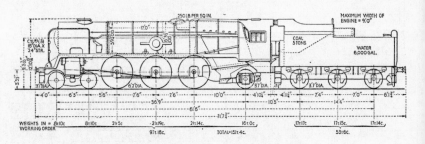

Fig. 3. Rebuilt *Merchant Navy* class

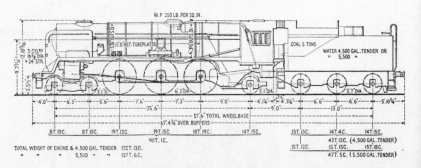

Fig. 4. Rebuilt *West Country* class

Chapter 2

A BROAD HISTORICAL ACCOUNT
OF THE LOCOMOTIVES

March 1941 promised to be yet another sombre month for Britain and the Commonwealth nations supporting her in the lone stand against the combined forces of Hitler and Mussolini. Understandably in such conditions, little public attention could be paid to the mundane matter of a new railway locomotive and consequently the consummation of much of the designer's work over the preceding two or three years had to go virtually unheeded. No. 21C1 *Channel Packet* had been turned out at Eastleigh works as the Southern Railway's first Pacific type in the February and run a few miles to Bournemouth and back on a test train before being christened. Obviously the war was no time to produce an express passenger locomotive (which this class undoubtedly was) so the subterfuge of classifying it as a mixed-traffic engine had to be resorted to so that the project might proceed relatively unhindered.

Accordingly in June it was placed, in company with sister engine No. 21C2, on freight train work between Salisbury and Eastleigh, where a close watch could be kept on the daily performance. The intention to keep the class constantly in steam whilst on shed was met by adapting two old locomotives (A12 Class 0–4–2 No. 646 and X6 Class 4–4–0 No. 657) to supply the necessary steam; No. 646 was stationed at Eastleigh and No. 657 at Salisbury for this purpose. By September the scene of the new engines' activities had become the Salisbury–Exeter route, and this resulted in No. 646 moving to Salisbury to replace No. 657, which took up station at Exmouth Junction shed.

By January of 1942 the first six engines of the initial order (No. 1068) for ten engines had been placed in traffic officially and, not surprisingly, it became difficult to employ all these engines on freight duties between Salisbury and Exeter. Therefore, in early January, No. 21C3 was rostered for the 11.7 a.m. Salisbury–Exeter passenger train, it being suggested that the

first occasion that one of the class worked an ordinary passenger
service was by this engine on this train on 9 January. From
March onwards the livery of the locomotives was altered to
black instead of malachite green. No. 21C5 was the first to be
repainted and No. 21C7 the first to be turned out new in that
garb. As 1942 progressed more passenger workings were taken
up by the new locomotives not only west of Salisbury but also
east thereof to Waterloo. By the summer, when No. 21C10 was
at work, it was possible to allocate five members of the class
each to Salisbury and Exmouth Junction depots. The engines
were then handling very heavy passenger trains between
London and Exeter in the order of sixteen or more coaches and
in December some regular trains were made up of no less than
twenty coaches and worked by No. 21C10.

1943 saw no new construction but sustained efforts to find an
efficient method to prevent smoke drifting down to obscure
forward vision from the cab. Eventually a solution was arrived
at and alterations involving side shields at the front and a hood
over the smokebox were standardised for the class. Also the
practice of using old engines to provide steam for Pacifics 'on
shed' was abandoned.

At the end of 1944 the first locomotives of order No. 1189
(for ten *Merchant Navy* class engines) appeared and were
allocated to Nine Elms; by January 1945 Nos. 21C11 and
21C12 were working on the Bournemouth route, and as further
new construction appeared more of the Bournemouth services
were turned over to the class. The order was completed with
No. 21C20 in June 1945 and, happily, the old malachite green
livery returned, the engines being repainted when coming into
works from about July onwards.

Meanwhile the *West Country* class had made its debut with
No. 21C101 running trial trips in May and being placed in
traffic in June. The locomotives were constructed at Brighton
(tenders were built at Ashford) and after running-in in the
Sussex area were allocated to Exmouth Junction shed, immediately taking over duties between Exeter and Ilfracombe, without
any of the hesitancy which marked the advent of the larger
companion class. Later in 1945, when the number of locomotives of the class increased, Plymouth saw the new design.
From the outset the engines took the malachite green livery.

With a sufficiently large stud of *West Country* engines available for services west of Exeter the Southern Railway decided to augment the motive power on the Kentish main lines. Posters having a photographic reproduction of one of the locomotives on a train and advising the public of the introduction of the class to South East England (a publicity channel first used in the West of England in connection with the advent of these engines there) appeared on stations throughout the county, and soon Nos. 21C117, 21C119 and 21C121 onwards were to be noted in action from Stewarts Lane and Ramsgate sheds. Order no. 2561 (for Nos. 21C101–30) was completed by May 1946 but building continued without a break with order no. 2885 (Nos. 21C131–45) and order no. 3213 (Nos. 21C146–70). During 1946 thirty-one of the class were put into traffic.

By the time No. 21C140 was allocated, the Eastern section had almost reached saturation point, so far as Pacifics were concerned, so the next members went to Western Section sheds at Exmouth Junction and Salisbury. No. 21C149 (later to become the first *Battle of Britain* class representative) emerged in December 1946 as the building programme continued unabated. The difference between *West Country* and *Battle of Britain* engines was no more than one of name grouping.

Throughout 1947 the flow was maintained until November, when No. 21C170 completed the order for the first seventy locomotives. The first naming ceremonies for those locomotives having *Battle of Britain* names, instead of *West Country* appellations, took place near the anniversary date of the battle in September that year. The radius of action of the class increased to include the Brighton–Plymouth through train, the Bournemouth route, Barnstaple Junction to Torrington, Southampton Docks, Bournemouth–Weymouth and Okehampton–Padstow. In June No. 21C164 became the 1000th engine to be built at Brighton works and entered traffic with modified cab as did all subsequent members of the class. Two months later the work of modifying cabs of the *Merchant Navy* class was started with No. 21C8 and of the light Pacifics with No. 21C152.

The plan to convert thirty *West Country* class to burn bunker oil proceeded slowly with No. 21C119 being the first, in July, to be altered. The first arrangement having one burner proved unsatisfactory and by the end of the year two burners had been fitted.

Nationalisation in 1948 did not put the brake on the Bulleid Pacifics immediately. No. 21C136 was converted early in the year as an oil-burner and in April No. 34071 left Brighton works as the first of order no. 3383 for another twenty *Battle of Britain* locomotives. This batch (as well as the final order yet to come) was built with 9 ft wide cabs and fitted with 5,500-gallon tenders. Meanwhile BR ownership was making its mark: Nos. 21C106 and 21C158 were the first Pacifics to leave Eastleigh and Brighton works respectively (in January) with the S prefix to the number. A few weeks later the prefix was abandoned in favour of renumbering the classes 34001–70 (for 21C101–70) and 35001–20 for the *Merchant Navy* engines. The Locomotive Interchanges were arranged and three large Pacifics (Nos. 35017, 35019, 35020) and three small (Nos. 34004, 34005, 34006) were fitted with LMSR tenders with water pick-up gear for working on other regions of BR. The three *West Country* engines and No. 35020 were fitted with extra-long smoke deflectors at the same time, as well as the modified cabs which were also acquired by the other two *Merchant Navy* engines selected. At about the same time No. 35005 was fitted with a Berkley automatic stoker for experimental purposes.

It was a busy and, in some ways, a bewildering year as the engines came out in varying letterings, such as BRITISH RAILWAYS in Southern style lettering or in Gill Sans style (mostly in medium—but a few in bold—Gill Sans) or without any lettering at all. In May–June Nos. 34011, 34056, 34064 and 34065 were repainted in an experimental apple green colour and the two *West Country* oil-burners were taken back into works for reconversion, not by reason of any failure of the design, but because the government of the day had bungled its calculations and could not afford to allocate currency for the purchase of oil from overseas. No. 34019 was re-converted quickly but No. 34036 was used for further trials for a period.

In September 1948 both Brighton and Eastleigh works were evidently under pressure because the former was fitting new construction Nos. 34082 and 34083 with repaired boilers while Eastleigh had to turn out the first few *Merchant Navy* engines of order no. 3393 (for ten engines) with light Pacific class tenders. Later 6,000-gallon tenders were fitted. By the end of the year Brighton had No. 34090 as the sole outstanding engine of order 3383 and Eastleigh had to produce Nos. 35029 and 35030 to complete its order. The last ten *Merchant Navy* locomotives were built complete with modified cabs and TIA equipment for water treatment. And BR decreed that the power classifications for the Bulleid Pacifics should be 7P for the large and 6MT for the small locomotives.

No. 34090 made its appearance early in 1949. In February No. 35024 was decked out in the new blue livery (with three red lines each side) for the premier express classes of BR (subsequently the lining out was amended) and in April the last *Merchant Navy* (No. 35030) was put into traffic. At the end of April No. 34059 was sent to the Eastern Region and during May ran test trips in the eastern counties, operating from Stratford depot, returning to home rails before the month was out. August saw the first *West Country* locomotive (No. 34039) to bear the standard BR green livery outshopped from Eastleigh works. Thereafter the new liveries were applied to the classes coming in for repair. New construction recommenced the same month with Brighton turning out No. 34091, the first member of order no. 3486 covering a further twenty light Pacifics. Hitherto Brighton had enjoyed the monopoly of building the smaller 4–6–2s, as Eastleigh had the larger class, but with the final order this was broken, with six engines coming out of the Hampshire manufactory. By November 1949 No. 34036 was back in service as a normal coal-burning unit after conclusion of trials of oil-burning apparatus.

New construction got as far as No. 34109 by mid-1950 and after that nothing else came but rumours that No. 34110 would appear without the Bulleid valve gear; the fitting of modified cabs continued and the ranks of engines still awaiting naming dwindled.

In January 1951 the final Bulleid Pacific, No. 34110, emerged from Brighton works complete with the valve gear usual for the class. March saw No. 34109 on a two-week test over the Somerset and Dorset line, complete with tablet exchange apparatus affixed to the tender, preparatory to the drafting of a few members of the class to Bath shed for duty on the

line. In April the Berkley stoker was finally removed from
No. 35005 and about the same time the Merchant Navy class
was reclassified as 8P. Three of the new BR standard *Britannia*
class were allocated to the Southern Region in May and to make
good the deficiency on the Eastern Region three light Pacifics
from the Southern (Nos. 34039, 34057, 34065) were sent over to
to Stratford shed. Also in May the blue livery for the *Merchant
Navy* engines was discontinued, with No. 35024 being the first
to sport the BR standard dark green. In August No. 35014 was
fitted with a boiler not having a thermic syphon, and just previously No. 35019 acquired a single blastpipe, both in connection
with BR investigations into the class.

1952 was the year in which the tender modification of remov-
ing the raves—to allow the water column bag to swing over after
filling without obstruction—was commenced. The first example
was tender No. 3310 attached to No. 34043, which was modified
in June. No. 35012 followed quickly and both classes started to
be dealt with in the same manner. Another minor alteration
adopted about this time was the removal of a small part of the
external casing between front buffer beam and cylinders.

The last Pacific in malachite green, No. 34070, was repainted
in March 1953. On the 24th of the next month, as No. 35020
was accelerating downhill through Crewkerne with the 4.30 p.m.
from Exeter Central the driving axle fractured, fortunately
without injury being sustained by anybody. This resulted in
examination of the whole of the Bulleid Pacific stud, during
which time motive power was loaned from other regions. Towards the end of the year the light Pacifics had the power
classification amended to 7P5F.

In March 1954 the Pacifics started to have the pressure of
their boilers reduced from 280 to 250 lb per sq in. The first
Merchant Navy to be treated was No. 35020, and of the lighter
engines Nos. 34013, 34014, 34033, 34052 and 34060 were all
dealt with in March.

1955 was an uneventful year until the closing months when
Eastleigh works started noting one or two locomotives arriving
for a general repair as being for modification. Nothing happened
however until, after a period of waiting, No. 35018 was taken in
hand on 16 November for conversion. It had run 225,873 miles
since its previous general repair and work on its conversion

occupied seventy-five working days, being released to the running shed on 14 February 1956. The next two (Nos. 35020 and 35013) to be converted took thirty-seven days (comparable with thirty-five for an ordinary general repair), but the final two of the first order for five fell back to forty-three days. There was a lull of about six months before further conversions were embarked upon. Meanwhile the reduction in boiler pressure from 280 to 250 lb per sq in, which had been going on for a couple of years, was completed with No. 34070 in June 1956. (The last of the *Merchant Navy* engines to be dealt with was No. 35007 in June 1955.)

The summer of 1957 marked the first modification of one of the light Pacifics (No. 34005) on similar lines to the larger engines. No. 34005 and subsequent early conversions were despatched to the Eastern Section just as work on the main line electrification commenced. In retrospect it appears that the expense of modifying the smaller engines was not really justified —certainly in such numbers as were done—with electrification so near. In any case the modified light engines were no longer as light and did not have the route availability enjoyed by the original design. The modified engines never were allowed to Barnstaple, Ilfracombe or Padstow. 1957 ended on a sombre note, with No. 34006 being involved in the ghastly St Johns accident on 4 December. The engine was relatively undamaged, the tender taking the brunt of the shock, felling a column of an overbridge in the process.

Rebuilding of the light Pacifics continued into 1958, with a considerable amount of tender exchange being involved, and recommenced in the spring for the *Merchant Navy* class.

In the spring of 1959 the equipping of locomotives with automatic warning system gear started. June of that year saw the Stage I Kent Coast electrification inaugurated and by October, with the rebuilding of No. 35028, the *Merchant Navy* class in its original form was extinct. A total of thirty of the light Pacifics had been modified by the end of 1959.

Modification continued unabated during 1960, with twenty-one engines being turned out in the revised form, and continued into 1961 until No. 34104 became the last—and sixtieth of its class—to be dealt with in May, leaving fifty of the type in the original form. Towards the end of 1961 the modified light Pacifics were reclassified from 7P5F to 7P6F.

The fitting of a Giesl oblong ejector together with spark arrestor to No. 34064 in April 1962 marked the last technical alteration to the Southern Pacifics whose fortunes were from thereon to decline, but not necessarily their performances. Indeed some of the finest were in the future. On 15 September 1962 all Southern lines west of Wilton were transferred to the Western region and with them, at the close of the year, seven *Merchant Navy* and thirty-seven of the small Pacifics. Their numbers were 35003/9/10/3/22/5/6, 34002/11/5/20/3/4/30/2/3/5/6/56/8/60/2/3/5/6/9/70/2/4/5/6/8/9/80/1/3/4/6/96, 34106/7/8/9/10.

On 22 April 1963 No. 34055 failed at Chichester while in charge of the 11.00 a.m. Brighton–Cardiff train and, in company with Nos. 34035, 34043 and 34074, shared the distinction of being the first of the original design of light Pacific to be withdrawn (in June by the Western region). By the end of 1963 ten of the original light Pacifics had been withdrawn, leaving the combined total for the classes at 130.

The first withdrawals of *Merchant Navy* engines (Nos. 35002 and 35015) were made in February 1964 and of a modified *West Country* locomotive—No. 34028—in the following May. The decline was rapidly gaining momentum. With the withdrawal of steam from the West of England main line to Exeter and beyond (apart from North Cornwall) in September the Pacifics were more than decimated.

To start the New Year of 1965 there remained twenty-three *Merchant Navy* engines and sixty-nine of the smaller class (twenty original and forty-nine rebuilt). Thirty-eight engines had gone in a year, including No. 35001. Fortunately No. 34051 *Winston Churchill* had survived the holocaust and was available to haul the funeral train conveying the body of Sir Winston from Waterloo to Handborough on 30 January. This, in more ways than one, signified an end of an era. No. 34051 survived until September, when it was withdrawn from service for preservation, thus avoiding the gathering of other members of its class at the South Wales scrapyard at Barry. On Summer Saturdays there were one or two returns of the light Pacifics on the Exeter road with relief trains, but it was a last fling.

Totals of engines to see in 1966 were: *Merchant Navy* sixteen and *West Country/Battle of Britain* fifty-four (of which forty were modified examples). During 1966 members of all three types were in demand for rail tours and appearances were made at Nottingham (more than once) and even Newcastle. Nameplates were removed from many of the engines still in service about mid-1966 (to prevent acquisition by unauthorised collectors) and on 3 October No. 34089 sallied forth from Eastleigh works as the last steam locomotive to be repaired there. At the end of 1966 there remained no more than ten *Merchant Navy* and thirty-six of the smaller engines (twenty-nine modified) in service.

With track works for electrification completed, making 100 m.p.h. running possible, 1967 witnessed enginemen working the run-down engines up to speeds of three figures. What was so amazing was not the speeds but the frequency with which it was done. During the last hundred days there were very few when 100 m.p.h. was not attempted and a high percentage of successes obtained.

The last of the steam-hauled trains ran on 9 July 1967 and there remained to be withdrawn that month twenty-eight Pacifics of which seven were *Merchant Navy* class, two were unmodified *West Country/Battle of Britain* engines and the balance nineteen rebuilt examples of the smaller class. All save two (Nos. 34023 and 35028 purchased for preservation and taken to Longmoor) were sent to scrap merchants and soon cut up.

Of the three engines set aside for preservation No. 34023 started to undergo surgery and restoration before it was removed from Longmoor to Liss on 28 May 1970 and then, in late September 1971, on to Sheffield Park, Sussex. No. 35028, maintained in good working order, remained at Longmoor until it too was moved to Liss on 28 May 1970, going on to Ashford (Kent) over the period 28–29 August 1971. No. 34051 languishes awaiting restoration and display.

At the giant ossuary at Barry, South Wales, where Woodham Bros. retained their scrap purchases for reasons best known to the company, modified No. 34016 was earmarked in 1970 for rescue and resuscitation, but surprisingly it was No. 34092 which was first (so far as Southern Pacifics were concerned) out of the graveyard, being conveyed by road to Ingrow on the

Keighley and Worth Valley Light Railway where it arrived on 27 October 1971. Later, on 7 November, it was towed along the railway to Haworth by No. 80002 for restoration work to be commenced. No. 34016 eventually left Barry in July 1972. Resurrections continued in 1973 with No. 34039 going to Loughborough (via Quorn) and No. 35005 to Carnforth while other dormant Pacifics were selected by prospective purchasers with a view to having the warmth of steam infused into the long-cold cylinders.

Some typical mileages run are:

No. 34005	720,000 (680,198 recorded until May 1962, of which 489,808 was prior to rebuilding)
No. 34100	575,000 (475,305 recorded until June 1963, of which 409,318 was before rebuilding)
No. 35006	1,132,416 (862,757 prior to rebuilding).

Chapter 3

WHAT MIGHT HAVE BEEN

For all practical purposes the history of the Bulleid Pacifics is
complete, for the remaining few examples of the classes are now
unlikely to add anything more than a postlude. But what might
have happened if...? Speculation on the course that events
might have taken is not entirely unrewarding if only to recall to
mind one or two events—or non-events—that had so much influence on the fortunes of the two classes.

Nationalisation unquestionably prolonged the life of the
Pacifics by several years—as well as being instrumental in creat-
ing the modified designs—because in the autumn of 1946 the
Southern Railway directors had approved a programme of
electrification and dieselisation which was to sweep away all
steam traction from the Eastern and Central sections of the
company by 1955. The hint was also dropped at the time of the
announcement that consideration was being given to extending
diesel-electric traction to the West of England. Within a year the
order for three such main line express locomotives had been
placed, their operational orbit being described as Waterloo–
Plymouth.

To hazard a guess, therefore, at events had BR not come into
existence it is suggested that, with the Eastern and Central
sections steamless by 1955, dieselisation of the West of England
route could have been accomplished by the same date, to be
followed by electrification of the Bournemouth line in 1958 and
the complete withdrawal of steam traction, if not concurrently,
at least by 1960. The *Merchant Navy* engines would have been
redundant by 1958 owing to lack of suitable traffic on unre-
stricted routes.

The next 'might-have-been' concerns detail rather than
principle and relates to the counter-order, in October 1947, by
the Government of conversion from coal to oil firing. Told, in
August 1946, to convert locomotives as quickly as possible the
Southern Railway selected, in the initial batch of 110 conver-

sions, twenty members of the *West Country* class. In the event
two were converted before the scheme had to be abandoned:
had the alteration been made to all twenty and the summary dis-
continuance not arisen it is not too fanciful to contemplate the
conversion of all the Pacifics to this type of fuel.

Shortly after nationalisation occurred (and possibly when the
construction programme for the diesel-electric locomotives was
retarded) consideration was given to installing water troughs to
allow non-stop running between Waterloo and Exeter and
between Waterloo and Bournemouth. So far as is known, no
Merchant Navy type tender was equipped with water pick-up
gear, although drawings might have been prepared for the purpose. Certainly plans for siting of water troughs existed: these
indicated proposed locations were Farnborough, Milborne
Port and west of Millbrook. The call for non-stop running to
Exeter was never great and the weight of such traffic really did
not warrant constructing the facilities at Milborne Port. The
Farnborough location was complementary to that at Milborne
Port although it would have been useful for Bournemouth
services. The duration of the stop at Southampton made by fast
trains could have been lessened if the Millbrook troughs had
been put in, and this also would have applied to the Portsmouth–
Salisbury and Bournemouth–Oxford services. However, the
installation would have been a luxury, as none of these services
was likely to omit the Southampton stop, and so it is not surprising nothing came of the investigation.

By 1958 reconsideration of future modes of traction on the
West of England main line must have been made because of the
decision to take the opportunity in the relining of Buckhorn
Weston tunnel (between Gillingham and Templecombe) to
lower the track formation—so as to obtain sufficient headroom
for overhead electric traction wires—despite the prolonged dis-
location of traffic which arose from the work. In retrospect the
proposition of an electric locomotive flashing through this tunnel appears more than a little whimsical but, in 1958, hopes
were obviously high. 1973 was the suggested date for electrification preceded by diesel-electric traction (once again!) in
1962.

In the summer of 1959 the first phase of the Kent Coast
electrification works was completed and modification of both

classes of Pacific was in full spate. Obviously steam traction was intended to last a long time. The plan, very simply, was to move progressively westwards with steam and, after the eventual Bournemouth electrification, to concentrate the most modern units in the 72 shed group with its headquarters at Exmouth Junction. Because the modified light Pacifics were not permitted to operate to Ilfracombe a stud of the original small design would remain.

At the start of the winter timetable in 1961 the schedule of the *Atlantic Coast Express* was cut to under three hours between Waterloo and Exeter. With the large number of locomotives recently rebuilt (mid-1961 saw the *West Country* class modification programme completed) thoughts, both within and without the railway service, turned to what might be achieved with this seeming excess of power. One of the external proposals propounded a regular interval service between London and Exeter with three-hour trains leaving Waterloo on the odd hours and at the even hours fast trains departing to serve the principal intermediate towns; dovetailed between would be smartly timed feeder services calling at all stations.

Although such a radical new timetable was not adopted, some very enterprising schedules were formulated internally to go forward for sanction for inclusion in the 1963 service. These included the acceleration of the 9.00 a.m. from Waterloo to Exeter to the unprecedented time of 2 hrs 48 mins inclusive of a Salisbury stop and an eleven-coach formation. The *Atlantic Coast Express* itself was to be speeded up by eight minutes to arrive at Exeter Central at 1.50 p.m. and the 7.00 p.m. down was to have had a sizeable lopping of its schedule. In the up direction there was to be a fast train leaving Exeter at 6.30 p.m. One could hardly wait for the inaugural run of the speeded-up 9.00 a.m.; but this prospect of brilliant performance was suddenly swept into oblivion one September Saturday in 1962 when Paddington awoke to find itself with a permit to kill the Salisbury–Exeter route and the fanned out tentacles beyond in recompense for the abduction of its own heritage in the Birmingham area. The 1963 accelerated timetable was one of the hardest 'might-have-beens' to have to forego.

The transfer of Exmouth Junction shed to the Western Region upset the Southern's steam motive power plans completely and some units returned eastwards in due course. Gone was the idea of a Southern steam élite in the West. After this blow there was more than enough modern steam power available for the Bournemouth services, and as a consequence no haste was evident in sanctioning electrification of that route. Had the Southern held sway in the West it is likely that Bournemouth would have seen a full electric service by 1966.

Finally the London Midland region cast envious eyes on the *Merchant Navy* locomotives and wanted no less than the whole class transferred to its jurisdiction. The pride of the Southern remained in the south, however, and no opportunity to see them regularly in action over Shap occurred. And, if none of these possibilities provide a spur to the imagination, then consideration might be given to what course events could have taken if it was the managerial chair at Waterloo, instead of that at Paddington, which had to accommodate, in 1962, Mr S. E. Raymond.

Chapter 4

HOW BAD WERE THESE ENGINES?

Critics of the Southern Pacifics appear to fall into one of three categories: those who consider both original and modified designs to be of little merit; those who acclaim the modified design and consider it overcame the considerable (to them) shortcomings of the original design; and those who affirm that the rebuilds were useless compared with the pure Bulleid design. Not unnaturally some of the arguments put forward by these various critics tend to cancel one another out. Nonetheless an examination of the major points of criticism may be made to see just how bad the engines were.

Slipping
The engines slipped very badly on starting and also at speed.

To this charge the plea of guilty is entered in respect of both original and modified types. But this is not so much a characteristic peculiar to the Southern Pacifics; it is inherent in high-powered Pacifics and *Mountain*-type locomotives the world over. On starting, weight is transferred to the rear of the machine, supported by the trailing axle, and the driving wheels 'lift' due to loss of adhesion. The lighter the engine the worse the problem, unless it is a low-powered locomotive. Because of weight limitations the two Bulleid designs, and indeed the subsequent rebuilt engines, were at a distinct disadvantage in this respect. The designer could not have it all ways, however, and to obtain high route availability (which was outstandingly attained with the light Pacifics) the adhesion factor had to be sacrificed.

Were the Southern Pacifics so much worse than any other 4–6–2 then? There is no proved technical comparative basis for measurement of slipping that can be applied to the case, so that one has to fall back on judgement (which so often is coupled with bias!) to provide an answer. The first British Pacific—the GWR *Great Bear*—is reported to have been a bad 'slipper'. The

Gresley designed 4–6–2s were by no means immune from this failing, nor were the LMSR engines of that wheel arrangement, as reference to the columns of the *Railway Magazine* will show. During 1944, 1954 and 1960 the subject was well ventilated therein and although variations existed according to the location there are on record some interesting observations. Two weeks' noting of the start of a train from Rugby platform 1 (gradient of 1 in 365 in favour) produced no clean start, even on a dry rail, with LMS *Duchesses*. Matters became so bad on the Eastern Region that an instruction was issued to drivers not to exceed 50 per cent cut-off on starting and, although considerable improvement was effected with the BR *Britannia* type, the LNER types did not benefit very much.

Probably the worst record of any was of a *Duchess* slipping for almost *one hour* (yes! hour) at Liverpool Lime Street trying to leave with a London train. The Southern engines used to slip, but the authorities took immediate action: for example, no. 7 platform at London Bridge was on a rising gradient and sharply curved and could cause trouble to London-bound trains which called there in the morning rush-hour. Ramsgate-based light Pacifics would sometimes have difficulty in starting and, if a shovel or two of sand from the sand box on the platform was of no avail, the following electric train was called forward to assist in the rear. The delay was seldom more than five minutes. When electric traction took over all traffic the stop was omitted!

Bearing in mind the Bulleid *Merchant Navy* class had 63 tons of adhesion, compared with 66 for LNER and 67 for LMS types, their propensity for slipping was really no worse than could be expected. It was the LMS engines which came out of it worst.

All this has dealt with slipping on starting. 'Ah!' says the critic, 'but what about slipping at speed?' (Thank you, sir, for admitting the speed—it was, like the slipping, not to be ignored!) It cannot be denied that both original and rebuilt Southern Pacifics slipped at speed, especially when climbing. 'Once they start slipping, and lose something of their way on a gradient, it seems that nothing can help them to regain mastery', wrote O. S. Nock in 1960, not of the SR machines, but, again, of the LMS *Duchess* class. Both of these types had a reputation for slipping at speed, more so than other 4–6–2s, with the difference that the Southern locomotives had bouts of slipping

rather than a continuous period of trouble, and to some extent
this may be traced to the chain-type valve gear. Usually these
slips at speed did not lead to great inconvenience except when
engineers wanted to take records. It has been suggested that
leaks from the oil-bath promoted this slipping at speed, from
which it might be inferred that the permanent way was very
oily. Many miles of walking alongside the track have never produced any evidence of this, although it did occur on the Rugby
Testing Plant where the locomotive was stationary and the oil
perforce accumulated in a small area.

Lightweight 4-8-2s in Czechoslovakia are also prone to
slipping at speed, and this appears to stem from the same causes
as slipping upon starting. Various remedies have been put forward to overcome this trouble, including equalised suspension,
but those who have had any experience of the Central of Peru
4-8-2s of 110 class, which were so fitted and were the most
notorious of 'slippers', will remain more than sceptical.

Eventually the oil-baths were made tight and so eliminated
trouble from that direction, and latterly little was heard of
slipping at speed with the original design. In any case its
occurrence was rare enough not to hinder day-to-day running.

Poor Steaming

Occasionally there were spells of poor steaming but usually this
was not a fault of the classes in either original or modified condition. There have been times when a depot has had a batch of
unsuitable coal—Nine Elms did once and timekeeping was
poor for a couple of weeks—or when inexperience in firing was
the cause. Generally, however, the boiler has been considered
the strong point of the locomotives, although the damper
arrangements were not always ideal.

Heavy on Repairs

It has often been inferred that the Southern Pacifics were heavy
on repairs. At one particular period this was probably fostered
by a diligent observer at Brighton, who used to record when
Pacifics entered the works there and publish his findings. These
nearly always resulted (and this is no reflection on the observer's
work whatsoever) in showing that the few 4-6-2s allocated to
Brighton were going into works almost monthly! The point of

this was that Brighton shed had a splendid gang of cleaners but few fitters and, to help out with minor running-shed repairs, the works would take an engine in for a day or two to remedy a defect.

A rather more reliable guide is the evidence given in a paper by R. C. Bond (then Chief Officer, Locomotive Construction and Maintenance, BR) to the Institution of Locomotive Engineers. For the year 1951 the average distance run between general overhauls was given, for some typical express types, as:

Type	Mileage
Eastern Region A1 4–6–2 (then almost new)	93,363
Western Region *Castle* 4–6–0	87,424
Eastern Region A4 4–6–2	86,614
Southern Region *Lord Nelson* 4–6–0	81,611
Western Region *King* 4–6–0	78,987
Southern Region *Merchant Navy* 4–6–2	75,687
Southern Region *West Country* 4–6–2	74,650
London Midland Region *Duchess* 4–6–2	73,188
London Midland Region Rebuilt *Royal Scot* 4–6–0	70,495
London Midland Region Class 5 4–6–0	56,969

Another source of information is the Eastleigh Works weekly record sheets in which the mileage was obviously compiled on a different classification of repairs basis to that above. In January 1960 unmodified No. 34069 entered works having run 305,808 miles since the last general repair and at the same time BR Standard class 5 came in with 173,165 miles (a good average for this type) to its credit. It must, however, in fairness be stated that the average for the *West Country* class was in the region of 225,000 miles.

Other mileages (picked at random) are:

35001 original condition June 1956	361,312
35027 rebuilt condition October 1963	375,836
34021 rebuilt condition October 1963	230,063
34105 original condition March 1956	309,545

The Eastleigh figures generally indicated better mileages for the *Merchant Navy* class than the smaller engines whether rebuilt or not.

The verdict must surely be that the Southern Pacifics were

neither the best nor the worst in the matter of workshop attention but about average.

Poor Availability

It was at times said that the Southern had so many Pacifics that
it could cover up the poor availability of the classes by substitu-
tions. At some depots this would be possible but generally it was
not true. What in fact would happen was that the 'good' sheds had
no need to cover in this way, while the 'bad' sheds (there were
some) never had any serviceable for covering anyhow! Everything hinged on the degree of maintenance handed out to the
engines.

To cite long lists of dates in this connection would be tedious
but, as an example, the 7.44 a.m. from Tonbridge (starting from
Ramsgate) to Charing Cross was noted for several years and
usually the same engine would appear throughout the week. In
one period, from 7 May to 27 June 1951, No. 34098 appeared
thirty-three times out of a possible thirty-five (there is no
evidence available to indicate if it was 'stopped' or merely
working another duty on the two days absent).

Poor availability was not the fault of the engines but if it
arose it was usually from other causes.

Uneconomical on Fuel

The original design incorporating the oil-bath for the valve
gear was expensive in oil due to leakage until matters were recti-
fied. More oil was lost than was used.

Coal consumption could at times be high as figures arising
from the Locomotive Interchanges indicated. This aspect, together with water consumption, is dealt with elsewhere in the
present volume.

Rebuilding of the engines had as one of its aims the reduction
in fuel consumption. Oil consumption was certainly reduced
but figures available for coal consumption are not impressive.
Also the water stops at Southampton Central still took place
even with engines not working west of Bournemouth.

Neither in original nor rebuilt form were the classes the most
economical of steam locomotives in so far as fuel consumption
was concerned.

Inaccessibility for Repairs

The criticism of inaccessibility for repairs is valid in so far as the idea of encasing parts of the locomotives—which was deliberate—failed on occasions. The valve gear was designed to be inaccessible in its oil-bath casing but, when it needed attention more than envisaged at design stage, this became a drawback.

The main air-smoothed sheeting was designed to be taken off as a complete unit, and the U-shape of it seen inverted on Eastleigh works floor on various occasions testifies to this. The snags came when small portions had to be removed for some purpose or other. All designs have some drawbacks of this nature and the Bulleid Pacifics proved no exception to the general rule.

The Valve Gear was Unsuccessful

The valve gear was not unsuccessful: rather it was a case of the degree of its success. The design of the chain valve gear was not the first choice (which was something more on the lines of poppet valve gear and had to be abandoned because of the difficulty of obtaining suitable gears during war time), being merely a substitute, and so it is in the light of that circumstance that the criticism should be made.

Various snags developed with the chains, although the manufacturer (a private commercial undertaking) denied that stretching of the links or chains was possible. What precisely—in view of this denial—was the fault is not clear but tangible evidence of something being amiss could be obtained from the stacks of discarded chains at some running sheds. The drawbacks were not sufficiently acute to demand the complete abandonment of the valve gear until rebuilding took place under BR direction.

The Steam Reverser was a Failure

It would be foolish to deny that the steam reverser was anything but a failure. The lack of accurate setting of the reverser in any engine other than one recently ex-shops caused the enginemen to fall back on driving on the regulator, with consequent higher coal consumption, and to playing things very much by ear. Early on in the life of the locomotives efforts were made to see if the fitting might be superseded but no reasonable solution was arrived at. As one engineman has said, 'I don't know why they had to rebuild the engines; all they needed was a decent reverser and they would have been fine'. And that about sums it up.

Where then do the Southern Pacifics stand in relation to other steam passenger locomotives of this country ?

The basic requirement of a passenger motive power unit is to move its load from point to point punctually and as economically as possible. The Southern Pacifics seldom, of themselves, failed the punctuality test, which was what mattered from the fare-paying passenger's point of view, as indeed it did from the operating viewpoint. And that could outweigh a lot of economic niceties.

To make an assessment of the Southern Pacifics of necessity requires judgement to be passed on the rival 4–6–2 classes and it invites the wrath of all 'blind' supporters of the other contenders. Here then, for better or worse, is such an assessment:

1. LNER A4
2. LMSR *Duchess*
3. BR(ER) A1 with roller bearings
4. SR *Merchant Navy* (in either form)
5. BR(ER) A1
6. LMSR 6200–12 class
7. LNER A3
8. SR *West Country* (unmodified)
9. SR *West Country* (modified)
10. BR *Britannia*

A few explanations may not be out of place if only in defence of the choice. The A4 class heads the list because of what it did and how it did it. Of all modern classes, the A4 was the one which was exploited almost to the limit and in so doing produced some superlative work. The place should have been claimed by the large LMS locomotives, but because they were not called upon to fulfil their potentiality with any regularity and because of their slipping characteristics they cannot take the premier place. They had the misfortune to operate over a line of poor timekeeping reputation and their grates were just too large for optimum hand-firing (despite a coal-pusher).

The BR(ER) A1 class edges in front of the *Merchant Navy*

class in respect only of the roller-bearing equipped members of the class, a refinement which proved very economical and reliable. The A1 class was a very much under-rated locomotive, or perhaps under-appreciated. The modified *West Country* class drops a place because of its lesser route availability upon rebuilding. The BR *Clan* class 4-6-2 and the LNER A2 variants and—worst of all—class A1/1 are very much 'also rans'. A rebuilt *Royal Scot* and a *King* could squeeze in between the LNER A3 and the original *West Country* design. Had the *Merchant Navy* class been fitted with roller-bearings the third place would have been taken by Bulleid's large creation.

Chapter 5

PERFORMANCE AND EFFICIENCY TESTS

Alone of the grouped companies the Southern Railway possessed neither dynamometer car nor stationary plant for locomotive testing purposes. Even if Bulleid had been inclined to obtain the former and less expensive item, it would have been extremely unlikely that the electrification-orientated SR board would have sanctioned expenditure on a vehicle which would have had nothing more than intermittent use. As it happened, Bulleid's designs came out during a war when the manpower situation was such that, had the car been available, it would not have been possible to expend a lot of time testing.

In the absence, therefore, of testing facilities assessments were made of the capabilities of the *Merchant Navy* class initially by running special non-revenue earning trains over selected routes to fast schedules. Little appears to have been attempted during the first few years when the wartime traffic and restrictions would have conspired against any fast non-stop running. In 1945 No. 21C2 was tried on a 116-minute non-stop timing from Waterloo to Bournemouth, with a seventeen-coach train weighing 517 tons. After passing Clapham Junction there was fine acceleration to 68 m.p.h. by Malden, rising to 77 m.p.h. at Walton-on-Thames, cut short by signals on the approach to Woking. Recovery from 30 m.p.h. on the rising grade was steady (48 m.p.h. at Brookwood and 54 m.p.h. at milepost 31); Worting Junction was cleared two minutes early in 52 minutes from Waterloo. The driver was content with a maximum of 80 m.p.h. down to Winchester—probably the highest speed generally allowable in view of the permanent way maintenance arrears—but even so Southampton Central was passed in 79½ minutes from the start. A slight signal check occurred at Totton and, for some unexplained reason, speed at Lymington Junction was reduced to under 45 m.p.h., although the top of

Sway bank was carried at 55 m.p.h. Elapsed time to Bournemouth Central was 112¾ minutes. With allowance for delays the net time works out at 109 minutes for the 108 miles, a creditable figure considering the load.

The same engine was not loaded so heavily (454 tons) for a 90-minute run from Victoria to Dover Marine: by Orpington 5½ minutes had been gained on the 26-minute schedule, but some of this was lost by a signal check before Sevenoaks, passed in 32 minutes. To reach Tonbridge occupied 39½ minutes, and, after a p.w. repair slack at Paddock Wood, speed soared into the eighty range. Pass-to-pass the 24·8 miles from Marden to Westenhanger occupied 18¾ minutes with a maximum speed of 86 m.p.h. near Pluckley. The minimum was just under 70 m.p.h. at Westenhanger, which was passed in 67½ minutes from Victoria. The conclusion to the run included another repair restriction and a dead stand for signals but, even so, the elapsed time was no more than 85 minutes (or 77½ minutes net) for the 78 miles.

Later two test runs were conducted between Exeter Central and Salisbury. The first train was powered by No. 21C14 loaded to twelve vehicles (389 tons) and, without producing fireworks, ran the distance in 86 minutes including signal checks in the Crewkerne locality. Net time works out at 82 minutes for the 88 miles. The second run was an extraordinary affair: No. 21C13, with a ten-coach load (325 tons), shot out of Exeter, passing Exmouth Junction in less than 3½ minutes, and was through Axminster in under 'even time' notwithstanding Honiton bank. This, according to the record, was due in part to a speed of 96 m.p.h. downhill from the tunnel which, bearing in mind the curve near the foot, must have been a hair-raising episode. Chard Junction was cleared in 30½ minutes from the start, Crewkerne in 37¼ for a stop to be made at Yeovil Junction in 44¼ minutes for the 48·9 miles. The continuation to Salisbury, with a couple of speed restrictions thrown in, was nothing like so mettlesome and calls for no remark.

With nationalisation came the Interchange trials of 1948. In many ways these were conducted on a haphazard basis—indeed a member of the BR Locomotive Testing Committee has summed it up in the term 'hit-and-miss'—with ordinary trains to generally unexacting schedules being used for test purposes.

Uniform instructions regarding the method of driving do not appear to have been considered, still less given to the crews. Some of the enginemen, such as a SR pair away from home, seem to have been encouraged to run hard and fast whilst others, from the London Midland region in particular, were acting as though orders had been given to save coal by not exerting the engines unduly, except downhill when dropped time might be regained without raising coal consumption unduly. Delays were encountered in such numbers on the West Coast route as to question the worthwhile nature of the operation, for surely BR did not propose to model their services on the punctuality standard of that particular line.

The performance of the Southern engines (*Merchant Navy* class Nos. 35017, 35018 and 35019 and *West Country* class Nos. 34004, 34005 and 34006) will be found in the relevant performance sections hereinafter, except that the Waterloo–Exeter trains are not detailed because the running was no more than typical of day-to-day operating.

Data relating to coal and water consumption, evaporation rates and power outputs have been published, and these may be conveniently examined, not in isolation, but in conjunction with the figures returned by the other contestants in the interchange trials.

When compared with the other contestants the Southern engines did not return very flattering figures for either coal or water consumption. An examination of the average evaporation rate figures, however, indicate that the fault did not lie with the

AVERAGE WATER CONSUMPTION FIGURES

Class		lb per drawbar horsepower hour
LNER	A4	24·32
LMSR	Rebuilt *Royal Scot*	25·81
LMSR	*Duchess*	27·08
LNER	B1	27·64
LMSR	Class 5	27·99
GWR	*King*	28·58
GWR	*Hall*	29·97
SR	*Merchant Navy*	30·43
SR	*West Country*	32·64

AVERAGE COAL CONSUMPTION FIGURES

Class		lb per drawbar horsepower hour
LNER	A4	3·06
LMSR	*Duchess*	3·12
LMSR	Rebuilt *Royal Scot*	3·38
LMSR	Class 5	3·54
GWR	*King*	3·57
LNER	B1	3·59
SR	*Merchant Navy*	3·60
GWR	*Hall*	3·94
SR	*West Country*	4·11

AVERAGE EVAPORATION RATE (lb OF WATER PER lb OF COAL) FIGURES

Class		Western Region	Eastern Region	London Midland Region	Southern (or Scottish) Region
GWR	*King*	7·41	8·73		
LNER	A4	7·73	7·76	8·18	8·01
LMSR	*Duchess*	9·03	8·45	8·59	8·61
LMSR	Rebuilt *Royal Scot*	7·60	7·55	7·42	8·24
SR	*Merchant Navy*	8·67	7·99	8·49	8·65
GWR	*Hall*	7·92	7·46		
LNER	B1	7·52	7·82	8·25	7·11
LMSR	Class 5	7·77	7·93	7·70	8·27
SR	*West Country*	7·95	7·81	8·85	7·13

boiler. The *Merchant Navy* figures compared well with those of the *Duchess*, with the *West Country* class not far behind. This points to a weakness in steam distribution in the Southern engines with the steam raising capacity of the boiler more than adequate for the purpose.

Great stress appears to have been placed on the fuel consumption figures and, although economy in working is a most desirable feature, it was odd that no comment was deemed necessary regarding an important facet of locomotive performance—timekeeping. In this respect, so far as can be gathered from external sources, because the official report does not help much, the Southern engines were good, with the timetable usually being honoured. The smaller Southern class did at times gain on the schedule to unusual extents (for example about 10 minutes between Taunton and Bristol) although this conferred no bonus points in the official reckoning. It would be nice to think that the railway authorities could persuade a passenger on the Marylebone–Manchester route, for example, to agree that his arrival 25 minutes late behind a class 5 engine was of more merit than a one minute early arrival behind *West Country* No. 34006 because the coal consumption had not been so great! Yet this is the implication in the report. From the public's point of view the timetable should be adhered to even if it requires greater fuel consumption.

Of all the classes taking part in the interchanges the one which constantly rose above its accepted performance level was the *West Country* 4-6-2. There are twenty-two records of equivalent drawbar horsepower figures in excess of 1700 (these exclude transitory figures) and of these no less than *eight* were provided by *West Country* engines including the *three highest*. Of the nine highest, eight were from the Southern Pacifics, which figure in the remarkable total of *fourteen* out of the twenty-two. Totals by classes were:

West Country	8
Merchant Navy	6
Duchess	6
A4	1
Rebuilt *Royal Scot*	1

The occasions when these figures were returned are indicated in the following table:

MAXIMUM EQUIVALENT DRAWBAR HORSEPOWER
(OTHER THAN TRANSITORY)
RECORDED DURING INTERCHANGE TRIALS

E.d.h.p.	Class	Location	Date (1948)
2010	*West Country*	Whetstone	11 June
1962	*West Country*	Annesley	8 June
1950	*West Country*	Druimuachdar	16 July
1929	*Merchant Navy*	Penrith—Shap	12 May
1920	*Merchant Navy*	Penrith—Shap	14 May
1912	*West Country*	Druimuachdar	14 July
1865	*Duchess*	Dainton	20 May
1860	*Merchant Navy*	Penrith—Shap	14 May
1835	*Merchant Navy*	Tebay—Shap	13 May
1825	*Duchess*	Bruton	21 May
1817	*Duchess*	Rattery	20 May
1790	*Merchant Navy*	Porton	2 June
1790	*West Country*	Etteridge	14 July
1782	Rebuilt *Royal Scot*	Crewkerne	18 June
1777	*West Country*	Wendover	9 June

1775	*Duchess*	Wrenthorpe	6 May
1740	*Duchess*	Hampole	6 May
1735	*Duchess*	Wrenthorpe	4 May
1730	*West Country*	Slochd	16 July
1728	A4	Rattery	4 May
1715	*West Country*	Stoke Canon	23 July
1710	*Merchant Navy*	Tebay—Shap	13 May

It is not implied that the Southern classes were the only ones capable of these high performances, as obviously the *Duchess* and A4 locomotives would be able to match them. The point is that, during the course of the trials, the *Duchess* and A4 classes did not do so to the same extent as the Bulleid designs, and this provides a clue to their more economical fuel consumption returns. The Southern engines—in particular the *West Country* representatives—were working above optimum level, which incidentally put no strain on the boiler, and consequently were harder on fuel. The Southern attitude seemed to be one of 'show off the prowess', and if any proof was needed the half-dozen equivalent drawbar horsepower figures in excess of 1900 provided it. So far as is known, these figures have not been collated in this manner before and consequently the Southern Pacifics' outstanding achievement in the trials has tended to have been passed over.

So much for the 'hit-and-miss' trials. Not unnaturally the Southern Pacifics, in the shape of the *Merchant Navy* class, were selected for further tests. These were conducted in three stages and at different times thus:

Series	Type	Date
1	As designed	March–November 1952
2	Having modified chimney and blastpipe	March–May 1953
3	Boiler without thermic syphons	December 1953–January 1954

Three types of coal were used: South Kirkby, Grade 1A and Blidworth, Grade 2B were fired on controlled road tests and on the test plant at Rugby in series 1; Bedwas, Grade 2A, described as friable with a considerable amount of small coal and fines—as normally used by SR Pacifics—was also used for plant tests. Series 2 and 3 were made using Blidworth coal.

For these tests, conducted at the Rugby Locomotive Testing station and between Carlisle and Skipton for the controlled road tests, the locomotive selected was No. 35022. This engine ran 1,115 miles after a classified repair before arriving at Rugby; for series 1 the mileage was 10,300 at Rugby and 3,840 on the road tests; for series 2 at Rugby 2,460 miles were 'run'. For series 3 the locomotive underwent a light repair, ran 1,140 miles before entering Rugby testing station and then clocked up 2,820 miles on test.

Having got No. 35022 to Rugby the testing engineers found considerable difficulty in carrying out the tests, so much so that the official report records that '. . . the test results cannot be regarded in all respects as being soundly established . . . must be taken as a general representation . . . rather than exact results'. This arose from the Achilles' heel of the design—the valve gear. The actual cut-off could not be related at all to the setting of the reversing gear, certainly for the locomotive as an entity and still less for individual cylinders. There was a tendency for the actual mean cut-off to lengthen with an increase in speed, albeit in an irregular manner. Random changes in cut-off occurred to no particular pattern and the power output on some occasions was theoretically impossible had the cut-off registered been correct. The reversing gear could not be prevented from creeping very slightly even by adjustment on the footplate, so to obtain uniform testing conditions, special clamped distance pieces had to be fitted for plant tests. Additionally, these speed fluctuations caused trouble with the plant's brake control system.

A further matter for concern was the leaking of oil from the oil-bath encasing the valve gear. This got onto the wheels and the plant rollers and induced some bad slips in which buckling of the coupling rods occurred, a far from pleasant happening within the confines of the testing station. Normally the locomotive in traffic did not stay still and the dropping of a large quantity of oil in one place would not arise, and in that case the testing station did not deal with a typical situation. Because of this slipping propensity it was deemed expedient not to attempt to find the limit of the boiler capacity.

On the plant tests were carried out at various constant

rates of evaporation, combustion and speed (between 15 and 85 m.p.h.). The regulator was fully open for most tests with cut-off nominally in the range of 10–50 per cent.

No more than 29,000 lb/hr as steaming rate was required to work to time a twenty-coach (594-ton) test train over the Carlisle–Skipton route, which load, incidentally, is stated to include the largest number of bogie coaches to be worked as one train over that road. At Aisgill, coming south with this train, the speed was 28 m.p.h. with a maximum of 73 m.p.h. near Lazonby.

The results and conclusions drawn from the series 1 tests were:

(a) Maximum steaming rates were sustained as follows:

With Blidworth coal	33,300 lb/hr
With Bedwas coal	37,000 lb/hr
With South Kirkby coal	39,000 lb/hr (for over an hour)
	42,000 lb/hr (for 20 minutes)

The limit could not be ascertained although the figure of 42,000 lb/hr is not far off the discharge limit of the multiple-jet blastpipe.

(b) The lowest specific steam consumption was just under 15·9 lb/IHP hr against figures between 13·2 and 13·8 for a variety of comparable locomotives.

(c) 'It is a most effective and capable engine but one that is relatively uneconomical. If operating, as they frequently are in service, with the reversing gear in a relatively long cut-off and with the regulator very little open, these locomotives will be still less economical. . . . The vibration, associated with full regulator and very short cut-off working, is also avoided.'

(d) '. . . combustion was never very good. . . . There was evidence that wider spacing of the grate bars and the provision of a deflector plate and admission of rather more air through the firehole door, with the doors closed, would effect some improvement.'

(e) Redesign of the chimney was desirable.

The last of these recommendations was acted on (as series 2) within a period of a few months and various experiments were made, mainly on empirical lines, with a single chimney. Eventually it had to be acknowledged that no variation of a single blast-pipe was as good as the multiple-jet originally fitted. No single blastpipe would allow a steaming rate of more than about 31,000 lb/hr. Additionally, it was stated that there was no evidence to suggest the multiple-jet blastpipe gave rise to the ejection of abnormally large amounts of unburnt coal from the chimney, as the losses from that cause were not seriously larger than from those of other locomotives.

Finally, in the last series of tests, no noticeable difference could be ascertained using a boiler without thermic syphons. The testing engineers were not certain whether the different brick arch necessary with a non-syphon-fitted boiler gave rise to such differences as were observed or not. This test, therefore, was inconclusive.

With the modification of the *Merchant Navy* class sanctioned and being carried out it was decided to test the redesigned model. The second engine to be dealt with, No. 35020, was accordingly allocated in mid-1956, immediately after modification, for testing. The preamble to the report is not entirely without interest, reading thus:

'Whilst the locomotives had given sterling service and demonstrated their ability to run to time, with an ample margin of power, due to their excellent steaming capabilities and free running characteristics, some of the features . . . (of design) . . . have proved troublesome, with the result that the locomotives were not entirely satisfactory from the point of view of availability. In addition, their consumption of coal, oil and water was high in comparison with other modern locomotives.'

and also

'The *Merchant Navy* class have long enjoyed a reputation for high performance under adverse traffic conditions . . .'

Much of the report was given over to an explanation of the modifications made rather than to details of the tests. What does emerge is that controlled road tests were carried out between Salisbury and Exeter in both directions, on special trains to fairly fast schedules with a highest rate of working of 32,000 lb of steam per hour with a coal rate of 4,780 lb/hr, and also service tests between Waterloo and Exeter Central on the 3.00 p.m.

ex Waterloo and 12.30 p.m. ex Exeter Central. No running details of the Salisbury–Exeter trains appear in the report, although such data does appear for the service tests. The loads (computed at tare weight plus 10 per cent) were 500 tons from Waterloo to Templecombe on 26 June, reduced to 466 tons two days later, and from Templecombe to Exeter Central 393½ tons on both occasions. On 26 June there was a late start of 1½ minutes with an arrival at Basingstoke in 51 minutes, 2½ minutes early. No great effort was made to milepost 31, speed at milepost 28 (Brookwood) being 55 m.p.h. From Basingstoke to Andover Junction 1½ minutes were dropped on the 21-minute schedule and on to Salisbury a further half-minute was lost. Speed at milepost 70 was 54 m.p.h. Matters woke up after Salisbury and, despite one severe and one slight temporary speed restriction, no more than a minute was dropped on the 34-minute hop to Templecombe. Leaving Templecombe 3½ minutes late, a minute early arrival was chalked up at Sidmouth Junction, giving a running time of 46½ minutes. Arrival at Exeter was a minute late despite another minute being wrung from the schedule of 14 minutes. Speeds were: 57½ m.p.h. at milepost 98½, 53 m.p.h. at milepost 107, 78 m.p.h. at post 124, 60 m.p.h. at post 132½ and 42 m.p.h. at milepost 152. Maximum equivalent drawbar horsepower was (west of Salisbury) 1686 at milepost 132½.

On 28 June the exit from London was not so quick despite a lesser load. Waterloo–Basingstoke occupied 54 minutes; to Andover Junction the schedule of 21 minutes was kept; and on to Salisbury there was a gain of half a minute. Speeds were 57 m.p.h. at Brookwood and 52 m.p.h. at milepost 70. The speed restrictions seem to have been more rigorously observed than on the previous test on the Templecombe length, which stretch took 37½ minutes. Five-and-a-half late away from Templecombe, No. 35020 really flew to arrive 2½ minutes early at Sidmouth Junction. The report gives 13 minutes to pass Yeovil Junction and 32 to pass Seaton Junction. Signal checks prevented a punctual arrival at Exeter Central. Speeds were 57 m.p.h. at milepost 98½; 75 at milepost 124; 80 at milepost 129, 63½ at 132½, followed by 95 at 145¾, 93 at 146¾, 74 at milepost 149 and 48½ at milepost 152. The maximum e.d.h.p. figure was 1691 at milepost 149; that at 145¾ was 1345.

The up journeys were made on the *Atlantic Coast Express*. Loads were: Exeter Central–Salisbury 399½ tons (25 June) and 436 (27 June) and 471 and 472 tons for the respective dates for the concluding section to Waterloo. Both runs were affected by temporary speed restrictions and signal checks. On 25 June Sidmouth Junction was left five minutes late and, with one slight restriction, Salisbury was reached a minute late in 75 minutes. Restarting 1½ minutes late and with a signal check at Basingstoke, No. 35020 reached Waterloo 4½ minutes late. Speeds were 42 m.p.h. at milepost 154½ (1603 e.d.h.p.); 64 m.p.h. at milepost 135½ (1328 e.d.h.p.) and 45½ m.p.h. at milepost 102 (1692 e.d.h.p.). Nothing of note occurred east of Salisbury.

The second test train got away 5½ minutes late from the Sidmouth Junction stop but had a halt for five minutes at Honiton to examine the train after a door had been found open. This gave rise to some excellent running, the arrival at Salisbury being no more than 4½ minutes behind schedule. From passing Yeovil Junction to the stop at Salisbury occupied 36 minutes: speed was 60 m.p.h. at milepost 133½ (1635 e.d.h.p.), 49 m.p.h. at milepost 103½ (1722 e.d.h.p.) and 47 m.p.h. at milepost 102 (1869 e.d.h.p.). These figures were returned with a 436-ton load. East of Salisbury the running was again not of any particular note.

Bedwas grade 2A coal, the usual fuel supplied to the Southern region, was used and the average figure of coal consumption per drawbar horsepower hour was 3·56 lb.

At this juncture it is instructive to refer to the 1948 Interchange running over the Waterloo–Exeter line with regard to the coal consumption of the contestants over the same route as the modified Pacific. The following figures indicate lb of coal per d.b.h.p. hr:

LMSR	*Duchess*	3·17
LNER	A4	3·20
LMSR	Rebuilt *Royal Scot*	3·24
SR	*Merchant Navy*	3·52
BR	Modified *Merchant Navy*	3·56

The modified locomotive certainly did not show any advance in this particular department of fuel economy.

Additional coal consumption figures (in lb per e.d.h.p. hr) for sections of the route with the modified locomotive were:

Section	25 June (Up)	26 June (Down)	27 June (Up)	28 June (Down)
Waterloo–Salisbury	3.21	3.29	3.54	3.33
Waterloo–Templecombe		3.24		
Templecombe–Exeter Central		3.97		
Waterloo–Exeter Central	3.51	3.44	3.77	3.53
Salisbury–Exeter Central	3.80	3.60	3.94	3.72

Comparative figures for the original design are:

1948	2 June (Up)	1 June (Down)	4 June (Up)	3 June (Down)
Waterloo–Exeter Central	3.44	3.44	3.49	3.72

It is not without significance that the report on the tests of the modified locomotive is silent on fuel consumption in particular and on all the other listed ills which were to be eliminated in the modified design.

Chapter 6

EASTERN SECTION
PERFORMANCE

BROMLEY SOUTH TO CHATHAM

The route from London to the Kent coast, due to its odd history of being built to London rather than from the capital, has never been an easy line to work from the traction engineer's viewpoint. Originating as the East Kent Railway and a local line, it had to adapt itself as best it could as it pushed westwards from the Medway; firstly it was compelled to make an almost frontal attack on the chalky heights overlooking Rochester and then cut across valleys cradling rivers down to the Thames and finally wend its way into the metropolis through growing suburbs. These same suburbs had to be served by local trains, the density of which services caused congestion through which main-line trains had to be threaded.

Consequently the pattern of services—with the few exceptions of businessmen's trains—was one of stops at Bromley South, Chatham, Sittingbourne and Faversham and then most stations to either Margate or Dover Priory. The *Thanet Belle* omitted some of these stops but ran to an undemanding schedule.

Soon after the advent of the light Pacifics on the route on ordinary, as opposed to boat, trains recorders discovered some lively running was happening between Bromley and Chatham. One driver in particular made his mark on the section, so much so that one tended to look upon it as the Gingell Line. It is fitting, therefore, that the opening run in Table 2 features driver Sam Gingell and No. 34066 *Spitfire*. The saw-toothed profile commences with a 1-in-95 rise from Bromley South to Bickley Junction, over which No. 34066 made a good start and then attained 51 m.p.h. in the dip before St Mary Cray Junction. Speed rose to 71 m.p.h. down the 1-in-100 to the bridge over the Cray valley and fell away on the climb up to Swanley.

An obstruction on the through line in Swanley station necessitated a diversion to the down loop and cost a minute in running but, even so, there was ample time in hand. At the bottom of the dip at the crossing of the river Darent, at Farningham Road, 80 m.p.h. was recorded and the minimum at the top of the 1-in-100 before Fawkham Junction was no less than 69 m.p.h., and on the similarly inclined length before Meopham speed did not fall below 64 m.p.h. By Sole Street the climbing is over and a descent of the 1-in-100 bank follows with a speed restriction at the foot round the curves before Rochester. There was a signal check before the junction so that eventually Sam Gingell brought his train into Chatham four minutes early.

But it was not only Gingell on this line, for a few months after this run driver George had No. 34017 with a ten-coach train which had the misfortune to be crossed over from main to local line on the 1-in-95 rise out of Bromley and, in the process, lose its feet so badly that the scheduled time of five minutes to Bickley Junction was doubled. Driver George set to remedying matters in no uncertain fashion with a ninety across the river Darent, and minima of 77, 66 and 71 m.p.h. at the three subsequent summit points, all of which exceeded those of No. 34066 with a lesser load. By Cuxton Road the train was within the schedule and amends had been well and truly made for the poor start, although signal checks spoilt the concluding mile or two into Chatham.

Detail C features Gingell again, although with No. 34065 as his steed. There was hard running throughout with Cuxton Road signal box passed in under even time so that, despite a ten-second signal stop outside Chatham, a $3\frac{1}{2}$-minute early arrival was recorded. The net time of $25\frac{1}{4}$ minutes might prove to be the fastest for the course. The same engine, but with driver Banton in charge, appears in detail D. They enjoyed the luxury of an unchecked run and so returned the fastest actual time in the table; the late start of 3 minutes from Bromley was converted to a $1\frac{1}{2}$-minute before-time arrival at Chatham.

The final run (detail E) with No. 21C135 was on the 10.35 a.m. from Victoria with a Ramsgate driver. The load was not far off 400 tons full, and although a moderate start was made the performance on the rising gradient after Farningham Road was impressive; despite a check near Cuxton Road, there was plenty of time in hand and Chatham was reached early. The larger Pacifics appeared very occasionally on these trains, and when the rebuilt engines came on the scene modernisation works were in full swing, so that Tables 2 and 3 relate solely to runs by engines of the original small design.

Westbound from Chatham was the harder proposition of the two. There was little chance to get up speed for the attack on the six-mile long Sole Street bank—mostly at 1-in-100—because of the curves at Rochester. Consequently net times were about two minutes more than in the down direction. In detail A (Table 3) No. 34102 had a comparatively light load and so had no difficulty in picking up the minute of a late start. Running was lively near Fawkham and because of this the slight check at Swanley was only remarkable in that it was not more severe. Matters were taken very easily from St Mary Cray; notwithstanding a further signal check Bromley was reached $4\frac{3}{4}$ minutes early.

No. 34092, in detail B, had the customary ten-coach train but was on a revised departure timing at Chatham, brought about by the Kent floods. A notable climb of the bank was made, especially in the initial stage, for a train of this weight. After that driver Webb did not press the engine but with a clear road and the easiest of running from St Mary Cray could not avoid stopping at Bromley $4\frac{1}{4}$ minutes early, in an actual time of $28\frac{1}{4}$ minutes.

The third of these up runs again features No. 34102, although with a normal load. The best part of the climb occurred near the summit; the maximum speed came not at Farningham Road but at St Mary Cray. Despite the permanent way slack before Bromley the arrival was $4\frac{1}{2}$ minutes early.

Driver Gingell with No. 34070 and ten coaches (detail D) had a good climb on the upper part of Sole Street incline and then flew away to 90 m.p.h. over the river Darent before getting signals at Swanley. Onwards the running was rather more decorous but did not prevent a net time of $27\frac{1}{4}$ minutes and a $1\frac{1}{2}$-minute early arrival being recorded. Finally No. 34091 with a coach extra and a relaying check found no difficulty in arriving early at Bromley.

On another occasion, recorded by Mr A. J. Baker but not tabulated here, driver Gingell and No. 34066 loaded to ten

vehicles (345 tons gross) attained 92 m.p.h. at the bottom of the
incline at Farningham Road, but because the climb to Sole
Street was not so outstanding did not return a net time of less
than 28 minutes to Bromley South.

CANNON STREET TO WHITSTABLE

The regular pattern of Kent Coast trains using Victoria as the
London terminus has been broken in the morning and evening
rush-hours for many years by a few services catering for the
City businessmen which have used the loops at Chislehurst and
made Cannon Street their terminus. There was skill required in
not running before time with these trains and, on the other
hand, not losing time. Exact timekeeping was appreciated by
operating authorities and passengers alike and over the period
of time from the introduction of the Pacifics to the commencement of electrification works beyond Gillingham the standard
was commendably high.

Not only was it important for the morning trains to be right
time, for the business fraternity looked also for timekeeping
going home. And it was usually forthcoming. The first and
second runs in Table 4 illustrate this: from Cannon Street the
local line was always used as far as Chislehurst, so that it was
unusual to have any fireworks in the first dozen miles. Both
No. 21C163 and No. 34013 were through Chatham at the
appointed time and each driver then proceeded to gain on
schedule. The unmodified engine was opened up at Rainham in
contrast to No. 34013 at Sittingbourne, where the eighty
mark was passed. Both trains arrived early at the first stop,
which in the case of the run on 12 June 1959 was especially
gratifying seeing that it was the last time the train was to be
operated by steam traction—a fine finish to many years of competent operation.

The third run, detail C in Table 4, was altogether different.
The fire which burnt out Cannon Street signal box in April
1957 caused various emergency arrangements to be put into
force, one of which was for the 4.44 p.m. train from the terminus
to start from platform 1 at London Bridge at 4.46 p.m. On the
day in question the empty stock arrived late, causing the departure to be 11½ minutes behind time, in heavy rain of tropical

nature and poor visibility. The only bright spot on this otherwise dreary evening was that the driver was Sam Gingell. He soon demonstrated that despite all setbacks he would run where he could: initially there was a dead stand for signals before Hither Green, followed by further signal checks at St Mary Cray Junction and Swanley. He got his eighty at Farningham Road then suffered a very severe check, caused by a U1 class 2-6-0 shunting empty stock at Sole Street, before chalking up another eighty down the bank. The Medway towns produced the usual cautionary signals, plus a dead stand, but this did not daunt Sam, who got 92 m.p.h. out of No. 34081 before delivering his Faversham passengers at their home station rather later than usual. At least they could not say he had not tried. Net time is difficult to assess but is probably in the region of 56 minutes.

VICTORIA TO DOVER MARINE

This was the route for which the *Merchant Navy* class was designed to haul 600-ton trains to a 60 m.p.h. schedule. That this was never achieved was due to one or two factors; with the exception of the *Night Ferry* no train loaded to 600 tons (this would have required trains composed of about seventeen vehicles which could not have been handled at Victoria Eastern) and, secondly, the traffic department never required operation at 60 m.p.h. Probably the nearest approach to this performance was one of the test runs by No. 21C2 in 1945, when a train of 455 tons was taken down to Dover in $77\frac{1}{2}$ minutes net. That the era of electric traction has not ushered in a 60 m.p.h. timing for the boat trains is some indication that the performance specification had been pitched unnecessarily high, although this is not to say that isolated runs of that calibre could not have been made. To become a matter of daily occurrence would have been well-nigh impossible, even if it had been desirable.

By the time *Channel Packet* appeared the war had put paid to its debut being made on the *Golden Arrow*, but eventually the boat trains returned: at first on 100-minute schedules, later pared down to 95 and 92 minutes, the light Pacifics worked the trains in company with the larger engines, without causing undue concern if a *Merchant Navy* was not available for one of the duties. Table 5 indicates the ease with which both classes handled the 450-ton trains without having recourse to any speed higher than 78 m.p.h. The climb by No. 35028 to Sydenham Hill was very creditable, the speed being 33 m.p.h. at the top of the 1-in-101 climb. There are some awkward pitches in the suburban area coupled with speed restrictions so that it was Dunton Green, about twenty miles from the start, before any speed could be made, and this possibly was one reason why mile-a-minute schedules have never come into force.

On the run under the head of detail B so much time was in hand that *West Country* No. 34091 had to coast down from Westenhanger to avoid an embarrassing early arrival. As it was it put in an appearance 6¾ minutes early!

CHARING CROSS TO FOLKESTONE CENTRAL

The principal task on the route from London to Folkestone lay in the climb out of the London basin to the summit in the North Downs—eleven miles with long stretches at the ruling grade of 1-in-120. From Knockholt to Dunton Green is a good downhill spin before a 1½-mile climb to the north portal of Sevenoaks tunnel, after which occurs the racing ground down the 1-in-122 to Tonbridge. Undulating for 25 miles to Ashford, the route then rises to a summit slightly east of Westenhanger before falling into Folkestone.

There was seldom opportunity to get a run at the rise, as witness the runs in Table 6. Checks bedevilled driver Croucher with No. 34079 on the Saturdays-only 12.55 p.m. from Charing Cross (detail A) so that speed was not higher than 44 m.p.h. at the end of the first 1-in-120 rise. A good recovery was made and Orpington was passed at 62 m.p.h.—a good figure—and Knockholt at 53 m.p.h., which was excellent. Matters were well in hand and needed the restraining influence of Tonbridge signalmen to act as a corrective. Even so, the train was still early at Paddock Wood and had to be eased at Pluckley to avoid running too early. Arrival at Folkestone was 3¾ minutes early, the minimum at Westenhanger being 61 m.p.h., the speed having been entirely within the 60–73 m.p.h. bracket for 35 miles between Paddock Wood and Shorncliffe.

No. 34075, in detail B, had a similar loading and did not suffer checks so badly as No. 34079 but did not put up so good a

performance to Knockholt. East of Tonbridge checks demanded
—and produced—harder running to give a net time of $69\frac{1}{2}$
minutes for the 69·2 miles from Waterloo. A rebuilt engine,
No. 34022, figures in detail C. Although having the same load
as the two unmodified engines, it did not match their performance on the climb, possibly because of an easier schedule. There
was a high speed of 82 m.p.h. at Paddock Wood but little else to
remark upon.

Finally, No. 34076, another locomotive in original form, had
a train heavier by one coach, and driver Shelvey, of Ramsgate,
enjoyed an unchecked exit from the metropolis. He did not
waste this opportunity and climbed well to Elmstead Woods.
The engineering works at Orpington hindered the ascent to
Knockholt, although at no time was the train behind schedule.
The gallop down to Tonbridge produced 82 m.p.h. and beyond
that junction speed was rather higher than the schedule demanded. Net time to Ashford works out at $59\frac{1}{2}$ minutes. Ashford to Shorncliffe occupied no more than 16 minutes for a
further gain to engine and crew of a minute, thus bettering the
rebuilt engine's time, despite the additional coach.

TONBRIDGE TO ASHFORD

On the Folkestone road the counterpart of the Chatham line's
Bromley–Chatham section is undoubtedly the Tonbridge–
Ashford length, not so much in the gradient profile as in the
nature of a sprint over a section of about 25 miles. On starting
from Tonbridge there is a climb at 1-in-258 for over a mile,
then a drop at a similar inclination to Paddock Wood; a rising
tendency to a summit a little beyond Marden follows, then a
couple of miles level before Headcorn precedes a rise (nothing
steeper than 1-in-244) to milepost 49 with a $1\frac{1}{4}$ mile long drop to
Pluckley, followed by a further rise to milepost $54\frac{3}{4}$ and concluding with a gentle descent to Ashford. Given a good start,
therefore, the locomotive can be worked up to speed over these
undulations.

The first run in Table 7 concerns unrebuilt No. 34098 on a
ten-coach train. Unfortunately the recorder rounded off the
speeds to 5 m.p.h. and therefore these have not been given. It is
evident, however, from the other runs that the line limit of

85 m.p.h. must have been attained for such passing and finishing times to have been recorded. On the second run (detail B) another unrebuilt engine got away to a good start, attained the permitted maximum speed and stormed home in $25\frac{1}{4}$ minutes.

The remaining runs in Table 7 are behind rebuilt engines. All these made slower starts than the unmodified locomotives, and it was not until driver Kennett opened out No. 34005 (detail C) that No. 34098's standard of running was approached. It was poor reward, therefore, to have a signal stop outside Ashford to spoil the run, which would otherwise have been completed at an average speed in excess of 60 m.p.h. All of the trains had left Tonbridge behind schedule and, enjoying the incentive of regaining time, had passed Headcorn ($15\frac{3}{4}$ miles) in even time or less.

The early morning departure from London was the only train which produced this sort of running over the length. In the reverse direction there did not seem to be a similar sprightly train, but in Table 8 an adaptation of a fast run has been made. The train in question had its departure time advanced because of heavy engineering works between Tonbridge and Sevenoaks which robbed the journey north of Tonbridge of all interest from the performance viewpoint. Not so east thereof, however! Admittedly the load was not heavy but within eleven miles from the start, inclusive of a slight permanent way repair check at the beginning, driver Longhurst had worked No. 34001 up to 91 m.p.h. and within 14 minutes even time had been comfortably achieved. A start-to-stop time to Tonbridge would have worked out at about $24\frac{1}{2}$ minutes net; the fastest schedule for an electric train for the same distance is 25 minutes and, in the down direction, 26 minutes. Certainly from Tonbridge to Ashford steam locomotives loaded to eleven coaches found no difficulty in maintaining times which were to become the standard for electric traction.

ASHFORD TO WATERLOO

From a performance angle the fifty-five miles from Ashford to Waterloo may be divided into three sections: an opening sprint, over undulating grades, to Tonbridge; the climb, in two parts, over the North Downs; and the fall into London punctuated by traffic delays. If the going was good as far as Tonbridge there was no guarantee that the remainder would be of the same standard but, if time was dropped on the first section, there was little likelihood of it being picked up on the climbs (four miles at 1-in-122 easing for two miles in Sevenoaks tunnel to 1-in-144 and then two miles at 1-in-143 up Polhill).

The opening run of Table 9 has unrebuilt No. 34078 getting off to a lively start, in falling snow, to pass Staplehurst in under even time and so have a couple of minutes in hand for the permanent way check beyond Paddock Wood. Consequently, Tonbridge was passed precisely at scheduled time and a competent climb to Sevenoaks was made, followed by an excellent attack on the grade from Polhill to Knockholt. The usual delays occurred approaching London Bridge but, despite these, the run was well within the time laid down.

In detail B No. 34099 faced the permanent way slack in the earlier stage of the run although by Tonbridge was on the right side of the schedule. Incidentally, Tonbridge was passed at a slightly higher speed than usual and with driver Gifford opening out, when crossing the river Medway, some valuable time was gained on the initial part of the climb to Sevenoaks. From Polhill to Knockholt the performance fell off; even so there was time to spare by Orpington.

With rebuild No. 34026 driver Kennett had no hindrances and therefore no need to extend the engine to any degree, especially as this was on an overall schedule of $66\frac{1}{2}$ minutes. In contrast, in detail D, driver Hurst had to push No. 34003 hard between delays as, for example, at Headcorn and Marden. He managed to keep the schedule in sight at least to Tonbridge, and then pull out a brilliant recovery from the Hildenborough slack on the 1-in-122 incline, followed it by a dash to Dunton Green and a fine assault on Polhill, all of which got the train $1\frac{3}{4}$ minutes inside schedule by Orpington. His reward was a string of signal checks into London—a poor recompense for a tenacious run.

Finally, in detail E, there is a train heavier than all of the foregoing, hauled by unrebuilt No. 34087, and starting from Ashford with a ten-minute deficit—and driver Card of Ramsgate. Who would have risked his money that the train would be right time at Waterloo (and even time into the bargain)? Yet so it was. Two minutes were recouped by Paddock Wood without

punishing No. 34087 and, with the aid of a splendid ascent to
Sevenoaks, three more minutes were picked up. The pressure
was still kept on to the extent that the 1-in-143 climb to Knockholt was at a rate of barely under a mile a minute and by Orpington eight of the ten minutes had been won back. Advantage
was taken almost to the full of the down grade to Hither Green
and with the minimum of signal delays Card triumphantly
pulled into Waterloo 'on the dot'. Net time for the 55·3 miles
works out at $54\frac{1}{4}$ minutes—with a 400-ton train.

DOVER MARINE TO VICTORIA

The up boat trains could prove to be frustrating to a recorder.
For example, if the cross-channel boat connecting with the
Golden Arrow was not dead on time then the train would run in
a timing 20 minutes later. Ordinary boat trains sometimes got
re-routed via Maidstone East—or would lose a path on the main
line—and therefore whilst sterling work might be done, it did
tend to lack the flair seen elsewhere.

Table 10 details three runs each of which was typical of its
period. No. 34088 (detail A) did not have a stiff task, the driver
being able to gain time in advance of the temporary restrictions
and, apart from the signal check at Tonbridge, avoid falling behind the clock. In detail B unrebuilt No. 35026 took advantage
of the fall from Westenhanger to get into the eighties and had
time in hand at Tonbridge, only to get checked on the climb of
the North Downs. Slow running in the suburbs was probably
due to the $1\frac{1}{2}$-minutes early start from Dover and although it
would appear that the *Merchant Navy* engine did no more than
scrape in on time it was indeed the same amount early on
arrival at Victoria as it had left Dover.

Driver Triggs with No. 34091 in charge of the *Golden Arrow*
had a slow start and slipping at Folkestone put the train
$1\frac{3}{4}$ minutes down in a dozen miles. By Headcorn, however, the
dust was flying with the *West Country* doing all but 90 m.p.h.,
and the climbing to Knockholt for a load of 470 tons was not
without merit. Inwards from Beckenham conditions conspired
against the train and a 5-minute late arrival was recorded, although the net time was no more than $89\frac{1}{2}$ minutes—a result
which must have been repeated many times down the years.

By comparison, Mr O. S. Nock had the luxury of a completely unchecked run (see *Railway Magazine* October 1959) when rebuild No. 35015 brought up the *Golden Arrow* in 87 minutes—also with a maximum of 88 m.p.h. at Headcorn—albeit loaded to 425 tons full. The honours here would seem to be in the favour of the smaller locomotive.

Chapter 7

WESTERN SECTION PERFORMANCE

1 WEST OF ENGLAND ROUTES

WATERLOO TO SALISBURY

Perhaps the hardest task set Southern motive power was the haulage of the *Atlantic Coast Express,* especially in the last year or two of its existence, when the schedules had been tightened up and locomotive maintenance was in decline. The first leg of this duty, from Waterloo to Salisbury, could be divided into two parts, of which the first comprised 50 miles of mainly up-hill 'collar' work and the second—of 33·7 miles—was mostly downhill save for a seven-mile climb from Andover Junction to Grateley. Once the first part had been accomplished the drivers could usually relax.

Opening the running in Table 11 is a modified *West Country* class engine. This was unusual, to say the least, because Nine Elms shed would always provide a large engine for its chief duty: on this occasion the prepared *Merchant Navy* locomotive became derailed in Nine Elms yard and No. 34095 was sub-stituted at short notice. A very capable run resulted—without any infringement of speed restrictions—in a three-minute under schedule timing. Detail B in this table relates to an unmodified small engine, but on the 7.00 p.m. from Waterloo. Quite ob-viously matters were not working too smoothly this Friday evening and a horrid exit from London was the result, including a dead stand of nearly two minutes at Weybridge. Once clear of Woking there was some resolute running well up to the faster *A.C.E.* standards, as witness less than thirty minutes for the 33·4 miles from Worting Junction to Salisbury.

A *Merchant Navy* engine in original form appears in detail C. This run was, of course, to the 83-minute schedule and suffered a 1¼-minute dead stand at Surbiton and a relaying restriction at Woking which put timekeeping out of reach. Anyhow, driver Letchford peeled off the last 33·4 miles in 28¼ minutes indulging in some high speed in the process at Andover Junction but not, it appears, down Porton bank.

Porton bank often did tempt drivers with time to win back, as the following extract from a run recorded by P. Balkwill on 9 January 1960 indicates. This was the *Atlantic Coast Express*, again on the slower schedule, with Salisbury's driver Cambray hurrying to make up for delays encountered before Andover with No. 35014 (rebuilt) and twelve vehicles weighing 397 tons empty or 430 tons loaded.

	Sch.	M.	S.	Speed
ANDOVER JUNCTION pass		67	43	90
Red Post Junction		68	41	85/89
Grateley		72	13	75
Allington S.B.		74	24	84
Porton		76	09	94
Milepost 81		—	—	103
Milepost 82		78	36	
Tunnel Junction (*50)	80½	78	57	
SALISBURY	83	82	04	

Cambray was neither fearful nor reckless in running at high speed and obviously had great faith in the brakes!

It would be easy to fill column after column with runs of net times in the region of 77 minutes; a two-minute gain on the 80-minute schedule was not at all remarkable, so it is somewhat higher up the scale that the target must be set. No. 35024 (detail D) in charge of a Nine Elms driver (because of the day being a Bank Holiday) had a late start of seven minutes and arrived in Salisbury but one minute down, having recouped six minutes on this exacting schedule. The interesting feature of this run—probably the finest made with such a load to Salisbury—is that it was made without recourse being made to any speed in excess of 90 m.p.h.

Last of the runs in Table 11 was also the last to the 80-minute schedule and proved a splendidly fitting *finale* to *A.C.E.* running. The key to this was the signal failure at Nine Elms which caused an early delay; thereafter the running was of a consistently high order with nothing more than 1 m.p.h. in excess of the general 85 m.p.h. speed limit.

The fast trains naturally stole the limelight and although semi-fast trains called for skilful handling (indeed some engine-men averred the hardest job out of Waterloo was the 1.00 p.m. train) such appeared to offer little appeal to recorders, despite the testing re-starts from intermediate stations. Three journeys are, however, recorded in good detail in Table 12. The first, as may be noted, was made very late in the steam era and was a special working on the Friday before Whitsun. Unfortunately the only clue to the schedule laid down which is available is a public notice and, therefore, the bookings have been deduced and must be treated with reserve. Just what could be done with steam on a semi-fast train was clearly demonstrated. The two middle stages were reeled off with great *élan* as would have also happened with the final lap in the absence of the relaying re-striction. This run amply repaid the recorder his fare as well as his curiosity.

On the first of the normally timetabled trains No. 34064 (in its pre-Giesl ejector days) suffered delays in the early stages of its run with the 3 o'clock. The sustained 55 m.p.h. at milepost 31 is worthy of remark with a train of such weight, bearing in mind the slight signal check before Brookwood. Neither was there much cause for complaint with the sprints to Andover Junction and Salisbury. By comparison No. 35007, by then rebuilt, did not shine: the climb to milepost 31 could not have been very brisk and 49 m.p.h. at Oakley was poor, although 54 m.p.h. at Grateley summit was slightly better, but by no means very good—perhaps the driver was overawed by the reputation of the 1 o'clock! On another occasion, however, the same rebuilt engine, No. 35007, with similar loading took no more than three seconds over 41 minutes for Woking to Andover Junction, which is a rather better story.

SALISBURY TO EXETER CENTRAL

In view of the attraction this 88-mile section had for performance recorders nothing more than a broad recapitulation of the principal features of the route is called for. Salisbury to Semley was almost an unbroken climb; then followed the first dip

(Gillingham); a climb at 1-in-100 to milepost $107\frac{1}{2}$; another dip before Templecombe; a climb (also 1-in-100) to milepost $113\frac{1}{2}$; a long descent to Yeovil Junction, and broken climbing to milepost $133\frac{1}{4}$ with the final length at 1-in-80; another long descent to milepost $146\frac{1}{4}$ before the formidable climb at 1-in-80 to Honiton summit; and then downhill to Exeter. Impetus was useful for the climbs but that alone would not take a train over the summits, especially Honiton.

Over this section it was the *Atlantic Coast Express* which stole the show and engaged most attention from recorders. As previously remarked, the smaller Pacifics seldom had an opportunity to appear on the premier train, and therefore Table 13 opens with a run by No. 34023 on the 11.05 a.m. relief from Waterloo. The recorder on this journey had been disappointed with a 96-minute run from Waterloo to Salisbury and had come to the conclusion that not much good would result beyond Salisbury. By Tisbury he had changed his mind and although not well situated to sight the mileposts recommenced his note-taking. Bearing in mind that the load was no more than 350 tons the summit speeds were not very exciting. This could not be said of No. 35012 in detail B, however; apart from a lightning recovery after the Buckhorn Weston tunnel slack to 80 m.p.h. at milepost $109\frac{3}{4}$ the record is sufficiently detailed not to call for further comment, although the '100' should not be overlooked.

In its original form No. 35005 (detail C) made an inauspicious start—to put it no finer—to Semley and the permanent way restriction hampered the descent to Gillingham but thereafter matters improved immensely and the driver demonstrated how the schedule could be toyed with. Rebuilt No. 34095, in detail D, was a replacement for the booked locomotive, and its fortune from London to Salisbury has already been noted in Table 11. Westward from Salisbury progress was no less notable than east of that city. That $3\frac{3}{4}$ minutes was dropped on the schedule of 73 minutes was no disgrace and of little consequence because the Western Region had by this time lengthened the duration of the stop at Sidmouth Junction for the purpose of detaching the through branch line coaches and at the same time decreed that no coaches be so detached! So the driver of No. 34095 could afford to drop a few minutes on schedule without turning up late at Exeter.

Last in Table 13 is another substitute engine, again a rebuilt light Pacific. The recorder states the engine was steaming badly throughout (Salisbury was left $6\frac{1}{2}$ minutes late) and driver Davey did well, despite a bout of continuous slipping between mileposts 152 and $153\frac{1}{2}$, to keep the further loss to no more than $4\frac{1}{2}$ minutes in view of the relaying restriction at Tisbury.

No difficulty would be experienced in collecting eleven-coach runs to the 75-minute schedule: for example, on 7 May 1962 driver Clements with engine No 35028 made a very consistent run in 73 min 36 sec with no higher speed than 80 m.p.h., and two days later his fellow driver from Exmouth Junction, Whitfield, with No. 35014 got to Sidmouth Junction in 23 seconds less time after some erratic running. Whitfield was more than $1\frac{1}{2}$ minutes behind Clements at Semley and then roared along—possibly touching 100 m.p.h. in the process below Sherborne—to get in front before Sutton Bingham, only to make a poor ascent to Hewish and so fall behind again before using the down grade through Axminster to establish the lead, which he nearly lost once more on Honiton incline.

However, one more eleven-coach load may be noted before passing on to a couple of twelve-coach train runs. In Table 14 No. 35012 was making a successful attempt to make up lost time suffered in the first stage from London, so much so that Semley was passed at 70 m.p.h. just short of even time. Buckhorn Weston tunnel repairs hampered progress but beyond Sherborne the pace quickened. No hundred at Axminster, but a fine sustained effort nonetheless for a net time of $64\frac{1}{2}$ minutes to Sidmouth Junction. In detail B No. 35028 did not have such a great incentive because the departure from Salisbury was no more than $1\frac{1}{4}$ minutes late. A very leisurely start was made before the slack at Dinton and then came the first indication of an increase in effort; by Templecombe matters were decidedly energetic with the summit beyond scaled at 65 m.p.h. At Sherborne it was evident that there were the makings of a record run and no diminishing of effort occurred—65 m.p.h. at milepost $133\frac{1}{4}$ (an excess on the 85 m.p.h. limit at Axminster must be admitted) and then came the simply magnificent climb to Honiton tunnel. By milepost $150\frac{1}{2}$ (passed in 59 min 2 sec) speed was not less than 62 m.p.h., and the next two miles occupied but one second over two minutes (with a load of 393 tons tare be it remembered). Directly No. 35028 entered the tunnel, driver Burridge eased off and coasted down to Sidmouth Junction to arrive 5½ minutes early. After detaching the branch coaches the train left 2¼ minutes early and arrived at Exeter Central 3½ minutes before time. The net time works out at 65 minutes to Sidmouth Junction: with a normal finish it could have been pared down to 64 and, with a livelier start also, to 62¾ minutes.

No. 35028 reappears in detail C complete with late departure and Buckhorn Weston tunnel slack. By an odd coincidence Sherborne was passed in precisely the same time as on the previously described run, but after that progress was much slower (!) so that, despite 98 m.p.h. near Axminster, nearly two minutes were 'lost' on the companion times over the next 35½ miles, even though it took but 28 minutes to cover the distance. This, then, is the measure of the quality of, in a sense, both these majestic efforts of No. 35028.

Table 15 records some heavyweight loads, all of which have great merit. At first glance the effort of No. 35029 (detail A) would appear to be no more than an excellent heavy load run; it was more than that because it was made into the teeth of a south-westerly gale, which increased in severity as the run progressed, and so reflected great credit on fireman Sloman no less than on driver Bennett. Next is an interesting example of a run in the earlier days before the schedules were tightened up and loads reduced: No. 21C2 with about 500 tons had a ten minute late start from Salisbury and arrived at Exeter 'on the dot'. Unfortunately the climb from Seaton Junction was interrupted by a p.w. check at milepost 149, the speed of 26 m.p.h. being noted three miles further on. Lastly there is a log of the *Devon Belle* with its awkward Wilton start with a heavy load. The best of the climbs on this particular trip would appear to be the final one to Honiton tunnel with a speed of 30 m.p.h. which was no disgrace with a 543-ton train.

Naturally—and rightly in view of the foregoing—the *Atlantic Coast Express* held the stage, but this was not to say that other trains were of insignificant interest. On the contrary, for the 7.00 p.m. from Waterloo could be a lively performer. Perhaps given ten minutes delay in the London suburban area, the

Exmouth Junction men would be eager to recoup the lost time and catch the reputed last 'bus home, so saving a walk. That last 'bus has probably been the spur for many a good performance, and some, such as No. 35013 reaching 100 m.p.h. on this train, have lacked adequate supporting data because of the unexpected nature of progress. With a light load and driver Whitfield in charge, No. 35026 (detail A, Table 16) ran like a stag until stopped outside Yeovil Junction, where the 6.00 p.m. from Waterloo was doing business. This tardy train put paid to No. 35026's frolics for the time being, and for a long stop at Sutton Bingham for signals driver Whitfield drew up his engine opposite the signal box to have a chat with the signalman! In detail B driver Clements took over a rather sulky No. 34015 from driver Cambray of Salisbury with the greeting of 'You're welcome to the old crab!' Clements was a fine engineman and proceeded to get a good performance out of the 'old crab'. With an original light Pacific also, but with a coach more, the same driver produced a better performance—90 minutes net with the two stops for the 88 miles which probably reflected the better condition No. 34002 was in, although hastily prepared by Salisbury as a replacement engine.

Towards the end of the steam era the 7.00 p.m. from Waterloo had extra stops to make and one of these runs appears as detail A in Table 17. This had the spur of a 30 minute late departure from Salisbury. The other run in this table concerns a rebuilt light Pacific on a Sunday train performing in commendable fashion. Tables 18 and 19 call for little remark save that the 54-minute schedule from Salisbury to Axminster was designed for diesel traction and was rather beyond a rebuilt light Pacific in the event.

EXETER CENTRAL TO SALISBURY

The up *A.C.E.* to Salisbury from Exeter attracted rather less attention than the down for a variety of reasons. First of all it was probably less easy to join for anyone residing east of Salisbury; secondly it could not offer the opportunity—however slight—of a tilt at a three-figure speed, and thirdly it did not seem to produce an equal brilliance of performance. This last was almost certainly an illusion: it did require a high standard with heavy climbing to Honiton, Hewish, Milborne Port and Semley with little useful in the way of dips to attain a high speed before starting the ascents. Some connoisseurs rated the required performance eastbound to be stiffer and demanding a higher degree of enginemanship than the corresponding westward run. It is a view difficult to refute.

The running eastwards opens with an unmodified large Pacific, No. 35023, in Table 20. Of note is the exceptionally fast conclusion to the journey made to the old schedule of 79 minutes. This is followed, in detail B, by an excellent run with an unmodified small engine handled by driver Davey. Now this driver, of charming disposition, did not always prosecute his running with the relentlessness of some of his *confrères* at Exmouth Junction, and this splendid run with No. 34002 is a little disappointing in that the advantage at Yeovil Junction was not pressed home to eliminate the half-minute late departure from Sidmouth Junction. The very next day driver F. Turner, who had not been on the duty for three months, demonstrated (detail C) in no uncertain fashion a determination to win back a 5-minute late departure from Exeter. Three minutes in arrears leaving Sidmouth Junction, the pressure was applied to such a degree that No. 35013 stopped in Salisbury $1\frac{1}{4}$ minutes early in $69\frac{1}{2}$ minutes. Any net time under 70 minutes for Sidmouth Junction to Salisbury was absolutely first class. In detail D the running was even finer: six minutes late at Exeter, the driver made a great effort to get into Salisbury on time but was thwarted by a signal check outside his destination and had to be content with a two-minute late arrival. Finally in Table 20 comes No. 35025, driver Gidley and six minutes to recoup. The start was well-nigh lackadaisical: then suddenly, at Seaton Junction, came a metamorphosis as though the fireman had bet the driver that Salisbury could not be reached on time. Capital though the running had been in the previous two details, No. 35025 gradually overhauled both those engines, although No. 35029 gave Gidley a run for his money. So far as can be traced No. 35025 set up a record time for Sidmouth Junction–Salisbury and if only (how often that occurs with locomotive performance!) the start had been good a net time of $66\frac{1}{2}$ minutes might have been recorded. If bet there had been, Gidley would have won with his quarter-minute early arrival.

The rebuilt light Pacifics, given the opportunity, seldom seemed to shine on the up *A.C.E.* An exception, however, was No. 34062 (Table 21) with a twelve-coach train. Driver Welling converted a 1½-minute late departure from Sidmouth Junction into a minute early appearance at Salisbury with a run of uniform excellence. The other run in this table records the progress of a railtour special and gives an indication of how steam could have operated a 2¾-hour 'Inter-City' service between Exeter and London with a Salisbury stop.

The semi-fast turns could provide interest, as witness Table 22. In detail A No. 34067 picked up some time on the schedule, as did No. 35009 with a heavy train (detail B) which the recorder indicates took on five tons more of passengers at Axminster. Net time to Axminster may be put at 31¼ minutes. Detail C has a rebuilt *Merchant Navy* in easy command on the 4.30 p.m. from Exeter, while the remaining two runs, on the same service, declare the superior running—weight for weight— of a *West Country* in original condition to a rebuilt *Merchant Navy*. It was this sort of performance with the smaller engines that made one wonder if there was any need for the larger design.

There is sterling running in Table 23 too. It has to be admitted that the loads were not severe for this route—although elsewhere in the country it might have been a different tale: first of all, No. 35009 left Axminster 8¾ minutes late to regain 5½ to Yeovil Junction. As a reward, it was held 14 minutes for the Yeovil Town connection and eventually arrived at Salisbury 6¾ minutes behind schedule. 68 m.p.h. at milepost 133¼ was rather a nice touch! The other three runs were all latter-day efforts in the diesel era. Driver Hoare with No. 34077 had a sulky engine which would not steam, and it was no small credit due to him that, but for a signal check outside Templecombe, there would have been an even time run (of 32¾ minutes) for the first section, if not the second. With equal loadings Nos. 34026 and 34015 were returning identical performances until signal checks in the Yeovil area rather put No. 34026 out of its stride. No. 34015 carried on well with some good minima in summit speeds.

Table 24 concludes the record for the Exeter–Salisbury length with three sprints in from Templecombe with trains of substance. Not the least noteworthy was the effort of No. 34013 due, probably, to the four minutes late departure, after awaiting a Somerset and Dorset line connection.

SALISBURY TO WATERLOO

The major test out of Salisbury was the climbing of the first thirty miles, after which all that was wanted was a free running engine and a clear road in the suburban area. There was little point in thrashing an engine up Porton bank and pulling the fire to pieces in the process because time could be regained more easily elsewhere.

Naturally the *Atlantic Coast Express* was the greatest test for the length and so Table 25 features that train. In detail A rebuilt No. 34062 seemed to be just a little too slow, even with only nine vehicles, to keep time, which was reflected in the driver's remark that it was 'stiff'. With a couple more coaches the same driver got unrebuilt *West Country* No. 34002 going rather better, and it was a thousand pities that a dead stand of $2\frac{1}{2}$ minutes at Pirbright Junction wrecked such a promising run. Next, in detail C, is an unrebuilt *Merchant Navy* engine manned by driver Letchford and fireman Holloway and a four minute late departure. In other words, all the ingredients for a fine run—and so it proved to be. Porton bank was taken with panache (and be it remembered this was a 400-ton train) for Andover Junction to be passed in under $18\frac{1}{2}$ minutes and the 33·4 miles to Worting to be covered well within even time. The descent culminated in 96 m.p.h. at Woking, and because he was running so early Letchford eased right off from Surbiton inwards but could not avoid arriving seven minutes before time. With the normal approach to Waterloo net time would have been $71\frac{3}{4}$ minutes.

Last of the twelve-coach trains comes No. 35020 with the summer relief portion of the *A.C.E.* crewed not by Salisbury men but by an unknown pair from Nine Elms. The whole run is breathtaking and, in computing a net time of $68\frac{1}{2}$ minutes, it has been assumed that had the p.w. check at Farnborough not been there progress would have been the same, but one wonders. Did the knowledge of that restriction cause the driver to mortgage the boiler previously? After this display of prowess on the part of No. 35020 and 35023 it would be anti-climactic to table any other run of less note, and so attention may be devoted to thirteen-coach loadings (Table 26).

These are both excellent runs with renowned drivers. With the unrebuilt engine Letchford had a 'right time' start which may have cramped his style a little: anyhow despite the p.w. check at Hurstbourne he was almost on schedule at Worting and then proceeded to press on—mercifully without a signal check—to arrive in Waterloo six minutes early. Hoare with the rebuilt No. 35009 gave a flawless performance which was so typical of his technique.

Opening the running of semi-fast trains in Table 27 is No. 34108 hastily summoned forward at Salisbury to take over from an ailing *Warship* diesel-hydraulic locomotive. Driver Fordrey then proceeded to show that the schedule laid down for the more modern type of traction was more than ample for steam. With a net time of $20\frac{1}{2}$ minutes between Basingstoke and Woking the net running time adds up to 85 minutes for Salisbury to Waterloo with three stops, or the same as the old schedule of the *A.C.E.* Unmodified No. 34056 loaded up to twelve vehicles (detail B) performed rather less well out of Salisbury but then proceeded to outpace—with two more coaches—No. 34108 on the next section. From Basingstoke to Waterloo the net time works out at $44\frac{1}{4}$ minutes for $47\frac{3}{4}$ miles and even in the electric traction era there is only one train time-tabled to beat this figure, and that by a mere $1\frac{1}{4}$ minutes. So there was little wrong with the performance of Mr Bulleid's design of light Pacific to return times such as these. Last in this table comes No. 35025 recovering all of a $6\frac{3}{4}$-minutes late departure from Andover without exceeding the 85 m.p.h. speed limit.

Table 28 records a couple of snippets on the 6.38 p.m. mail train from Salisbury, in the first of which No. 35008 got up to 102 m.p.h. at milepost 69, while Table 29 continues with both these runs as far as Basingstoke and introduces a couple of original light Pacifics on rather heavier trains.

One train ran non-stop between Andover Junction and Woking, and in Table 30 four of those occasions are recorded. The ten-coach trains were briskly handled, although No. 35007 eased off to 60 m.p.h. around Basingstoke, suggesting a signal caution which may have escaped the recorder. The twelve-coach trains were dealt with competently but none of the engines was really extended, which would point to timekeeping journeys to a comfortable schedule.

WEST OF EXETER

West of Exeter the switchback character of the route from Salisbury gives way to a long climb—almost without intermission—to milepost 200¾ just beyond Meldon Junction. Starting fairly gently at 1-in-305 through Newton St Cyres the gradient stiffens to 1-in-125 after Yeoford, increases to 1-in-80 before Bow (which station is situated in a dip) and continues at 1-in-100 or 1-in-80 nearly to North Tawton, where there is a fall for about a mile, after which climbing continues at 1-in-77 most of the way to Okehampton. After that point the 1-in-77 gradient extends to the far end of Meldon viaduct where it changes to 1-in-58 up, before giving way to 1-in-80 to the summit. Then all the height gained is lost by Plymouth down gradients of 1-in-75.

Not many trains were heavily loaded over the Exeter–Plymouth section, five or six coaches usually sufficing for the traffic. An exception was the through train from Brighton and Portsmouth which included a refreshment car and mustered ten or eleven coaches on occasion. The booking for the 25-mile run non-stop from Exeter St David's to Okehampton was 38 minutes, well within the capabilities of the *West Country* class, which engines would usually return times of between 35½ and 37 minutes.

Table 31 sets on record an above-average run: the incentive for this was a six minute late start from Exeter St David's. Permanent speed restrictions at Cowley Bridge, Crediton and Coleford Junction hamper the first half of the stage to Okehampton and it was on the second half, from Coleford Junction, that No. 34057 made the greatest gain on schedule. The combination of the adverse gradient and speed restrictions at Meldon provided an obstacle to a speedy start from Okehampton but, after Bridestowe, it remained only to use the brakes, except for the rise up to milepost 217¾ which brought speed down from 55 to 43 m.p.h. Long stretches of the route from Bridestowe to Devonport were subject to speed restrictions but by Bere Alston the engine had regained the six minutes deficit and fast running did not have to be indulged in thereafter.

In the up direction trains usually left Plymouth on time, so the locomotives were seldom extended on the climb, especially as the schedules laid down are not strenuous. From Okehampton into Exeter matters could be frisky on occasion and, although the route was nearly all downhill and no high power outputs were involved, the timing of a train could be rewarding for a recorder. Table 32 demonstrates this: in detail A No. 34059 galloped away with a ten-coach train to such purpose that, despite the speed restrictions at Coleford Junction and Crediton, even time was attained between Newton St Cyres and the junction with the Great Western main line.

No. 34031 (detail B), with half the load, managed to equal the times in the preceding column although in a rather erratic fashion which included a maximum speed of 82 m.p.h.—almost the maximum permitted and one of the best, if not the highest, recorded west of Exeter. The second part of detail B (noted as B/1) was not a continuation of the run with No. 34031 but another, behind No. 34043, with a similar load giving a net time of 13¼ minutes from Yeoford to Exeter St David's. The fastest time claimed for this 11·6 mile length is 13 min 29 sec (net 12 min due to signal checks) by No. 34065 on 28 September 1962 with a five-coach load weighing 170 tons gross, but beyond that there is no further information in support of the times. No. 34011, in detail C, performed in a lively manner and enjoyed the luxury of an unchecked run into St David's. In view of the load the honours in this table undoubtedly go to No. 34059 in the run first described.

It has been fashionable in the past to pour scorn on the use of *West Country* locomotives on two-coach trains on the North Cornwall line and, in the process, overlook the question of locomotive utilisation. It will not be inappropriate, therefore, to place on record a run with such a locomotive loaded to ten vehicles in the days when holidaymakers patronised the rail service to reach the resorts of their choice. No. 34035 had the task of lifting its well-loaded train (see Table 33) from almost sea level at Padstow to the summit at Otterham on Bodmin Moor, 800 feet higher, in a distance of under 25 miles. The start

9. Footplate view of one of the first batch of *Merchant Navy* locomotives.

10. Footplateman's view—after dismounting—of No. 35020 *Bibby Line* at Crewkerne on 24 April 1953 on the occasion of the fractured driving axle (see Chapter 2).

11. First of the class, No. 21C101 *Exeter*, with short smoke deflector wings.

12. One of the last batch, No. 34101 *Hartland*, at Stewarts Lane shed, having long smoke deflector wings, modified cab and bottom hinged circular covers to sandboxes.

13. No. 34019 *Bideford* running light at Southampton Central as an oil-burner.

14. No. 21C162 at Shorncliffe with experimental turned-in smoke deflector wings.

15. A later smoke deflecting experiment. No. 34049 *Anti-Aircraft Command* in February 1960. By this time modified cab and tender had been acquired.

16. No. 34006 *Bude* approaching Marylebone on 11 June 1948 in charge of Driver Swain and Fireman Hooker during the Locomotive Interchanges. Engine fitted with modified cab, extra long smoke deflector wings and (temporarily) LMS tender.

17. No. 34090 *Sir Eustace Missenden Southern Railway* in special finish approaching Folkestone Junction with up Margate train.

was marred by a delay outside Wadebridge; leaving there
1¾ minutes late No. 34035 reached a maximum of 39 m.p.h. before falling to 33 m.p.h. on the 1-in-73 climb to St Kew High-
way, where speed was reduced for the loop through the station,
and then accelerated to 31 m.p.h. to arrive 'right time' at Port
Isaac Road. The 1-in-73 climb to Delabole was taken at a
steady 29 m.p.h. to gain a minute on schedule. In the next
section there was considerable delay before the train could be
admitted to Camelford station where enginemen were changed.

The new crew left Camelford with 9½ minutes to regain. The
gradient becomes as favourable as it was adverse before Otterham, so that skilful use of the brake was the main requirement
(even if the speed limit of 55 m.p.h. for the North Cornwall line
was slightly exceeded in the process) to cut the schedule to
Launceston by 3½ minutes. Departure from that stop was
10½ minutes behind time but speed was kept within the limit
down the 1-in-94 to Tower Hill, then fell to 31 m.p.h. for the
station, rose before Ashwater, passed at 26 m.p.h., to rise
further to 52 m.p.h. With full regulator and 40 per cent indicated cut-off the 1-in-82 and 1-in-73 banks were attacked and
surmounted without speed falling below 41 m.p.h., so that
2¾ minutes were won back by the time Halwill was reached.
This sort of performance indicated just how useful the light
Pacifics were on secondary lines which had weight restrictions
coupled with, at times, heavy traffic requirements.

One of the routes which never became open to the rebuilt
West Country class (and still less the *Merchant Navy* class) was
Coleford Junction to Ilfracombe, where the original light 4-6-2s
held undisputed sway. The route from Exeter is, of course, the
same as the Plymouth road as far as Coleford Junction, the
climb finishing a little short of Copplestone. There follows a
long descent to Barnstaple, a few miles of mainly level ground
to Wrafton, then the 1-in-40 climb to Mortehoe rounded off by
the precipitous descent at 1-in-36 to Ilfracombe. Speed restrictions were:

Coleford Junction–Umberleigh	55 m.p.h.
Umberleigh–Barnstaple Junction	60 m.p.h.
Barnstaple Junction–Braunton	55 m.p.h.
Braunton–Mortehoe	40 m.p.h.
Mortehoe–Ilfracombe	30 m.p.h.

In addition to these restrictions, there was single line from
Copplestone to Umberleigh which meant slowing down for the
stations.

Naturally light loads did not extend the locomotives and,
therefore, in Table 34 the main interest centres on a couple of
runs of the down *Devon Belle*. This train, however, features in
the first detail: this particular instance with the Friday evening
departure from Waterloo shows a driver determined to win
back a $4\frac{1}{4}$ minute late start from St David's. Indeed most of it
was won back before the single track started at Copplestone, and
the slack for permanent way repairs at Lapford was contained
within the running to Umberleigh where, owing to a failure,
hand signalling was in force. To make up for this the driver exceeded the 60 m.p.h. speed limit by a wide margin and pulled
into Barnstaple Junction with over half a minute to spare.
Detail B records a run with the Pullman train which was not
without incident, for firstly the observation car had had to be
removed at Wilton and then there was a stop at Crediton to examine the train because a door was thought to be open. This
stop lasted $2\frac{1}{2}$ minutes so that the time of $7\frac{1}{2}$ minutes from the
restart to passing Yeoford could hardly be said to be brilliant.
No. 34018, in the last column, had a bad check before getting
on to Southern metals, although by Copplestone it was within
schedule time. Some of the intermediate timings beyond
Morchard Road were distinctly tight (e.g. four minutes Lapford–Eggesford, a distance of 3·8 miles) when slowing at
stations for the tablet is taken into consideration and demanded
good acceleration with a 400-ton train, even on down grades.

North of Barnstaple the 1-in-40 and 1-in-36 gradients meant
that heavy trains had to be assisted. The distance of 5 miles
70 chains from Braunton to Mortehoe was scheduled to be
covered, by the *Devon Belle* for example, in 17 minutes. Some
specimen times are: No. 21C147 with 130 tons—14 min 3 sec;
No. 21C146 with 100 tons encountering a very strong wind—
13 min 53 sec; No. 34081 with 100 tons—11 min 49 sec (an
exceptional effort); and No. 34017 with 400 tons banked by
No. 1834—15 min 11 sec.

More severe is the climb out of Ilfracombe with the 1-in-36
starting almost in the station. Times for the 3 miles 9 chains to
Mortehoe are: No. 21C146 with 90 tons—10 min 45 sec;

No. 21C147 with 125 tons—11 min 32 sec; and No. 34017 with
400 tons banked by No. 1834—11 min 14 sec against a schedule
of 12 minutes.

Table 35 gives two runs on the uphill length from Barnstaple
to Copplestone. In detail A No. 34034 got away to a fine start
but, despite some good running, failed to keep the schedule
precisely between Umberleigh and Copplestone. The figures
against the stations on the single line relate to the speed in the
section previous to the station rather than at the station, which
points to good acceleration and finely judged braking. Inwards
from Copplestone on the down grades running became lively
and thus the schedule was considerably bettered.

Proportionate to its load No. 34020, with the up *Devon Belle*,
did better than No. 34034, for it was slightly swifter over the
single track length, although not putting quite so much vigour
into the start. If the checks at the end of the run had not occurred the 53-minute schedule would have been kept with ease.

Chapter 8

WESTERN SECTION
PERFORMANCE

2 BOURNEMOUTH AND OTHER ROUTES

WATERLOO TO SOUTHAMPTON CENTRAL

London to Southampton is a classic example of a finely en-
gineered railway route: long straight lengths, sweeping curves to
vast radii and constant gradients are the hallmarks. Consequently speed restrictions are few, the most severe at Northam
Junction to 15 m.p.h. being due to a connecting chord diverging
from the original route on the outskirts of Southampton; elsewhere reductions had to be made at Clapham Junction, Basingstoke and from the down main line at Worting Junction. On the
other hand, the summit of the line at Litchfield tunnel meant
that there was almost continuous work against the collar for 56
out of the 79 miles, and this could prove very trying with an
ailing locomotive on a heavily loaded fast train. The 23-mile
balance was all downhill and could be taken very easily. During
the years of the two-hour Bournemouth expresses there were
always tight margins in the Southampton area, involving in
particular the diesel trains crossing over to Alton at Winchester
Junction or using the section from that junction to Shawford,
and this meant that very fast running down from the summit
could not be indulged in except with this factor in mind. High
speed down through the chalk of Wessex was, of course, exciting
but the real test was to pass Worting Junction with time in hand.

Table 36 commences with a ten-coach load: No. 35028, under
the able guidance of driver Hooper, might have cleared Worting
Junction in 47 minutes but for the p.w. slack at Wimbledon and
delays near Basingstoke. With an extended schedule to take into
account engineering works there could be no excuse for indulging in high speed, especially as the train was eight minutes early

by Winchester. Detail B of this table records an 81-minute schedule run; both No. 35030 and driver Letchford were in fine fettle this day, as had become evident as early as Hampton Court Junction and was underlined by the high figure of 75 m.p.h. at which milepost 31 was passed. Good as it was this figure was toppled fourteen months later when No. 35018, with the same train and load, went over the summit at 76 m.p.h., but both figures were some way above the customary performance. Unfortunately no record appears to be in existence of the summit being carried at 80 m.p.h. with a substantial train for, given an unchecked passage through Woking at 85 m.p.h., it would have been feasible. After milepost 31 Letchford did not press No. 35030 too hard, but even so he was $6\frac{1}{2}$ minutes early at Worting Junction and, after establishing a record of getting out to that junction in $45\frac{1}{2}$ minutes, Nemesis could not be far away. Anyhow he pressed on until stopped for $3\frac{1}{2}$ minutes at Wootton signal box and then, shortly after, for another minute which was used in going round the engine with the oilcan! The offending freight train was passed in the Weston–Wallers Ash loop after which the driver felt justified in opening out No. 35030. The effect of this was to regain 2 minutes in the final $12\frac{1}{2}$ miles and to arrive no more than $4\frac{1}{2}$ minutes late. The recorder, incidentally, was placed in the second coach, so slightly earlier passing times were to be obtained by anyone timing in the leading vehicle. The net time of $70\frac{1}{2}$ minutes is based on the standard of running as far as Worting being continued. This is a conservative estimate as subsequent runs with this driver indicated that a figure of $69\frac{1}{4}$ minutes could be considered more appropriate. How Letchford managed to pull into Bournemouth Central on time, despite a dead stand for signals in the final stage, is recorded in detail E of Table 51.

No. 35005 (detail C) soon demonstrated that No. 35030's run was by no means a freak by beating it to the tune of $1\frac{3}{4}$ minutes to Hook before signal checks sadly cut short progress. This run took place in the last week before decelerations for electrification works came into force and obviously was an attempt to see just what could be done with an engine opened out. Beyond Hook the run was completely wrecked by checks but not before there were pointers that steam, with eleven coaches, would not find it impossible to keep the 70-minute electric timing introduced in

1967. Of particular note in this 1965 run are the speeds at milepost 31 and in the Fleet–Hook area.

Whatever follows these two runs cannot fail to be bathetic. However, No. 21C20, in detail D, on an 85-minute schedule did not disgrace itself in any way. There was a frustrating series of checks (five in all) spread out over almost the whole run, but the driver stuck to things well with 65 m.p.h. at milepost 31 and good acceleration after Shawford, to say nothing of an odd gallop on the approach to Woking which was rewarded by a signal check. Last of all in Table 36 is a run which had the incentive of a four minute late departure. Driver King handled No. 35012 with skill to gradually win back time and, after Worting Junction, to get some in hand: perhaps he should not have been so greedy for he was rewarded with a signal check to 18 m.p.h. after Swaythling and so got into Southampton a minute late.

Table 37 goes on up in the load scale starting at 400 tare tons, with unrebuilt No. 34040 on the 6.30 p.m. from Waterloo. The dip in speed at milepost 31 was a little pronounced, the more so in contrast to the 70s from Walton-on-Thames to Basingstoke; a little more hurry down from Worting would have offset the p.w. restriction at Swaythling. No. 35021 in charge of driver Horne (in the second column of the table) put in an impeccable timekeeping run with great economy of effort. In detail C unrebuilt No. 34095 started well enough but encountered a signal failure at Hersham which prevented normal running until after Woking. Driver Pragnell managed to claw back some of this lost time until a 1½-minute stand at Allbrook put paid to a punctual arrival at Southampton. The net time of 76¼ minutes is worthy of notice. Fourth in the table is the 8.30 a.m. ex Waterloo on a 93½-minute schedule. Driver Hooper took No. 35008 out of London well enough although the drop in speed up to milepost 31 was rather more than customary. The Farnborough–Basingstoke section was subject to a 40 m.p.h. restriction as far as Winchfield, at which point the train was switched to the local line regaining the through line outside Basingstoke. After Worting all was plain sailing until a signal check outside Eastleigh caused heavy braking. The signal cleared but the brakes could not be released quick enough to prevent a dead stand. Concluding this table is No. 34048 on the 6.30 p.m. down from

Waterloo. This was a very steady heavy load run which unfortunately paid the penalty of running ahead of time in its later
stages.

Continuing up in the load scale Table 38 starts with the 445-
ton *Bournemouth Belle* in charge of No. 35007. Notwithstanding
early signal checks No. 35007 was on time by Woking and
followed this up with some excellent running onwards to
Basingstoke. Just after that station there was a signal check
followed by a 15¼-minute stand because of an obstruction. A
reversal took place for the train to run forward on the up line to
Micheldever where it regained normal running. Next (detail B)
comes a heavily loaded—465 tons—train entrusted to unrebuilt
No. 34109, albeit on a 91-minute schedule. Slipping was the
cause of a poor start, then followed a p.w. slack at Surbiton and,
at Woking, a check to walking pace. Beyond Micheldever speed
rose and time was gained in anticipation of the p.w. slack at
Allbrook, but with 88 m.p.h. at Shawford the fierce braking
necessary brought speed down so rapidly that the engine was
stalled! All was well, however, and No. 34109 put in an early
appearance at Southampton. An almost identical load was
handled by rebuild No. 34010 (detail C) with driver Letchford
in charge. The early loss of time because of a p.w. check was
soon regained and then Letchford set about getting ahead of
time as was his wont. The signal checks duly cropped up in the
Southampton area but did not prevent a punctual arrival.

Up in the heavyweight category comes the *Bournemouth
Belle* with two runs (details D and E). The first of these had rebuild No. 35005 which the recorder notes as 'steaming well but
sluggish due to worn piston rings. Sanding gear not operating
(broken pipe dragging on rail). Partial lubrication only to right-
hand cylinder'. These ailments might be taken as fairly representative of the state of Bournemouth engines at the time as
maintenance at that shed appeared to lag behind Nine Elms or
Exmouth Junction. It was all the more meritorious therefore
that driver Rabbetts regained time with the train, although poor
reward for him that signal checks on the outskirts of Southampton caused a quarter-minute late arrival. The other run—on an
85-minute schedule with a load limit of 400 tons (how that
could be with the *Belle* nobody explained)—was with unrebuilt
No. 21C18. The aftermath of an accident in the outer London

area caused heavy delays as far as Woking. After that No. 21C18 ran much faster than was usually necessary at that period covering the Woking–Northam Junction length at less than the later faster schedule of 50 minutes, despite the slow rate at Woking.

WATERLOO TO WINCHESTER CITY

Waterloo to Winchester trains had most of the disadvantages affecting the fast Southampton services without the advantage of a reasonable run down from the summit, during which time could be won back. It was, therefore, even more essential that Worting Junction should be passed within a minute or so of schedule.

The running in Table 39 opens with the 4.22 p.m. from Waterloo, only moderately loaded, in charge of No. 34034 and driver Fordrey. This smacks of an all-out effort planned from the start, and between Hampton Court Junction and Woking No. 34034 appears to have been snapping at the tail of another train. Milepost 31 was carried at 75 m.p.h.—an acceleration all the way from Woking—and 90 m.p.h. was attained at Newnham siding, although these high figures must be tempered with a consideration of the load. A further good acceleration occurred from Worting Junction right up to Litchfield tunnel and it was a pity a three-figure speed down the bank was missed. 56 minutes seems a fair assessment of the net time. In detail B No. 34108 on a heavier train returned a reasonably good time on what might be termed a typical run for the length. Much the same could be said of the next run, with unrebuilt No. 34007, although the recovery from the check at Basingstoke was a slow business, but a before-time arrival was accomplished nonetheless. The first of the *Merchant Navy* runs was a lively affair made in the last weeks of steam traction. The signal checks around Basingstoke were a nuisance, but did not prevent a gallop through Wallers Ash. Last in Table 39 is another rebuilt *Merchant Navy* with Ernie Rabbetts of Bournemouth as driver enjoying his last few months before retirement. This was a fine continuous effort all the way spoilt by signals at Pirbright and on coming down from Wallers Ash. Rabbetts did not relax after Winchester as witness detail D of Table 52.

The twelve-coach loads spill over into Table 40 with Ernie

Rabbetts again performing on the 6.30 p.m. down, this time with No. 35030. It was not such a good run as with No. 35029 (perhaps practice was helping by then!) and it was a pity about leaving the 100 m.p.h. attempt a trifle late. How much brake dust Rabbetts caused to accumulate on the track north of Winchester about this time it would be difficult to calculate.

The run in detail B is probably the fastest exit ever made with steam from Waterloo to passing Basingstoke with a load of this magnitude (other runs approaching this feat are in Table 36, details B and C) yet it was virtually unpremeditated. The mainspring for this effort was the fireman—Gallen of Bournemouth —in more ways than one. He was not driver Woods' regular mate and furthermore this was his last week as a main line fireman because of promotion to driver. He saw it as a last chance to enjoy himself and to this end there was much badinage on his part at Waterloo to get his driver to capture some of his enthusiasm. Woods was his usual genial self and gave nothing away: however, before a dozen miles had been covered he had shown his hand. Doubtless as he raced down to Woking he had a chuckle at calling Gallen's bluff. Anyhow even time was bettered before West Byfleet (21¾ miles) but the rise to milepost 31 pulled the speed down rather drastically. Fireman Gallen afterwards admitted he was not prepared for driver Woods taking him at his word and if he had known he would have planned matters in rather more detail (it would have been interesting to see what *that* would have produced). The permanent restriction at Basingstoke had a rather liberal observance but signals shortly afterwards had to be carefully observed and hard as Gallen might wave his arms at the signalman at Worting Junction it was of no avail. Doubtless that worthy in his box considered the fireman slightly mad for wasn't he six minutes before time anyway? He had sent a freight down in front and seemed, as well he might, somewhat nonplussed at some reproachful glances he attracted. After all the haste it was rather sad for Woods to draw into Winchester five minutes late on what had been an unusually exciting run.

In detail C driver Jones caught up the 6.22 p.m. twelve-coach train headed by a *Lord Nelson* which had also been checked. To conclude the running on this section there are two fine performances with heavy trains by unrebuilt light Pacifics.

Apart from a check at the start driver Gould had the luxury of a
clear road and did some very consistent work. With No. 34107
driver Pragnell was rather more variable, producing a greater
range of speeds, but would have kept the schedule without
difficulty if the final signal checks had not intervened.

WATERLOO TO BASINGSTOKE

It might be thought that truncating the Winchester service at
Basingstoke would give an even harder run than that from
Waterloo to the Wessex capital. Had the same sort of schedules
obtained such would probably have been the case, but the timings were liberal at 55 minutes with no less than 27 of those for
the last $23\frac{1}{4}$ miles. Departures were usually made at the correct
time from Waterloo so that there was not a lot of point in rushing
out to Basingstoke, merely to stand outside or in the station to
let the schedule catch up, and expend a lot of effort in the process. Consequently running tended to be adequate rather than
exciting. Detail C of Table 41 and detail D of Table 42 readily
confirm this. In the first unmodified No. 34006 suffered a
signal check to 20 m.p.h. and then ran steadily to regain the lost
time without having recourse to any undue exertion. The rebuilt larger engine met with slight delay on leaving Waterloo in
getting the proper main line route and then had a clear run to
draw in at Basingstoke a full six minutes early after holding
71 m.p.h. on the final 1-in-249 pitch before the stop. There was
no apparent reason for the haste displayed by No. 35025 with
this heavy train.

All the other runs in these two tables were made either just
before electrification works commenced or during such works
(when schedules were lengthened by an additional 8 minutes
between Woking and Basingstoke). Rumours were rife then,
and one of these was that the electric schedules were to include
a timing of 45 minutes from London to Basingstoke. What
could be done with electricity could be done with steam was the
opinion of some of the locomotive crews, and so Waterloo–
Basingstoke in 45 minutes became a challenge. That timing was
beaten on an actual basis more than once and several times on a
net time basis. In detail A, Table 41, rebuilt No. 34090 and
driver Saunders had a medium-weight 5.30 p.m. train to cope

with and lost no time in leaving the capital. Circumstances were
against them, however, because of crossing from main to slow at
Farnborough and back again at Winchfield: even so they
sauntered into Basingstoke 12 minutes before time. With a
similar load a larger rebuilt engine and driver Hooper fared
rather better. After the p.w. restriction had been cleared Hooper
really opened out No. 35005, some of the most astonishing
running coming west of Farnborough, including a ninety at
Newnham siding. This resulted in an arrival at Basingstoke
$11\frac{1}{4}$ minutes in advance of time on the 55-minute schedule
($41\frac{1}{2}$ minutes net). Passing over detail C which has already been
remarked upon, the 5.30 p.m. ex Waterloo hauled by No 35029
comes next under observation. This train was switched to the
local line outside Brookwood and back again at Farnborough,
after which the acceleration was most energetic and accom-
panied by a raucous exhaust. Last in Table 41 comes unmodified
No. 34102. In this case the driver had not entered the '45-
minute Stakes' but still finished up $8\frac{1}{4}$ minutes in hand on the
extended schedule. The rise in speed beyond Fleet should not
go unnoticed, being very fine for the smaller type of Pacific. It
was not achieved without some cost as the recorder notes that
'. . . 34102 produced many rockets . . . one of which entered my
compartment and burned a hole in the upholstery'!

First in Table 42 is driver Saunders again, this time with
No. 35017. This was one of three fine runs made on the
5.30 p.m. during the week by this driver, all of which were
deliberate attempts to get to Basingstoke inside three quarters of
an hour. A boat train, hauled by a standard class 5, was running
seven minutes in advance of the 5.30 p.m. and, by arrangement,
the driver of that engine promised to try to keep out of the way.
But the rise to milepost 31 told against the smaller engine and so
reacted on the 5.30 p.m. After the last of these checks the exhaust
noise was deafening—even in the fourth coach—to get up to
80 m.p.h. by Fleet. The finish was quite slow but, even so, the
train came to rest in $44\frac{1}{4}$ minutes ($41\frac{1}{2}$ net) with plenty of time
for any steam deficiency to be made up.

Detail B features a rebuilt *Battle of Britain* engine with a sub-
stantial load on a very steady run, and in detail C driver
Saunders is recorded again, with rebuilt *Merchant Navy*
No. 35005. Saunders was going even better than with No. 35017

before he was stopped in his tracks before Hersham. Recovery was good but without a storming finish it was not possible to return less than 41¾ minutes net.

Few drivers would indulge in 'fireworks' with a heavy train on the first leg of a long journey: if they had there would have been a justifiable lack of enthusiasm on the part of their fireman and the probability of the fire being pulled apart. Fast exits from Waterloo always risked checks from the preceding train running on a 3-minute headway, but this was hardly likely to cause driver Hendicott any concern with the newspaper train on 19 March 1966 (detail A, Table 43). The train was switched to the local line at the west crossing at Waterloo and therefore was able to pass through Clapham Junction at a higher rate than on the down main, although this benefit was more than wiped out by the reduction at Wimbledon to gain the main line. The apparent lack of acceleration between Surbiton and Hampton Court Junction was due to the brake being inadvertently applied and the run-in to Woking included crossing to the local line again. Assuming a run on the main line throughout, the net time is calculated as 26 minutes.

The next run (detail B), again by a modified *Battle of Britain* engine, benefited from a 4-minute late start which driver Robinson managed to wipe out by the time he reached Woking. This run was most energetic and worked up to a fine climax. Detail C shows a *Merchant Navy* getting away very quickly but, lacking the incentive supplied by a late departure, not being pushed beyond Surbiton. Rebuilt No. 34018 next features in an extraordinary start with a 400-ton train; aided by a higher than normal speed through Clapham Junction, coupled with a very fast exit through Vauxhall, it returned an unusual time of 16 minutes to pass Hampton Court Junction. Either the locomotive was winded, or more likely, the driver realised the hurry he was subjecting the train to, for thereafter there was a marked easing down. Despite that the stage was completed in 26½ minutes.

Finally in Table 43 there is an example of a *West Country* in original condition loaded to twelve vehicles with the 5.00 p.m.

West of England train. There was a slow start to Clapham Junction, after which the running was not markedly short of the *Merchant Navy* effort in detail C.

Table 44 places on record some Surbiton–Woking snippets with the 8.35 a.m. from Waterloo in the closing months of steam traction. With a light load No. 35023 rather steals the show (detail A), although probably the run of greatest merit was made by the smaller engine No. 34036 on 28 October 1966 (detail D).

WOKING TO BASINGSTOKE

Less than two of the 23½ miles from Woking to Basingstoke are downhill. At the start there is the climb to milepost 31 on gradients around the 1-in-300 inclination and then follows a generally rising road with some level stretches, so the section could fairly be described as against the collar for the locomotives.

Table 45 is confined to runs made in 1967 when the payment-by-results scheme initiated by a group of performance recorders was in operation. The schedules laid down were of academic interest only and therefore have been omitted from the table. The first three runs were on newspaper trains when the powers-that-were were tucked up in bed and dreaming of the new electric trains purring over the summit at milepost 31 at 80 m.p.h. They would have had nightmares if they had known steam was doing just that with a motley collection of vans and three coaches filled with railway enthusiasts! Detail A records No. 35008 with three coaches and two vans: at the start the train had to cross over to the local line but then was opened up to three-quarters regulator at 27 per cent cut-off, which produced the acceleration beyond Brookwood. Riding on the local line was very rough and the driver deemed it advisable to ease off, otherwise the summit might have been carried at 85 m.p.h. Steam was shut off for Farnborough and easing took place at Winchfield, the run concluding with a crossing from local to main line. Despite all the easings Basingstoke was reached well within even time. So it was on the mornings of 4 and 8 July! Even time by Farnborough by No. 34001 was especially noteworthy. Not far behind this standard of running—considering the heavier load—was No. 35003 in detail D. No. 35007's run was the continuation of that in Table 44, detail C.

Going back a year or two detail A of Table 46 indicates how an unmodified light Pacific performed on the nocturnal newspaper train. Things had not been worked up to such a pitch as just noted and so the climb to milepost 31 was rather more sedate but good for the 350-ton load. This run was made on the local line all the way, the speeds beyond Fleet being remarkably steady. Another unmodified engine, No. 34051, features in detail B. There was heavy slipping at the start but otherwise it was a good run. Rather better were the two runs by rebuilt engines made in July 1966, especially that by No. 34036 when a very good start was made. It was a pity that the signal stop outside Basingstoke spoilt the run, although it must be conceded that the stage was completed within the schedule at that time. By comparison the effort put up by No. 35030 on 3 July 1967 looks a little feeble.

BASINGSTOKE TO SOUTHAMPTON

The first four miles out of Basingstoke, on the Southampton road, were uphill slog all at 1-in-249 nearly to Wootton signal box; then came a couple of miles slightly falling to Steventon signal box, two more up at 1-in-600 to the summit in Litchfield tunnel and then a glorious fall for over twenty miles, which was conducive to fast running not requiring high power output.

Detail A in Table 47 is the continuation of the last down steam-hauled newspaper train (Table 45, detail C) and driver Porter's own swan-song with that type of traction. The start to Wootton was fairly brisk but, of course, the load was light and no difficulty was encountered in stopping in Winchester well within even time. Porter did not loiter on the next two stages, getting No. 34095 to sprint along nimbly enough. Driver Hendicott (Table B) had a respectable load which caused the ascent to Wootton to be taken at slower gait than No. 34095's effort. As soon as 95 m.p.h. was reached at Wallers Ash steam was shut off and the locomotive was coasted to the relaying slack at Shawford Junction. After regaining speed the train got on the tail of something in front; a probable net time would be 31 minutes or just over 60 m.p.h. average.

Table 48 details some gallops to Winchester. No. 34001 (detail A), one gathers, was nominally in the hands of driver Anderson. With a reasonable load a violent attack was made on the up grades, as witness 4 minutes to Worting Junction, 6 to Wootton and 8¾ minutes to the summit at Litchfield tunnel. The fire then went out of No. 34001's belly (or chimney ?) and the descent paid due respect to some non-bogie stock included in the train formation. Going up the weight scale, No. 35012 had a 75 m.p.h. restriction van in the consist which the driver obviously forgot in his effort to see no time was dropped due to the signal check; No. 35008 with an eleven-coach train in the less competitive days of 1964 put up a very rapid climb to Litchfield tunnel and bowled along in easy fashion thereafter; No. 35003 with an eleven minute late departure from Basingstoke plus a p.w. restriction provided tailor-made conditions for the driver, and finally No. 35005 with driver Rabbetts, whose days to retirement could then be easily counted, had to get a move on below Wallers Ash to attain 100 m.p.h. With 2 minutes 42 seconds from passing Winchester Junction at 99 m.p.h. to the stand at Winchester and a signal check and 100 m.p.h. maximum thrown in for luck one cannot but be impressed by the efficiency of the brakes and the coolness of the driver. The three high speed runs down the grade must have been thrilling to record but none required a power output of a very high order so much as an ability to run freely.

In Table 49 the scene of action moves down the line. The advantage gained by fast running in the region of Allbrook could easily be lost by coming into Southampton cautiously, as witness No. 35029 in detail E compared with, say, No. 34007 in detail C. No. 34107 (detail G) took a long time over the last mile especially as the speed at Northam Junction was higher than normal. Even swifter than anything in this table was the run of No. 34071 in Table 50, when a lightning start was evidently made and braking at St Denys delayed for as long as possible. The other two runs in the table relate to the snippet introduced by the opening of Southampton Airport: driver Dente with No. 34044 managed to clock under even time start-to-stop, and without the signal check it would seem No. 35023 could have repeated the feat.

SOUTHAMPTON CENTRAL TO BOURNEMOUTH CENTRAL
On the face of it a 34-minute schedule for 27¾ miles is not over-demanding so far as motive power is concerned. There was a

little more to matters on this route however; firstly, there was a 40 m.p.h. restriction $2\frac{1}{2}$ miles from the start; secondly, a 60 m.p.h. restriction at the half-way mark at the foot of the 1-in-103 climb to Sway; thirdly, there was the 60 m.p.h. restriction at Christchurch in the dip between Hinton Admiral and Pokesdown. Taking all this into account an elapsed time of 32 minutes for the stage could be considered good. All in all, the standard of running was consistently high over this section of line, a fact borne out by the large amount of data available, which has made the task of selection of noteworthy runs tantalisingly difficult. Accordingly the records have been tabulated in weight groups, the first (Table 51) being eleven-coach trains in the 375–400 tons bracket.

To open the running is a record of unmodified No. 34040, in the hands of Bournemouth's driver Sprague, with the very lightly patronised 2.30 p.m. from Waterloo. The departure was five minutes late and even with a slip on starting Redbridge was cleared in the first five minutes; Sprague had gained three-quarters of a minute by Lymington Junction (the 17-minute schedule might have more realistically been 18) but, on this August Bank Holiday, he did not push the engine down from Hinton Admiral. Instead no braking took place for the Christchurch slack and this helped the climb up to Pokesdown, on which the speed did not fall below 60 m.p.h. A little over two years later the same recorder sampled the train again with modified *West Country* No. 34029 and a three-minute late departure. A signal check—virtually to a stop—opened proceedings and acceleration from this was not hurried, the driver probably judging it best to let the obstruction get well out of the way. In the forest, however, the train moved in no uncertain manner and Sway bank was breasted at 62 m.p.h., doubtless with the help of a higher than regulation speed at Lymington Junction. There was no restraining No. 34029 down Hinton bank nor yet at Christchurch (recorder's note says '. . . the riding of the curve at 82 m.p.h. did not seem rough to me') and, notwithstanding a slight check at Bournemouth Goods, an on time arrival was made.

The remaining three runs in this table belong to the modified *Merchant Navy* type. The first of this trio (detail C) had the luxury of no checks and the speed restrictions were not treated

with any great degree of disrespect. The whole run was one of a
sustained effort throughout—a good start, strong up the banks
and free running downhill. Next comes No. 35007 in the hands
of driver Evans of Nine Elms No. 1 Link. Despite two slight
checks, No. 35007 was level with No. 35005 in the previous run
at Lymington Junction and then drew away to attain even time
by Hinton Admiral. Evans by now was well before time, which
would account for the easing up Pokesdown bank. Even after
the stop outside Bournemouth—and a 20-second slip on restarting—the arrival was $4\frac{1}{2}$ minutes before time. It is on record
that the exhaust noise on climbing Sway bank was 'absolutely
phenomenal'. The net time works out at $28\frac{1}{2}$ minutes for the
$28\frac{3}{4}$ miles.

Detail E is the continuation of the run tabulated in Table 36
(detail B) which had a bad delay above Micheldever. Time had
to be made up to the tune of four minutes. Driver Letchford did
not initially 'push' No. 35030 but after Woodfidley the dust was
really raised, culminating in a 70 m.p.h. attack on Sway bank.
This was followed by 80 m.p.h. at New Milton and a rousing
85 m.p.h. at Christchurch—to say nothing of 70 m.p.h. at
Pokesdown! The reward for all this was a one minute signal
stop outside Bournemouth, but even so Letchford drew into the
platform there at booked time after a run which is probably the
fastest ever with steam from Southampton Central to passing
Boscombe or for a net time of 28 minutes (the present booking
for electric traction) for the whole distance.

Moving into the twelve-coach grade (400 tons tare) driver
Hutton's run with No. 35028 needs no elaboration; Hutton was
a most reliable man whose running was always very steady, fireworks being resolutely eschewed. Detail B of this table (52)
features an unmodified *Merchant Navy* getting away to a very
brisk start and gaining on No. 35028 in the first column until
signal checks wrecked proceedings and put paid to what could
have been a 30-minute run. No. 35014, a rebuilt engine, had a
very poor start from Southampton (detail C) with no less than
seven slips, as well as a 6-minute deficit to recoup. Matters improved across the New Forest and with a thundering approach
to Christchurch there was a very good chance of cutting arrears
substantially: unfortunately the 9.30 a.m. ex Waterloo was not
out of the way and a crawling approach through Boscombe was

the result. Detail D places on record an effort of Bournemouth's driver Rabbetts, well served by fireman Wright, to offset a 10 m.p.h. restriction near Beaulieu Road which resulted in some livery progress downhill from Hinton Admiral. The net time assumes a fast flight across the forest.

Table 53 features the *Bournemouth Belle* with its heavy stock. Driver Elston demonstrated the good climbing abilities of No. 35007 although, with about six minutes in hand, things were not pressed for the final rise to Pokesdown. On the second of these runs there was a signal failure at Millbrook and a relaying slack at Sway, neither of which daunted the driver. Some slipping occurred on wet rails on Pokesdown bank. No. 35017 (detail C) was hampered by signals near Totton but ran very steadily to keep within the schedule. In detail D there is a record of a run by a modified *West Country*. A lot of slipping in leaving Southampton put the train behind time; although this was regained the not unusual stop outside Bournemouth prevented a punctual arrival. The last of these *Belle* runs was during the period when electrification works were at their zenith. No. 35007 was two minutes late away from Southampton and went well enough until Sway where single line working (on the up line) was in progress as far as New Milton. Again checks were met in the concluding stages of the run and the arrival was five minutes late at Bournemouth.

The final table of non-stop runs (54) between Itchen and Bourne concerns trains loaded to twelve and thirteen vehicles. The first of these relates to the *Pines Express* diverted from its original Mendip route. Unrebuilt No. 34041 is recorded as being allowed to make its own pace almost the whole way. It would have been more interesting if it had been pressed! A large modified engine appears in detail B with a thirteen-coach load and seems to have coped without any trouble as far as Christchurch. Inwards from there no great verve was displayed, although this might have been due to cautionary signals which the recorder did not observe. Another thirteen-coach train, the *Pines* again, appears under detail C in charge of No. 34044, which dealt with the load in competent style. Despite the dearth of speeds in the log it may be deduced that the restrictions at Brockenhurst and Christchurch were observed and that the climb to Sway was fractionally better—the more so when weights are compared—than No. 34041's effort in the first detail.

Driver Cooper and Fireman Gallen with No. 35011 (detail D) were badly delayed north of Winchester and in consequence left Southampton $8\frac{3}{4}$ minutes late. The recorder in this case was travelling in the tenth vehicle from the engine which affects the passing times, more especially when compared with other logs, in giving a slow start and a fast finish. With this load and an engine which the crew described as 'stiff' there was some fine running between Lyndhurst Road and Brockenhurst and up Pokes-down bank. Fortunately the finish was not delayed and a good time of $31\frac{1}{2}$ minutes was returned. Heaviest of all the trains in Table 54 was the down *Bournemouth Belle* allocated to which was No. 21C11. The schedule was a couple of minutes more than that faced in detail D and so the demands on the engine were not so heavy despite the increase in loading. The start was rather better than that of the previous run but thereafter the running reflected the easy schedule. How could a crew spin out 36 minutes with one of these engines—even if loaded to 500 tons?

Lightly-loaded trains on semi-fast duties could provide some fast running, as one observer found with the 7.30 p.m. ex Waterloo. Table 55 illustrates this: indeed *with* a stop at Brockenhurst the running time between Southampton and Bournemouth could still be less than the 34 minutes allowed for the non-stops. In the first run the time inclusive of the stop came to $33\frac{1}{2}$ minutes, brought about possibly by a ten minute late start from Southampton. No. 34108 had been by no means sluggish as far as Brockenhurst but, upon restarting from there, fairly flew after a good climb to Sway. Another original *West Country*, this time driven by Rabbetts of Bournemouth, had a seven minute late start and got going well enough, especially between Totton and Lyndhurst Road and west of Beaulieu Road, to pull back four minutes in the initial stage. The restart with No. 34105 from Brockenhurst was nothing like as good as that of No. 34108, nor was the climb up from Christchurch. Detail C has a train with seven coaches rather than the six of the previous two runs and rebuilt *Merchant Navy* No. 35022 as the locomotive. Departure was eleven minutes late and despite an eighty in the forest it had its work cut out to compete with driver Rabbetts and No. 34105. A relaying check at Christ-

church was carefully observed, the net time being estimated as
$17\frac{1}{2}$ minutes from Brockenhurst to Bournemouth.

On a damp May evening driver Varney and fireman Ellement
had a rather more substantial load of eight vehicles with unrebuilt No. 34106. Four minutes arrears were nearly wiped out
by Brockenhurst and the remainder, despite slipping on getting
away from the intermediate stop, was easily recouped. Arrival
at Bournemouth was three minutes early after a particularly
good climb from Christchurch.

By way of contrast the final detail is of a heavy load handled
by a modified light Pacific. There was some very bad slipping at
the start, after which the engine settled down to a spell of competent running. Brockenhurst was a terror of a place to start a
long down train owing to the super elevation of the track. This
occasion proved no exception and cost $1\frac{1}{2}$ minutes, although it
probably gave rise to the performance that followed; especially
good were the climbs to Sway and Pokesdown, the latter with its
fine minimum of 62 m.p.h.

Next comes, in Table 56, a selection of Southampton–
Brockenhurst snippets. Nocturnal newspaper trains often were
productive of good sprightly running, as witness No. 34077
driven by Hendicott in detail A. A good start contributed, as
likely as not, to the check at Totton which was thought to be
due to tardiness in getting the level crossing gates open.
Apparently the train was not considered to be as near as it in
fact was. It would seem reasonable to reckon the net time as
$14\frac{1}{2}$ minutes for the 13·6 miles. Rebuilt No. 35013 with a light
load also had a quick start and the delay came on the approach
to Brockenhurst, again possibly because of the crossing barriers;
83 m.p.h. was a high figure for running in the forest. Next
comes unmodified No. 34002 with a heavier load and a good
steady running to knock five minutes off the booking. If No.
34002 had done well then rebuilt No. 34036 did even better
(detail D) in beating $15\frac{1}{4}$ minutes with 70 tons greater load. Last
of these snippets is detail E, wherein No. 34104 left Southampton $23\frac{3}{4}$ minutes late and without trace of a slip. A very fine exit
was made—especially in relation to the substantial load—and
was followed by some good driving on the part of Rowe.
Two minutes were regained to Brockenhurst and although
not shown here further time was regained to Bournemouth.

To conclude this section Table 57 records five runs with trains having calls to make beyond Brockenhurst. The final steam-hauled 2.45 a.m. newspaper train figures in detail A with No. 34095 and driver Porter; the record speaks for itself. Net time Southampton–Brockenhurst is reckoned as being 13¾ and the figure for the Christchurch stop is for the over-run stop 250 yards beyond the station, after which the train set back into the platform—doubtless 93 m.p.h. down the bank was a contributory factor in this miscalculation. The same train at an earlier date and same type of engine appears in detail B, under the supervision of driver Hooper. The remaining three runs all concern the eleven-coach 5.30 p.m. ex Waterloo. That in detail C was eleven minutes late on leaving Southampton; slipping occurred on starting at Southampton, Brockenhurst and New Milton, and at Christchurch it was necessary to set back. Maximum speed on Pokesdown bank was 28 m.p.h. and despite poor coal there was no lack of steam. A not dissimilar run to this is recorded in detail D with unmodified No. 34039; in this case there was a thirteen minute late start of which seven had been regained by Pokesdown. Slipping was noted at the last three stopping places and maximum speed on Pokesdown bank was 35 m.p.h. Last of all comes rebuilt *Merchant Navy* No. 35008 in a hurry although running to time. 84 m.p.h. *with this load* was remarkable in crossing the forest and 72 m.p.h. on the approach to New Milton is noteworthy. Speed rose to 35 m.p.h. on the climb to Pokesdown.

BOURNEMOUTH CENTRAL TO SOUTHAMPTON CENTRAL

The up Bournemouth road as far as Southampton was not so much a hard road as an awkward one with which few liberties could be taken. At the start there was a curving rise past the goods yard which meant caution had to be exercised to prevent slipping: the Christchurch dip carried a speed restriction of 60 m.p.h. which prevented Hinton Admiral bank being rushed and the same thing happened going downhill from Sway with a restriction to the same speed between Lymington Junction and Brockenhurst. At Woodfidley the limit was 75 m.p.h. and then, three miles from Southampton, a 40 m.p.h. slowing was necessary. It is hardly surprising, therefore, that even time does not appear to have been recorded for the start-to-stop journey with a train of significant weight.

Before considering in detail the runs for this section the reader may care to indulge in a slight test of judgement (or luck!) by getting a piece of paper at least the width of Table 58 and placing its lower edge immediately above the horizontal line giving the number of vehicles in the train. Having done this he is invited to note down which of the four variations of Pacific (the Giesl-ejector member is not included) he considers, based on the performance details, most likely to have hauled each particular train and then check the result by moving the paper up one line. The fact that each and every one of the five was hauled by an unmodified small Pacific underlines the even performance which was to be found on this length of line.

Passing to the details the first, A, records a Sunday afternoon run with driver Kiff in charge of No. 34006 when milepost 100 (the summit of the climb from Christchurch—at that point 1-in-103) was passed at 65 m.p.h. With the aid of a slight transgression of the restriction at Brockenhurst even time was returned by Beaulieu Road, and with an unchecked entry to Southampton a net time of 30 minutes would be not unreasonable for this sprightly run. With a coach more driver Allen and No. 34023 (detail B) did even better; the start was faster, although the climb up through Hinton Admiral was slightly slower—but fine nonetheless; the slight signal check at Brockenhurst put No. 34023 behind No. 34006 for which a storming finish made amends and gave a net time of under 30 minutes.

With a train of 400 tons No. 34044 in detail C could hardly be expected to be so lively as the two previously described but, after one minute had been conceded at the start, there was nothing between No. 34006's 14 min 33 sec from New Milton to Redbridge and the 14 min 38 sec of No. 34044 for the same distance with 80 tons more. Rising up the tonnage scale, detail D has No. 34094 with 475 tons on the *Royal Wessex* and a neck-and-neck run with No. 34044 as far as Sway, where the Bournemouth driver of No. 34094 deemed a less hurried passage of Brockenhurst to be the order of the day. Unfortunately a check to walking pace at Ashurst Crossing prevented an on-time arrival at Southampton.

Finally (detail E) in this table No. 34109 had the *Bournemouth Belle* loaded to almost 500 tons. It being a Sunday there was a lot of luggage to be stowed away in the vans and, without a trace of slip, No. 34109 left two minutes late on a foul afternoon. Three quarters of a minute was picked up by Lymington Junction but this was not sufficient to offset the slack at Ashurst Crossing where the gates were being replaced.

The *Bournemouth Belle* was undoubtedly as good a test as any for a locomotive over this section. Table 59 is devoted to runs with this train. In detail A driver Porter of Nine Elms had No. 34047 (which, due to poor steaming, he had in exchange for No. 34093 used on the down train) on what was officially the last time steam was to be booked for the job. As might be expected with this driver, the running was of good quality with the Hinton Admiral incline being climbed at nothing less than 60 m.p.h.

In some quarters the unmodified engines were considered to be slower off the mark than the rebuilt members of the class, but little of this can be detected from detail B, wherein No. 34041 was ahead of all other runners as far as New Milton. Indeed, the recorder makes mention of this start and from his notes it seems that on an afternoon of miserable conditions No. 34041 brightened up matters with a fine pyrotechnic display up Hinton Admiral bank. One injector was giving trouble and the blastpipe had partly disintegrated so that driver Pope had his hands full for the occasion. With a similar load No. 35011 and driver Hendicott were a little slower off the mark due to slipping and had the hindrance of a distant being 'on' at Lymington Junction. Here it may be apt to quote the recorder's note: '. . . a good run because the relevant pages in my notebook have the tell-tale grime of fine cinders in the folds—always indicative of hard running in warm weather!'

If Harry Pope had a difficult engine in No. 34041 then No. 35016 must have been in fine condition on 4 August 1963 (detail D). This run stands out as the finest from Bournemouth to Southampton, yet by Brockenhurst there was no marked superiority. Time was literally grabbed between Lyndhurst Road and Southampton and one hopes that the riding in the vicinity of Totton did not cause any upsets at the tea tables! Last in Table 59 there is an unrebuilt *Merchant Navy* effort exhibiting a slow start, a good climb from Christchurch and an exact timekeeping finish on what was the fastest-ever schedule for the length. This was a finely judged performance in which the speed of 75 m.p.h. occurred before, rather than at, Totton otherwise the results might have been even more colourful than on No. 35016's run.

The final Table (60) dealing with Bournemouth–Southampton non-stop runs is of a comparative nature, all with trains over the 400-ton mark. In detail A, No. 34001 had a $10\frac{1}{4}$-minute late departure to recoup and was dealt with well enough to win back over half of the arrears under the able hand of driver Davis of Weymouth. This run took place at the end of the steam era and the engine could not have been in pristine condition. It was otherwise in the case of the other two runs, made on the same day in June 1965, for both engines were recently ex-shops and in first class condition. Detail B features an interloper in the shape of class 5 No. 73092 in charge of one of Bournemouth's best enginemen. It is as well occasionally to see how the Pacifics compared with other classes, especially as one Bournemouth driver averred that if one could do London–Bournemouth in two hours with a Bulleid Pacific it could be done with anything else! It is considered that driver Dean had his standard 4-6-0 at full stretch for most of the way in an endeavour to adhere to the schedule. The start was, as might be expected, better than many by the Pacifics and, again as might be expected, the climb from Christchurch pulled speed down considerably. Beyond New Milton there was a noticeable lack of recovery to Sway but No. 73092 hung on gamely and did not disgrace itself. No. 34044 and driver Bevis of Bournemouth had a very heavy train to cope with and although the net time was a shade over 32 minutes it was evident that the engine was worked easily, there being little noise in the ascent of Hinton bank. In any case Bevis would not, by nature, work an engine unduly hard.

Turning to the semi-fast trains, the section from Bournemouth to Brockenhurst is dealt with in Table 61. In detail A No. 34040 was $6\frac{3}{4}$ minutes late away and put up a good performance. Sister engine No. 34044 was $5\frac{1}{4}$ minutes late off Bournemouth but lacked the verve displayed by No. 34040 or by No. 35011 in detail C. With a much heavier load rebuild No. 35017 (detail D) managed to pull back some of the five minute arrears which had arisen by the time Bournemouth was left.

At times the Brockenhurst–Southampton Central section would be the scene of some lively work. The runs in Table 62 illustrate this. With six coaches and a van, driver Porter shot out of Brockenhurst in startling fashion with unrebuilt No. 34015. After the check before Totton matters were taken very easily. The same driver with another original design engine— No. 34006—almost repeated the rapid exit made with No. 34015 and ran with vigour throughout, despite signal checks, to more than regain the $1\frac{1}{2}$-minute debit against the train at the start. Detail C features the Giesl ejector fitted locomotive, No. 34064 on a time-regaining run; similarly, in detail D, No. 35011 regained time with a 15-minute incentive on leaving Brockenhurst. Detail E is the continuation of detail D in Table 61, illustrating some very steady work with a good load marred only by the final signal check. Before passing on, reference may be made to a rather freakish run with No. 34006 when loaded to seven vehicles ($228\frac{1}{2}$/250 tons) which has not been tabulated. It took place six days after driver Porter's effort with No. 34015 (detail A) and the object was to beat that engine's time to Woodfidley. This was done with 10 seconds to spare at 72 m.p.h.; other times and speeds were Beaulieu Road 5 min 23 sec (61/69 m.p.h.), Lyndhurst Road 7 min 50 sec (60 m.p.h.), Totton 10 min 51 sec (51 m.p.h.), Redbridge 11 min 39 sec (31) and, after signal checks, Southampton Central 16 min 57 sec. The driver was Giles of Nine Elms and the run was recorded by Mr A. Wild.

To conclude the review of Bournemouth to Southampton running Table 63 contains a variety of semi-fast examples, all with reasonable tonnages. Unrebuilt No. 34012 in detail A had 23 minutes to win back on a summer Saturday evening and managed by Southampton to cut that down to a quarter of an hour. Slipping occurred at the starts from Bournemouth, Pokesdown and New Milton. Driver Porter with No. 35028 also had a late start (ten minutes) which was wiped out by the time Southampton was reached. The delay at Beaulieu Road was due to crossing over from the down line, due to single line working, which probably yields a net time of $15\frac{1}{2}$ minutes from Brockenhurst to Southampton. In detail C No. 35020 was obviously not under pressure and by comparison No. 34087 (detail D) did rather better on the Christchurch–Brockenhurst length. Lastly No. 34078, well loaded, put up a good performance especially through the forest, assisted probably by having been recently outshopped from Eastleigh works.

SOUTHAMPTON CENTRAL TO WATERLOO

This route needs little introduction: a climb of nearly twenty-five miles followed by a long racing descent to the capital is the bones of it. The tradition, so far as Bulleid Pacific driving was concerned, was steady up the bank just under the 60 m.p.h. mark and steady inwards from Basingstoke at a rate about 20 m.p.h. higher.

The running opens, in Table 64, with driver Porter of Nine Elms and rebuilt No. 35028 aiming a little higher than the tradition, although with a not very heavy train. Signal checks in the Eastleigh area hampered the start and no huge effort was made up the bank but thereafter there was a marked *joie de vivre* in the running despite a check before Woking. Four hundred tons gross was considered to be a minimum load for any self-respecting driver to demonstrate his steed's capabilities on this length and all the runs to be described meet this criterion. In detail B driver Prior took the *doyen* of the West Country class up to the summit in Litchfield tunnel at well above average rate but attempted nothing more than normal running thereafter. At Farnborough the train was switched to the relief line regaining the main line at Brookwood. After the signal check at Surbiton progress became sedate.

There was some lively running by rebuilt No. 34044 in detail C. As an incentive there was a departure 8½ minutes late, and from the commencement it was evident a special effort would be made. In addition to the relaying restriction at Winchester Junction there was a signal check just after Winchester itself. The recovery from the slack was most vigorous and speed kept on rising right up the climb to Roundwood. The crew appeared to be in rather a hurry to leave the county of Hampshire, as witness the progress at Fleet and Farnborough. A signal check at Woking sobered up proceedings for the following permanent way slack at Weybridge. Arrival at the terminus was 1½ minutes early and a good time had been enjoyed by all.

Not all running was like this, especially before the announcement of the execution of steam, and bearing this in mind attention may be given to a run by an unmodified *West Country*
No. 34041 made in 1957. Southampton Central was left
$4\frac{1}{4}$ minutes late and with a temporary speed restriction in force
at Malden matters were judged perfectly to bring the train into
Waterloo on the dot of time.

Behind the figures of detail E of Table 64 there is a tale.
Driver Ernest Rabbetts had determined to have a shot at a
three-figure speed on the up Southampton run before his retirement. As many another driver has done (the classic case being
Clements of Exmouth Junction with his last down *Atlantic
Coast Express*, when his record-breaking attempt was cut short
by a locomotive derailing itself at Yeovil Junction and blocking
everything), Rabbetts left things a bit late and, suddenly finding
his date for retirement was earlier than he had thought, was
obliged to make his attempt with the 12.40 p.m. from Bournemouth Central on 30 April 1964. As it turned out a better choice
could have been made because No. 35029 was handed over at
Bournemouth with a poor fire and low in steam. Attention was
immediately given to the fire by fireman Wright, and by
Southampton, despite the poor coal, matters were a little
brighter; there was a good start and an equally good climb to
Roundwood, although the regulator vibrated down between
Winchester Junction and Micheldever on a couple of occasions,
so that by Worting Junction there were several minutes in
hand. A slight signal check at Basingstoke did not set matters
back too badly and Rabbetts started to build up his speed. By
Brookwood he was up to 94 m.p.h. when the 1.30 p.m. down
came along, like a destroyer, laying a smoke screen. There was
little or no wind and, although Rabbetts hung on as long as
possible, the pall persisted: he dare not risk missing a signal—
because he was about seven minutes before time a clear road
through Woking might well not be available—and therefore he
had no option but to ease down. In the event the road was clear
but No. 35029 was not steaming too well on the dross being fed
in and Rabbetts had to content himself with a $75\frac{1}{2}$-minute
actual time or $73\frac{3}{4}$ minutes net.

Continuing, in Table 65, the pre-1965 running, a couple of
twelve-coach trains handled by *West Country* class engines may

next be considered. The first of these, with modified No. 34039, had the incentive of a seven minute late start which appeared to put driver Purchase on his mettle sufficiently to make an above average climb to Roundwood and regain time to the extent of $4\frac{1}{2}$ minutes by Worting Junction. On the other hand, the arrears unmodified No. 34044 had to make up was no more than $3\frac{1}{2}$ minutes and so nothing more than an average climb ensued. After Basingstoke, however, the faster running was made by the unmodified engine and with a signal check only of a moderate nature at Woking an on-time arrival was made. No. 34039 and driver Purchase got a nasty signal stop outside Woking which put paid to a right-time arrival. The good climb to the summit gave No. 34039 a net time of $77\frac{1}{2}$ minutes compared with 79 for the unmodified No. 34044. To counter the tendency to record the more spectacular performances, that of No. 34050 has been included (detail C) as a typical run—55 m.p.h. up the bank, 65–75 m.p.h. beyond Basingstoke, 80 m.p.h. in the vicinity of Woking and signal checks in the suburban area. A clear road in would have avoided a $1\frac{1}{2}$-minute late arrival.

A couple of *Bournemouth Belle* journeys complete the table. No. 34005 had to contend with a relaying restriction in the tunnel at Southampton and a slight signal check after Eastleigh (which brought speed down by about 5 m.p.h.) before the attack on the incline. This could be made in vigorous style because of the temporary speed restriction at the summit. At Worting Junction the relief line was taken as far as Winchfield and then came a gallop to the suburban area. The net time is difficult to calculate with regard to the Roundwood slack but, assuming the boiler had not been mortgaged on the ascent it works out at about $76\frac{1}{2}$ minutes. The unrebuilt *Merchant Navy*, No. 21C14, with a heavy load made a very leisurely recovery from the check at Shawford Junction and fell back rather on the approach to Roundwood. There was time to spare at Worting, nonetheless, and with a sprint thrown in afterwards it was asking for a signal check—and it came. Indeed, there were three in all, but an early arrival was not prevented.

To round off this length of line comes Table 66 with what are five classic performances. First in date order comes No. 35027 in charge of Bournemouth driver Sprague on a special eighty-minute schedule. About this time the authorities were examining the possibilities of an hour and twenty minute booking each way between London and Southampton, and for this purpose test runs were carried out with the 10.30 a.m. down and the 3.15 p.m. up. One minute off the down schedule presented no difficulty and was duly accomplished. The real interest came in the up run. Timing was undertaken from the rear of the train and has accentuated the apparent slow start. Once clear of Eastleigh Sprague opened out and an unprecedented speed— for that time—of 70 m.p.h. was recorded at St Cross. The climb to Roundwood was taken very steadily with speed falling off slightly on the higher ground. A rapid acceleration followed a check approaching Basingstoke and an equally quick recovery was noted after the Woking caution. No relaxation in running was allowed so that Sprague pulled into Waterloo with 1½ minutes in hand on the test schedule, or 5½ early by the public time, giving enough margin to nip round for the down *Royal Wessex*! Net time works out at 74¾ minutes which, in 1960, was considered to be a very good performance. Actual running time is within the mile-a-minute rate.

Moving on three years to detail B, driver Rabbetts again appears and with a nine minutes late start to recover. He immediately set about the task with No. 35021 and the help of fireman Wilson and went up the bank to such good effect that over half of the arrears were wiped out. Pressure was kept up by both driver and fireman and the speed limit of 85 m.p.h. more than once transgressed before the problem of Woking arose. The check was severe enough to put on on-time arrival at Waterloo out of court, otherwise Rabbetts and Wilson might well have pulled into the terminus early. Within a month this effort had been surpassed, as detail C indicates. Driver Pope of Nine Elms No. 2 Link had already brought No. 35016 to Southampton from Bournemouth in 29 minutes (see detail 59D) and immediately followed this up with a restart unparalleled for a load of such magnitude, so that the possibility of an error of one minute in the starting time cannot be entirely ruled out. Be that as it may, there followed an excellent climb to Roundwood summit and a finely judged descent to the capital, the speed limit being only fractionally exceeded near Fleet. Happily there was a clear road almost to the end, and whether the net time be 73 or 74 minutes it was a most notable performance.

The last two runs were made in the spring of 1965 when the
writing was on the wall for steam. Both were on the *Bournemouth Belle* with worthy loads and had the advantage of good
weather conditions. Driver Hooper with No. 35012 was making
a deliberate attempt to extend the locomotive from start to
finish. The engine was accelerated the whole way to the summit
at an unprecedented rate for the load. The summit was reached
before 80 m.p.h. could be recorded but if the climb could have
been elongated this figure would not appear to have been un-
obtainable. A signal check before Worting Junction fortunately
did not herald an obstruction and the headlong dash for
Waterloo may best be seen from the range of speeds (81–
93 m.p.h.) between Winchfield and New Malden. This run was
pre-meditated, but Hendicott's effort with No. 35011 was not.
It was not until he had passed Eastleigh that he was mildly
challenged to beat with No. 35011 the effort that driver Hooper
had made the previous month. At such short notice the result
was remarkable. With a difference of 16 m.p.h. in speed at
Eastleigh Hendicott narrowed the gap to 4 m.p.h. at the summit
before deciding to call it a day. By any normal standards the remainder of his run was splendid, but it does suffer when placed
next to Hooper's flight with No. 35012. On both of these runs
the time for Litchfield tunnel is the mean of entry and exit times,
as was the habit employed by this recorder.

WINCHESTER CITY TO WATERLOO

There were not many non-stop trains from Winchester to
Waterloo, and those that there were usually got involved in
signal checks approaching the suburban area if before-time
running was indulged in. Consequently the main aim of most
drivers was to keep to schedule and avoid checks and the usual
running pattern was a steady start up to Worting without any
fireworks and an equally steady run in to London with fast
running to Woking if arrears had to be made up. Because of the
slow start it was very seldom possible to record any substantial
improvement on a 60 m.p.h. rate for the net time.

In Table 67 the record opens with rebuilt No. 34037 bringing
back the Sunday excursionists. It was not a heavy load and this
gave driver Myles the opportunity to indulge in some sprightly

running. There was good acceleration from the relaying slowing just after the start and, with nothing more than two slight reductions in speed beyond, there was every chance of a 64 (actual)-minute run. Waterloo was full up and Myles had to join the queue and waste eleven minutes. With the same load *Merchant Navy* No. 35028 did not display like energy (detail B) at the start, although the speed near Fleet was a bit high for a morning train. According to the driver the locomotive was so rough that he decided against trying for a three-figure speed. For the run in detail C the clock goes back ten years and to the traditional 50 m.p.h. climb to Roundwood. What was not quite so traditional was the romp east of Woking with the unmodified engine living up to its name of *Hurricane*, but for this the penalty of a signal check was paid and the train delayed. The last of the four runs in this table was, like details A and B, made to an extended schedule rather than to the standard 72 minutes of detail C. The start was immensely brisk considering that the arrears on leaving Winchester was nothing more serious than $1\frac{3}{4}$ minutes. There is a slightly better effort on record when No. 35030 with nine vehicles (300/320 tons) got past Micheldever in $10\frac{1}{2}$ minutes at 71 m.p.h. and into Litchfield tunnel in just under $12\frac{1}{2}$ minutes from the start at 74 m.p.h. at the behest of driver Hooper but, considering No. 34044 had a heavier load, the laurels rest with the smaller engine. After Worting Junction No. 34044 had a chequered run and so many slight checks make an estimate of net time difficult: probably $64\frac{3}{4}$ minutes is not far wrong.

Table 68 is devoted to the *Royal Wessex*, the heavy fast morning train which was a testing assignment for a *West Country* engine when loaded to thirteen vehicles. Not a lot of comment is called for in the case of No. 34001 in detail A—the record speaks for itself—except to note that the fog was thickening as the journey progressed. Just why driver Saunders ran so fast with No. 35026 in detail B is not revealed: whatever the reason this combination gained 4 minutes by Worting Junction, and with the assistance of 90 m.p.h. running another 4 by Woking, making the estimated net time of 63 minutes seem rather conservative, especially when compared with the previous effort of No. 34001. The last three runs are all by locomotives in original condition and display the tradition of running this train.

No. 35030 got signals before the p.w. check at Hampton Court Junction and, possibly because of severe braking, stalled as the signals cleared. The small engine, No. 34107, showed at the hands of her driver complete mastery of the heavy load and put in an appearance at Waterloo three-quarters of a minute early. This run, some slipping on starting apart, was a model of economic operation combined with good timekeeping.

SOUTHAMPTON CENTRAL TO WINCHESTER

The slow passage of Northam Junction, with a restriction of 15 m.p.h., always prevented a time of under $16\frac{1}{2}$ minutes from being returned on the $12\frac{3}{4}$-mile hop to Winchester. With a moderate load No. 35030 was worked up to a climax of 71 m.p.h. (detail A, Table 69) by driver Hooper before the stop at Winchester. No. 35013 on the Sunday excursion from Weymouth well loaded put up a very similar performance when the slight p.w. check is taken into account. In detail C an uneven performance by No. 35005 is noted; the start to St Denys was very smart indeed but the effort flattened out by Eastleigh to be rounded off by a very fast run in from St Cross when the brakes must have been applied very late to bring the train to as smart a halt as its start. No. 35014 more than recouped a minute late departure from Southampton on a steady, not untypical, run for a heavy train, but the show is stolen by the last of the five tabulations to be considered wherein unrebuilt No. 34078 set a standard which none of the larger rebuilt engines could better. There was a quick start and sustained effort by this engine; unfortunately the recorder had to alight at Winchester and although his hope that someone recorded matters on to Waterloo may have been fulfilled, nothing has come to hand to see what transpired.

WINCHESTER TO BASINGSTOKE

Before 1965 anyone who might have contemplated a 60 m.p.h. start-to-stop run from Winchester to Basingstoke with steam traction would have been dismissed as a dreamer, at best. With time running out for steam traction some drivers did have a tilt at such a target and but for p.w. or signal checks might well have managed it. Table 70 illustrates five gallops: in these cases the schedules have not been included because it would be rather meaningless, but, solely for the record, a typical one was 5½ minutes to pass Winchester Junction, 25 to pass Worting Junction and 29 to the stop at Basingstoke. In detail A No. 35003 had the disadvantage of a p.w. slack at Winchester Junction but this did not stop the '80' mark being reached; No. 34087 had the advantage of no hindrances on the climb and so surmounted the summit in excess of 80 m.p.h., Roundwood signal box being passed in less than even time—a deliberate, but nonetheless praiseworthy, feat. The last of these runs was by an original light Pacific with a heavier task of a train exceeding 250 tons. A right-time departure was made, and in trying to hurry the engine along the driver was faced with continuous slipping for the whole length of the ascent.

BASINGSTOKE TO WOKING

Although this stretch of 23½ miles largely favoured the engine the traditional running was pedestrian but usually adequate to keep the schedule of a minute or so under the half-hour. Right at the end of the steam era this length was 'discovered', and being fettled up for 100 m.p.h. running there were no qualms about the riding to be encountered at such speeds. Could steam then, with the advantage of good track, keep the 19½-minute schedule laid down for the electric trains? Provided the loads did not exceed 300 tons and there were no out-of-course checks, the runs in Tables 71 and 72 certainly demonstrated it could be done. Indeed some of these exploits seemed to have caused the recorders to become too excited to total accurately the tare weight of the trains: for example, no less than five logs of No. 34021's run in detail C were received, the number of vehicles and weights being given as 6/175; 7/-; 7/225/240; 7/200/220; and 7/187½/205. Yet the difference in the elapsed time for the run ranged no more than *two* seconds from 19 min 15 sec to 19 min 17 sec which demonstrated good application to the task while the train was in motion! Because of this, estimated gross weights are given for two details.

Running is opened by No. 35003 with a very light load and speeds in excess of 100 m.p.h. in the Fleet area. This same engine is credited with one or two very similar runs giving net times of $18\frac{1}{2}$ minutes. In detail B No. 35008 had already exceeded 100 m.p.h. coming up from Salisbury under the hand of a Basingstoke man, and the Nine Elms driver seemed determined to show he could do as well. In the event it appears he may not have succeeded for, although he may have touched three figures, it was not maintained for a measurable distance. 100 mp.h. was claimed as the maximum for No. 34021 but the claim cannot be substantiated from the data supplied; for all that it was a well sustained run giving a splendid actual time of $19\frac{1}{4}$ minutes.

By the time these capers—and capers they were indeed (although by no means detracting from the ability of the machines and men to produce such performances)—were being enjoyed the metamorphosis of the *Merchant Navy* class had long since been complete. But not so the smaller class of Pacific. Details D and E of Table 71 give an indication of what could be done with the original design and a moderate load. For No. 34102 a speed of 100 m.p.h. at the site of Bramshot Halt is claimed. The pass-to-pass time Fleet–Bramshot is stated as 32 seconds which, for the distance of 68 chains gives an average speed of 95·6 m.p.h. Once again the century may have been reached although the supporting data is too lean to establish the point without question.

Heavier loads are featured in Table 72. Little comment is necessary save to notice driver Rickman's late attempt with No. 35023 (detail A) to reach a high speed and to pass the observation that No. 34087, at the hands of an Eastleigh driver, gave a performance with a twelve-coach train which was certainly not the least meritorious of the nine examples under consideration.

WOKING TO WATERLOO

The last stage of the semi-fast or stopping trains on the main line was usually non-stop from Woking to Waterloo and it seldom produced anything more than adequate performances because of the blanket speed restriction inwards from New Malden, the permanent slowing called for at Clapham Junction and the increasing volume of traffic as the terminus was approached. Schedules ranged from 29 to 32 minutes for the

24·3 miles, which called for some energy to be exhibited in the first dozen miles at least.

In retrospect, the smaller Pacifics always seemed to make a better fist of this length than the *Merchant Navy* class and this is borne out by the selection in Table 73—all small engines. Rebuild No. 34077 had a trifling load and wasted no time in heading for home: the recorder noted that 'this is probably record time to pass Hampton Court from Woking start with steam' and certainly tremendous activity was demonstrated as far as New Malden. Whether driver Gale made a habit of approaching Waterloo in the same way as his Nine Elms *confrère* Evans is not known, but if he did the net time could well be reduced to 24 minutes. As it was, Gale brought his train to a halt 7¾ minutes early. No. 34015 (detail B) clearly demonstrated that the reputation the unrebuilt engines had in some quarters for slow starting was unfounded, but unluckily it got signals badly at Weybridge, otherwise more of the 13¾ minutes of a late start would have been regained. Driver Evans had the luxury of an unchecked run with No. 34100 and put it to good effect with an under even time run. With a similar load and the same driver, No. 34057, an unmodified engine, was able to return an even faster net time due solely to a very fast run into the terminus and skilful brake handling. Last in this table the well-known No. 34023 put up a splendid performance with a 300-ton train of an even time journey. Had it come in as fast as No. 34057 it would have taken the honours completely.

Table 74 presents four runs with trains of substance featuring each variety of Pacific. It is a nice point, and one which could be argued *ad infinitum*, as to which is the finest run of the four. A recital of additional detail may assist in such consideration: No. 35027 left Woking 14½ minutes behind time; No. 34019 was noted as being 'driven with energy, not thrashed'; No. 34104 left Woking 2½ minutes early, whilst No. 35004 was merely noted as being a good engine—not, it would appear, without some reason!

BOURNEMOUTH CENTRAL—WEYMOUTH

Locomotive performance between Bournemouth and Weymouth has never excited attention to any marked degree. The particular feats associated with this route are the fifteen-minute booking of LSWR days between Dorchester and Wareham and the 95 m.p.h. gallop of a *Schools* class 4–4–0 over part of the same length in the pre-1939 era. Whether or not T9 Class 4–4–0 locomotives achieved the even time booking (the purist will rightly point out the distance is but 14 miles 79 chains!) is not clear; what is certain, however, is that the Pacifics have done so—in the opposite, and uphill, direction.

Before coming to examples of such runs the general features of the route may be recalled. The exit from Bournemouth is against the grade (about 1-in-300) for the most part to Gas Works Junction, followed by a 1-in-120 rise to Branksome station and then a steep drop at 1-in-60 to nearly sea level at Poole. Beyond Poole there is a short, sharp rise at 1-in-100 to Hamworthy Junction, a corresponding fall at a lesser inclination and then a level section through Holton Heath. After Wareham there is a 1½-mile climb at 1-in-200 past Worgret Junction (where the speed restriction is a greater handicap to up trains than to those to Dorchester), a short dip and then a rising tendency to Wool; a mile west of Wool the climb steepens at 1-in-200, -180, -100 almost as far as Moreton. A short falling length occurs after that station followed by another climb of a couple of miles, a mile down at 1-in-200 and a final climb at 1-in-110 into Dorchester station.

Lightweight loads, possibly coupled with a late start, could provide the incentive for a driver with a liking for speed, as may be seen in Table 75. In detail A No. 35026 restarted so briskly from Wareham that it was necessary to ease the locomotive at Worgret Junction to acknowledge the speed restriction; acceleration was rapid and the maximum of 81 m.p.h. was attained before topping the 1-in-100 rise at 73 m.p.h. to pass Moreton well within even time. No. 35022, also a rebuilt locomotive, indicated that similar times could be returned with one coach more; in this case the maximum speed occurred on the rise to Dorchester rather than in the dip.

With the tonnage increased to 175 rebuild No. 34098 returned similar times as far as Wareham. For the stiffest section the running between Worgret and Wool was not so hard as with the larger engines and so a start-to-stop even time was missed by a handful of seconds. The following day, which was damp and windy, one of the original small engines, No. 34066, was in sprightly fettle with a similar five-coach load but, despite an 'eighty' after Moreton, could not get inside 15 minutes.

Last in the table come the energetic sprints of unrebuilt No. 34010, again with a 175-ton load. The driver of this engine returned the best times of any on the first two stages and seemed well set for the final stretch; his very swiftness was probably his own undoing, in that he seems to have surprised the signalman at Moreton who, presumably, had not closed the level crossing gates in time to allow for an unchecked run. An undelayed run would have doubtless yielded a time of $14\frac{3}{4}$ minutes.

Loads in excess of five coaches seldom had such swift passage between Wareham and Dorchester. The running in Table 76 pales somewhat in comparison with that in 75, although the run of No. 34028 (which had the incentive of heavy delays as far as Poole) stands out as a fine effort, especially when compared with No. 35008's running. The last run in Table 76 concerns one of the BR 'Farewell to Steam' specials; the drop in speed at Worgret Junction was necessary to avoid transgressing the speed restriction.

Eastbound journeys hardly ever produced such interesting running as in the down direction. For one reason or another, it was deemed necessary to call at Wool going up and so there was no opportunity for a tilt at the legend of 15 minutes Dorchester to Wareham. Somewhat strangely, records show running in this direction to be patchy, for seldom can a log be picked out with energetic running in all stages. For example, detail A of Table 77 records a lively performance as far as Wareham but well below standard thereafter. No. 34044 (detail B) produced a rather more consistent run; No. 35016 on the Sunday excursion with nine coaches did well to stop in Wareham 37 seconds over even time but thereafter compared poorly with No. 34044. Unrebuilt No. 34006 gave a very good display with a heavy train but got into trouble on Parkstone bank with a signal stop and eventually called for banking assistance. The detail shown for this last stage relates, therefore, to No. 35027 with a four-coach load (132/145 tons) and has been included to record a fast run up the bank. Another snippet (untabulated) concerned No. 34109 (unrebuilt at the time) with a four-coach train covering Wool to Wareham in 6 min 24 sec.

The Channel Islands Boat train provided an opportunity to sample a non-stop run between Weymouth and Poole and, moreover, to a distinctly sharp timing of 23 minutes from passing Dorchester Junction at 15 m.p.h. to the stop at Poole 22·4 miles away. This schedule was dictated by the necessity of getting the train through the Bournemouth area with some tight margins. In the event it often appears not to have been kept, which is hardly surprising in view of the awkwardly-placed speed restrictions, and perhaps could be said to be unrealistic in conception. Of the three runs in Table 78, the first came nearest to pulling it off, making as fast a run as possible within the speed limits. The comparatively poor effort of No. 35023 may be laid at the door of the driver, who said, 'We never keep time to Poole but make it up later', which was indeed possible with the slack schedule between Lymington Junction and Southampton.

By the time the boat train started running between Waterloo and Weymouth all the *Merchant Navy* class had been rebuilt, and as no record is available of an unmodified Pacific on this train the run detailed in Table 79 is included as the nearest possible comparison. The train, the 9.10 a.m. from Llanelly, reversed direction just south of Dorchester Junction and therefore the starting time is not strictly comparable with the times of the boat trains passing the signal box at the junction. The recorder probably passed the signal box between 1 and $1\frac{3}{4}$ minutes after starting; possibly the distance of 22·4 miles is slightly short for this particular train also. Giesl ejector fitted No. 34064 appears to have had the load in easy control, although a liberal interpretation of the 45 m.p.h. restriction at Worgret Junction is evident from the figures.

PORTSMOUTH DIRECT

A speculative railway, as the Portsmouth Direct was, seldom proved easy from the locomotive point of view as there usually was a preponderance of steep banks and sharp curves, arising from the desire to keep engineering costs to a minimum. The line from Godalming to Havant proved no exception to this generalisation. There are long climbs at 1-in-80, from the

northern side to a summit at Haslemere and from the south to
Buriton and northwards from Liss, as well as curvature restrictions at both extremities of the section. Electrification resolved
much of the traction problem some years prior to the advent of
the Bulleid Pacifics and thus there was no opportunity to sample
running behind these locomotives over the route, unless there
was a diversion or a special train operated. Such a railtour was
run from Waterloo which incorporated a 90-minute run (not to
Portsmouth but to Fareham) in simulation of the steam service
operated by the *Schools* class in the mid-1930s, to see how good
a tilt a *West Country* engine could make at the phenomenal time
of $35\frac{1}{2}$ minutes Guildford–Havant (pass to pass) returned by
No. 931 *King's Wimbledon* and recorded in the February 1936
issue of the *Railway Magazine*. The result will be found, together with details of how the engine was worked, in Chapter 12
(see Table 94).

Of the two runs in the northbound direction set out in
Table 80, the first concerns a railtour returning from the West
Country and passing through Havant on the through road. Unfortunately, delays of a non-railway nature had been incurred
and, although some time had been regained, the train narrowly
missed its path from Havant and delays were experienced from
an all-stations electric train in front. There was a steady
climb by No. 34032 on the 1-in-80 rise to the summit near milepost 58, a good ascent of the 1-in-100 incline to Haslemere
followed by a maximum of 80 m.p.h. down to Witley, but the
run suffered too many delays to provide a good record for
posterity.

Better by far, from the point of view of lack of delay, was the
run under the head of detail B. This was a heavier train, of
400 tons, diverted from the main line route between Southampton and Waterloo. Although booked to call at Havant, in the
event it ran slowly through the platform road. No. 34039 made
a good climb to milepost 58 and, after the relaying restriction at
Liss, climbed well enough to pass Haslemere with three minutes
of the schedule in hand. The descent was not made in the same
hurricane fashion as indulged in by the crew of No. 34032;
nonetheless, Guildford was reached well within the booked time
despite the permanent way slack encountered. The train had,
therefore, been worked within the normal allowance for the

comparable electric train service and incidentally equalled, in the net time, the schedule laid down for the lighter railtour special. It would appear that the *West Country* engines could have well coped with 400-ton trains on a 90-minute timing between Waterloo and Portsmouth.

Chapter 9

EX-LNER ROUTES
PERFORMANCE

The first ex-LNER route to be traversed by Southern Pacifics was London (King's Cross) to Leeds during the course of the 1948 Locomotive Interchanges. The locomotives involved were Nos. 35017 and 35019. Because of an overall restriction of 60 m.p.h. between King's Cross and Hatfield and 70 m.p.h. elsewhere there was not a lot of zest in the work of any of the competitors and tabulated details of running over the testing ground tends to tedious reading.

Suffice it, therefore, that a few of the notable points are touched on. Mr R. N. Clements recorded the down run on 25 May 1948 when No. 35017, in the hands of driver James, hauled a train of 503 tons net (535 tons gross) weight. Driver James surprised a lot of observers by getting through Finsbury Park in 7 min 32 sec, admittedly taking second place to a $7\frac{1}{4}$-minute start by the GW *King* but putting the other contestants in the shade. Later in the run there was good climbing from Little Bytham to Stoke summit, for which the official report gave an equivalent drawbar horsepower figure of 1,528 (this compared with 1,395 and 1,294 for *Royal Scot* and A4 classes respectively). Table 81 details this climb.

In the up direction matters were a degree more lively. One of the best runs was in the acclimatisation period, on 18 May, with No. 35019 between Retford and Grantham (see Table 82). A very good start was made and after a maximum of 75 m.p.h. at Crow Park there was a reduction to 55 m.p.h. to obtain water at the track troughs. A high minimum of 47 m.p.h. was maintained at Peascliffe tunnel and, but for a momentary signal stop outside, a time of 37 minutes Retford to Grantham could have been returned.

The other piece of excitement came on 28 May when No. 35017 cleared Stoke signal box from the standing start at Grantham in $9\frac{1}{2}$ minutes returning an equivalent drawbar horsepower figure of 1,659 in the process. This was head-and-shoulders above the other competitors and ranked with the best performances of the home line engines. The racing ground down from Stoke was ignored.

After this came *Bude* (No. 34006) with the London (Marylebone) to Manchester (London Road) test train. Driver Swain was in absolute command and returned some never to be forgotten figures with loads just under the 400-ton mark. The official report records 1,639 and 1,962 equivalent drawbar horsepower for Chalfont and Annesley banks in the down direction on 8 June 1948; that same day *Bude* reeled off the 31·2 miles from Aylesbury to Woodford in $31\frac{1}{2}$ mins (start to stop), and the 19·9 miles from Rugby to Leicester in $20\frac{1}{4}$ mins. Returning next day there was some energetic running, first between Staveley Town and Heath where the e.d.h.p. figure was 1,695 and then up Wendover bank where 1,777 was recorded. A couple of days later all these figures were eclipsed when No. 34006, worked at full regulator and 27 per cent cut-off, went up Ashby Magna bank at $67\frac{3}{4}$ m.p.h. to return 2,010 e.d.h.p.

After the interchanges the next visit to the old LNER territory occurred at the end of April 1949, when No. 34059 appeared in East Anglia on test tuns; these were conducted during May and included trips between Liverpool Street and Norwich with the *Norfolkman*. It is to some of these trips that G. F. Fiennes refers in his book *I Tried to Run a Railway* (Ian Allan, 1967) when he writes '. . . first run with 400 tons behind us we topped Brentwood Bank at 56 m.p.h. . . . BLOWING OFF. (his capitals!) What a change from B1s at 42 . . .' and 'On another we deliberately ran down the fire till we had 100 lbs of steam only. The fireman then hurled Grade 3 coal into the firebox for 15 minutes until it was up to the firehole door. Such treatment would have killed a B1 or indeed any Thompson or Gresley engine stone dead. The Can just ate it all. The gauge was up to 180 lbs and we were making up time hand over fist.'

Nothing more happened for two years and then, in May 1951, Nos. 34039, 34057 and 34065 were transferred to Stratford (30A) shed to work in company with the BR *Britannia* class Pacifics. Difficulties developed and as far as possible the

Southern locomotives were kept as reserve engines. Later Nos. 34076 and 34089 went to Stratford. By the spring of 1952 all had returned to the Southern Region.

Mr R. V. Coates has communicated some of the reactions of two Eastern Region firemen, one from Ipswich and the other from Harwich. Both tell a similar story; they agreed the Bulleid machines were fine engines but said they never mastered the technique of firing nor could their fellow firemen. On occasions they would leave Ipswich with a full tender of coal only to call at Chelmsford to replenish supplies before going on to Liverpool Street. This sort of comment was to be echoed on other regions also from time to time, and explains the lack of performance details for these engines during their sojourn at Stratford.

After regular working of Southern engines on ex-LNER metals ceased in 1952 occasional visits were made. Special railtour trains understandably used ex-LNER types where possible, and the opportunity to have a 'fling' down Stoke bank was missed. However, in the closing months of the Southern engines' existence No. 35026 did head a special train from York to Newcastle and back (Table 83). This was a nine-coach formation loading to 325 tons gross, the engine being handled by North Eastern men. Outwards from York they got the feel of No. 35026 fairly quickly and returned a not unreasonable time of 83½ minutes (net) to Newcastle.

On the return there was an attempt, across the Plain of York, to see what the *Merchant Navy* could produce; some steady running at 90 m.p.h. was the result. It was said at the time that full regulator with about 18 per cent cut-off was used to obtain this figure, very much in the way that A4s used to be driven. It would have been good to have had an opportunity to see what slightly less regulator and 25 per cent would have produced. Nonetheless the 80½ min (net) time between Newcastle and York together with the canter on the level through Thirsk bears comparison with the best of North Eastern Pacific running.

Chapter 10

EX-LMSR ROUTES
PERFORMANCE

In the Locomotive Interchange Trials of 1948 one of the routes selected was Euston–Carlisle and so during the first two weeks of May No. 35017, in charge of driver Swain, was to be found on the West Coast main line. Some supporters of the Southern cause seemed to think that there was a deliberate conspiracy afoot to place obstacles in the way of driver Swain, such as signal checks and the sending, on one occasion, of a slow train ahead from Crewe and not letting the Southern engine have the road until Leighton Buzzard. This was no conspiracy—merely LMR operating, which was suffered as a matter of course by regular travellers.

So numerous were the speed restrictions, apart from any other delaying factors, that south of Preston the runs could have contributed little data of significant value. Interest is therefore confined to the northernmost ninety miles: on the preliminary runs driver Swain, to whom a duty of 300 miles was a new experience, was out of luck. On 3 May the water pick-up scoop was damaged, and two days later a series of checks culminated in a dead stand north of Tebay in appalling weather and it proved a hard task to get the 500-ton train on the move again. However, on the test run of 13 May with a 501/530 ton load No. 35017 made a good climb to Shap after passing Tebay at 57 m.p.h.; at milepost 34 on the gradient of 1-in-75 the speed of $41\frac{1}{2}$ m.p.h. was recorded, the equivalent drawbar horse-power being 1,835, and although three miles further on the speed had fallen to $27\frac{1}{4}$ it rose to 29 m.p.h. by the summit. This increase in speed was made with full regulator and cut-off indicated as 43 per cent.

Both similarly loaded southbound test runs were notable in the climb from Penrith to Shap; the better of the two performances, although only marginally so, was that of 12 May when the allowance of 27 minutes from starting at Penrith to passing

Shap summit was cut to ribbons in a time of five seconds over 20 minutes. Two days later the same distance of $13\frac{1}{2}$ miles took $20\frac{1}{2}$ minutes. These efforts resulted in a speed of just under 50 m.p.h. at the summit and gave figures of 1929 and 1920 equivalent drawbar horsepower—achieved on 33 per cent cut-off with fairly wide regulator openings. As driver Swain made purgatorial progress from Crewe to Leighton Buzzard on 14 May he at least could reflect with satisfaction on the splendid efforts in surmounting the Cumbrian Fells from the north.

With driver James in charge the performance of No. 34005 between St Pancras and Manchester Central was of a consistent nature without any outstanding feats. The tare loads were slightly in excess of 300 tons and on nearly all stages there were net gains to the locomotive. Power outputs were not high, being in the range of 1,100 to 1,200 e.d.h.p., the highest figure noted (1,370 on 24 June) coming between Rowsley and Millers Dale, for which cut-off was 34 per cent and nearly full regulator was employed.

In July driver Swain returned to the fray, this time with No. 34004, to do battle with the Highland line between Perth and Inverness. If the long haul from Euston to Carlisle had been unusual to him how much more so the tablet exchanging on a heavily graded mountain line? However, after some initial difficulty in this direction and in interpreting the pilotman's tongue, some astounding attacks were made on the Scottish banks. Going northwards from Perth the best running was made up the inclines with extremely restrained progress down the gradients, so much so that time was more than once lost on the descents. Nonetheless, net gains to No. 34004 ranged from 15 to 20 minutes, which reflects the quality of the work performed. Equivalent drawbar horsepower figures for 13 and 15 July runs included 1548 and 1585 at Dalanraoch and Struan.

If No. 34004 had attacked the banks going northwards then on the return trips they could be said to have been overwhelmed. On 14 July there was a strong side wind to contend with on the climb to Druimuachdar; using less than full regulator and 30 per cent cut-off an e.d.h.p. figure of 1912 was recorded, but even this was eclipsed two days afterwards, when the cut-off was advanced to 35 per cent and with 235 lb in the steam chest a figure of 1950 was returned. Gain in time was of the same order as on the northbound trips and, of course, without any assisting engine to push the train up the hills (as was alleged not too seriously in some quarters had occurred in the opposite direction!). By any standards the *West Country* performance in the Highlands was impressive and rang down the curtain on the visits in a fitting manner.

After the interchanges of 1948 the Southern Pacifics had no reason to penetrate LMR preserves until the last days of steam, when some railtours were arranged with this in view. Usually LMR men would crew the engines and their unfamiliarity with the type of motive power almost always gave rise to lacklustre, or even downright poor, performances.

The organisers of a tour in June 1964 fortunately had the foresight to import the SR engine complete with its crew. Table 84 places on record the attack rebuild No. 35012 made on Shap in the hands of driver Hooker. Admittedly the load was of no vast magnitude but, even allowing for this, the speed of 57 m.p.h. at Scout Green was worthy of remark. For this lack of awe for the gradient Nemesis came swiftly, in the shape of a signal stop at Shap Wells, and effectively wrecked what could have been a notable ascent. Doubtless pertinent remarks about LMR operating were made within the train but on the footplate driver Hooker must have recalled the incident just over sixteen years previously when he was firing to driver Swain, and ruminated on the peculiar coincidence.

Later the same day Hooker had a tilt (Table 85) at Ais Gill from the Carlisle direction. The start again was leisurely, if not lethargic (Hooker never indulged in rapid exits), and with a hindrance before Appleby it took 42 minutes to pass that station. From there to the summit 17·6 miles, a lot of it at 1-in-100, occupied 17 min 46 sec, being run at an average speed of a shade under 60 m.p.h. The liberal schedule was toyed with and then, to curb these frolics, came a signal stop at Settle Junction (just as the 19½-minute late start had been wiped out) and, upon restarting, leaking brakes seemed to be another reminder of the displeasure of the northern routes for the disdain which No. 35012 and driver Hooker had evinced that day for the two famous inclines.

Chapter 11

EX-GWR ROUTES
PERFORMANCE

Away from home the Bulleid Pacifics performed best on the routes of the neighbouring Great Western (later Western Region), particularly when handled by Southern crews. Prior to being merged into British Railways the Southern engines had regular duties over the GW coastal route from Exeter to Plymouth, balancing with the GW locomotives' duties over Southern metals (via Okehampton) between those two Devonian cities. This was an arrangement to ensure that, in the event of a blockage on one route, the other could be used by both companies' men without the necessity to provide pilotmen, and it continued for many years after BR had been established. However, such duties were not of the most exacting type and, for the present purpose, it is convenient to turn to the Locomotive Interchanges of 1948.

No. 35019 was the *Merchant Navy* class engine chosen for the Paddington–Plymouth runs in late April and it returned a very even and consistent performance on the down trains, being slightly above the average of all competitors. On 27 April there was a good ascent of Brewham bank at 48 m.p.h. (1430 equivalent drawbar horsepower), and an excellent climb to White-ball (30 m.p.h. minimum with 505 tons). Some slipping occurred on the banks in south Devon without causing time to be dropped. Two days later a not dissimilar run was made, except that there was rain for the first part of the journey.

On the return from Plymouth on 28 April No. 35019 made a good climb of Hemerdon bank and followed that by a good, although checked, effort between Exeter and Taunton. Leaving Taunton nine minutes late and with a gross load of 525 tons, No.35019 recovered $3\frac{1}{2}$ minutes to Westbury; station overtime occurred there, which lengthened the debit to $6\frac{1}{4}$ minutes, all of which—and $1\frac{1}{2}$ minutes more—had been regained by the time Paddington was reached. The other run, a couple of days later, did not produce such lively running, possibly because there was not the incentive to make up for delays.

No. 34006 was the light Pacific engaged on the Bristol–Plymouth test length. On the opening run from Bristol matters conspired against the engine, about 30 minutes being lost *en route*. Despite this, with a gross load of 440 tons, Whiteball was topped at 30½ m.p.h. and Dainton (with the load reduced to 255 tons gross) at no less than 33½ m.p.h. A more satisfactory run was made on the second occasion in the down direction, when a good speed of 35 m.p.h. was recorded at Tigley on the climb from Totnes. With the misfortunes of the first down run still fresh in their minds, the Southern crew 'pulled out the stops' on the first up run on 21 July. There was a competent climb of Hemerdon and this was followed by a brilliant run with 475 tons gross from Exeter to Taunton. No. 34006 returned e.d.h.p. figures of 1631 at Stoke Canon and 1565 at Cullumpton, passing Whiteball in 22¼ minutes from the start nearly 20 miles away. No other engine—large or small—in these tests came near this performance over this particular section. From the re-start at Taunton No. 34006 was hard at it with 1585 e.d.h.p. as early as Creech. Then, for mile after mile, the speed was kept between 70 and 75 m.p.h., save only for a drop to the mid-sixties around Brent Knoll, so that even time had been re-corded in about 17 miles and so far behind had the schedule been left that there was a considerable wait outside Bristol Temple Meads for it to catch up! The *West Country* had certainly made amends for the delays the previous day. The re-maining up run could hardly be expected to be so lively; even so, driver Snell could not be dubbed a sluggard because the overall running time was six minutes more, for he returned even higher figures at Stoke Canon with 1715 e.d.h.p. (at 57 m.p.h.), the engine being worked at 25 per cent cut-off and with 195 lb per sq in of steam in the steamchest.

Turning next to regular workings, there were two duties for Bournemouth men and locomotives to Oxford, and in Table 86 a couple of such runs with the *Pines Express* between the uni-versity town and Reading West are set out. In the last decade of steam traction this train included a lot of heavy stock so that a twelve-coach formation could weigh 450 tons gross. In detail A driver Dean handled unrebuilt No. 34103 very well, producing

some speeds along the Thames Valley which would have been
of remark had a South Wales express of equal loading returned
them. The customary signal stop concluded proceedings: nonetheless 3½ minutes actual had been regained or about seven
minutes on a net time basis. The larger rebuilt engine (detail B)
did not lack incentive in a 37½-minute late departure. Perhaps
the magnitude of the arrears became rather more of a disin-
centive, but, whatever the reason, No. 35002 did not produce
running as good as that—let alone better—of No. 34103. By an
odd quirk of circumstance the running time was slightly less
but not, of course, the net time.

One of the routes to pass from Western to Southern influence
was that between Salisbury and Westbury (or Dilton Marsh
Halt to be precise) and at the time the journeys recorded in
Table 87 were made it might be said that the Southern men were
as well acquainted with it as their own metals. Despite this it
was, and still tends to remain, a Western route. The first run
(detail A) was admittedly with a load of no great proportions for
the *Merchant Navy* class engine hauling it. But it was very
lively for those participants of the railtour who troubled to take
notes. The Salisbury driver—a very competent man, Oxborrow
by name—soon had the engine in its stride up the Wylye valley.
The line rises from Salisbury all the way to Warminster, although there are some dips at one or two places, mostly within
the limits of 1-in-93 and 1-in-198. Inwards from Dilton Marsh
the engine was restrained; discounting this easing the net time
might be put at 29 minutes. Naturally with a 400-ton load
(detail B) unrebuilt No. 34038 could not be expected to go off
at such a dashing pace and in the event the schedule of
33 minutes proved too tight.

No. 34038 continued from Westbury to Swindon Works (this
was the Railway Correspondence and Travel Society's East
Midlander No. 7 Special) gaining the main line at Thingley
Junction. Speed was raised to 60 m.p.h. by Chippenham and
further to 73 m.p.h. in the dip before Christian Malford. The
up grade (1-in-660) pulled the speed down to 69 m.p.h. but
then No. 34038 was opened out a little to get up to 72 m.p.h.
before striking the 1-in-100 incline. Speed fell from 70 m.p.h. at
milepost 87 to 60 m.p.h. at the top of the bank (milepost 86) and
dropped to 57 m.p.h. before recovering to 60 m.p.h. at Wootton

Bassett. The passing times are given in Table 88. Comparable times by the home line's trains are not easy to trace and GW partisans may rightly point out that No. 34038 could afford to have a tilt at Dauntsey bank in view of terminating at Swindon, whereas a driver of a main line train running through to London might hesitate to attack it in this fashion.

Retracing steps to Westbury there are two runs booked non-stop from that station to Exeter St David's (Table 89). Driver Parsons was driving on each occasion and the recorder was the same person, which is helpful in making comparative assessments. In detail A No. 34019 (an unrebuilt engine) travelled via Frome, whilst No. 35026, in detail B, ran by on the avoiding line giving a shorter overall distance of 15 chains (0·2 miles). Neither train was heavy although No. 34019 had the handicap of negotiating the junctions into and out of Frome which it did decorously and got behind the clock. Running was steady and, without exceeding the 80 m.p.h. limit, No. 34019 was right on time on passing Taunton. On the other hand, No. 35026 was finding the schedule over-generous and by Taunton, with no undue effort, had $7\frac{1}{4}$ minutes in hand. No. 34019 suffered badly from signals and slacks up to White-ball and afterwards could not win back the lost time. No. 35026 went gaily on and cleared the formidable Wellington bank at an average rate of about a mile a minute with the greatest ease, passing the summit no less than twelve minutes early and, even with two severe relaying checks, was still able to pass Cowley Bridge Junction with eleven minutes in hand. At the time the railtour was planned the Western Region did not see their way clear to accede to a request of a 75-minute schedule from Westbury to Exeter: proposed passing times were Castle Cary 21 minutes, Taunton 45 minutes and Whiteball 57 minutes. On the day No. 35026 fully vindicated the organisers' original pro-posals and probably set up a record for the fastest ascent of Wellington bank with steam hauling a 275-ton train.

In the opposite direction two runs with the same engine—No. 35023—feature in Table 90. The loads were not dissimilar at about 330 tons and again both trains were enthusiasts' specials. In detail A a good start was made only to be cut short by a very bad signal delay at Tiverton Junction. Anyhow speed was whipped up to 45 m.p.h. by Whiteball and with running almost up to the speed limit down the bank the lateness of the train was kept within reasonable bounds. On the trip in detail B the ascent to Whiteball was unhampered and a slack at Wellington did not adversely affect timekeeping. The $40\frac{1}{2}$ miles to Blatchbridge Junction from Taunton occupied slightly over 40 minutes, with a minimum of 48 m.p.h. at Brewham, and an early arrival at Westbury was possible. In detail A the same $40\frac{1}{2}$-mile distance took $35\frac{3}{4}$ minutes, the lowest speed being 56 m.p.h. at Brewham. Of necessity the running over this length was greatly superior to the other run of eight years previously.

Finally there are one or two runs in south Devon which are not without merit. In Table 91 No. 35023 appears again with the same train as in detail B Table 90, on its first stage. Speed was quickly worked up to 56 m.p.h. at Plympton for an all-out attack on the 1-in-42 Hemerdon incline, but once on the bank speed fell alarmingly to 14 m.p.h. only to recover powerfully to 20 m.p.h. within a mile. It transpired that the regulator had stuck when driver Gidley wanted to open up for the bank. Being a man of small physical stature he had great difficulty in raising the regulator and had to summon his mate to his aid. Their combined efforts saved the situation just after milepost $240\frac{1}{2}$ and thereafter the run was made in easy manner. With six minutes in hand at Newton Abbot and 30 minutes to cover the 20 miles to Exeter, Gidley killed time by giving his passengers a slow journey over the most scenic section of the famed coastal route.

Just over a year before, this Southern driver had performed with great *élan* over this same route with unmodified light Pacifics. There was a 'bus strike in progress locally and the trains were packed—nay crammed—tight with passengers, as the recorder is at pains to stress in assessing the gross weight. The 4.32 p.m. from Plymouth was one of the regular turns for the Exmouth Junction men and locomotives but was seldom loaded or patronised to this extent. The rise starts at 1-in-111 at the platform end at Plympton and after a short distance changes to 1-in-41, -47 and then -42 for a $1\frac{1}{2}$-mile stretch almost to Hemerdon siding. There was no trouble with the regulator this time as Gidley put his engines to the climb, as Table 92 bears witness. Undoubtedly the effort with No. 34023 and nine coaches was worthy of the highest praise. Admittedly with No. 35023 the regulator stuck, but the comparison of No. 34023's time of 7 min 12 sec start-to-pass Plympton–Hemerdon with No. 35023's of 6 min 54 sec pass-to-pass is not too flattering to the rebuilt locomotive.

Table 93 records driver Gidley and No. 34023 a little later in the same run going up the grade to Dainton without any embarrassment and nothing lower than 22 m.p.h. on the 1-in-38 at the summit. On such a high note it is appropriate to close the record of Bulleid Pacific performance away from home.

Chapter 12

ON THE FOOTPLATE

Very few of the runs detailed in the preceding pages have been recorded other than from the inside of the train and therefore lack information concerning the working of the locomotive. On occasion it was possible to obtain some idea of the regulator opening and cut-off at a particular place by questioning the driver after the event but this could be taken to be little more than a general guide. It will be useful, therefore, to examine one or two examples of the general manner of working.

Before considering this it may not be out of place to remark on one or two characteristics of the footplate and cab layout. On the *Merchant Navy* class the spaciousness of the cab was most noticeable; even in the smaller class it could still be termed commodious. Although not of the advanced type favoured on the Gresley A4 Pacifics of the LNER, seats hinged from the in-side of the cab side sheets were provided for each of the crew members. Underneath that for the fireman were the injectors whilst another refinement incorporated in the original design for his benefit was the foot-operated treadle which actuated the steam valve to the cylinder for opening the firebox doors, a gadget which seemed to have had greatest appeal to Devonian footplatemen.

The firebox door opened in a sliding bi-parting motion. When closed it was still possible to observe combustion by means of peep-holes in the door; it was also possible to keep the door partly open.

Great care was given to the layout of the controls, those for the driver's use being grouped on the left-hand side of the cab with those under the care of the fireman being placed on the right hand. The whistle could be operated easily by either crew member, being sounded by pulling on a cord suspended at high level across the cab. Another fitting arranged for common operation was the sanding lever which was a bar placed horizontally above the firebox door of sufficient length to be within the grasp of either man from his seat.

The driver's vision was hampered by the position of the brake valve and even in its later amended position it was not ideally placed. The regulator was arranged to move in an upward arc; when closed the lever was in a vertical position. It was opened by pulling upwards and outwards until the full-open position was horizontal and high up in the cab—hence the exhortation seen on a lineside bridge in the last months of Southern steam which read 'UP IN THE ROOF!'

With the modified locomotives it was not unusual to find a bundle of newspapers on the footplate awaiting the crew when they took over at the shed. This was not to suggest that rebuilding had effected such economies in working that there was time to spare for reading but rather to afford some comfort, in particular for the driver; the cab front sheeting was not by any means a tight fit around the firebox profile and, because the gap induced a howling gale, the newspapers were used to fill the opening. From time to time this improvised plugging would ignite to provide additional illumination in the cab and have to be promptly dowsed by the fireman.

In the roof of the cab on the driver's side was affixed the 'garlic plate', altered under British Railway's regime to aniseed. When these smells permeated the cab they indicated a hot middle big-end and the driver was enjoined to follow the instructions on the plate to bring his engine in with the least damage. Neither of these odours could be said to be an outstanding feature of Southern locomotive performance.

The reverser for the original design was a lever operating in a quadrant and mounted parallel to the cab side sheet on the driver's side, being pulled toward him; that in the modified design was the BR standard drum indicator type but not steam-operated as previously with the Bulleid type.

In running, the enclosed cab tended to trap the finer dust particles; riding of the locomotives was generally very smooth and more than sufficient to enable the sound of rail-joints to be picked up as easily as in a coach. The speedometer was placed on the driver's side and, when checked against rail-joints as to accuracy, these seldom gave an error in excess of 2 per cent.

Compared with some other classes on the Southern lines, both types of Pacifics gave an impression of size and power from the footplate and whilst most enginemen were happy with the locomotives there were some, in particular from the remoter sheds of the Central Section, who were overawed by the machines at their disposal. Some even refused to take them out! Generally, however, the attitude was one of satisfaction which could be summed up in the phrase used by a driver, some-time Mayor of Eastleigh, that 'they're big enough, aren't they?'

So much for the general impression; how were the engines worked? The short answer to this could be half regulator and 20 per cent cut-off. Records of locomotive working were almost always made by someone other than one of the two crew and it might be said such occasions were not truly representative of normal working as the men were under observation. This could be a valid comment but it is only relevant in the context of what was normal procedure.

Regulator openings are rather rough and ready guides to the working, and inasmuch as the Bulleid Pacifics were fitted with steamchest pressure indicators such readings will be referred to in preference to regulator positions. Thus, on an ordinary service train (the 1.00 p.m. from Waterloo to the West of England) a modified *Battle of Britain* class engine loaded to 399 tons tare (430 tons gross) was worked from Salisbury to Templecombe in six seconds over 32 minutes (scheduled 34 minutes) on 20 per cent cut-off throughout, apart from the start when 55 and 40 per cent was used coming down to 25 per cent by Wilton. On the rising grades to Semley 180 lb per sq in was the steamchest pressure; after the summit this was reduced to 120 or 100 p.s.i. Speed was 58 and 66 m.p.h. at Dinton and Tisbury respectively. After Templecombe the load was reduced to 302/325 tons and the same 20 per cent cut-off used until Seaton Junction, where it was advanced to 30 per cent for the climb to Honiton tunnel in conjunction with full regulator working (180 to 190 p.s.i. in the steamchest) giving a speed of 41 m.p.h. upon entering the tunnel.

A fully detailed log of working appears in Table 94. This records the first leg of a special railtour in which an attempt was made to see how a modified *West Country* would fare on the old 90-minute steam booking from London to Portsmouth; in this case an equivalent stopping place was found in Fareham, 2·7 miles further from Waterloo than Portsmouth. The old schedule allowed 81 minutes to pass Havant, whereas the timing to this point for the special was clipped (by five minutes) to 76.

The locomotive inspector detailed to travel on this train gave very close attention to the handling of the locomotive. He cautioned the driver at Wimbledon not to exceed the suburban area speed limit and also required early reduction in speed upon the approach to the crew's home shed station. Twenty per cent cut-off was again the standard employed and the only point where full regulator working occurred was at Worplesdon where steamchest pressure was up to 220 p.s.i. Fireman Hewson maintained good boiler pressure and with a minute lost due to signals at Woking there was a good incentive, once the 60 m.p.h. restriction at Farncombe was passed, for time to be regained. At Godalming the engine was blowing-off and driver Edwards accordingly opened the regulator. For the climb at 1-in-100/82 up to Witley he altered the cut-off to 30 per cent but had to reduce this to 25, much to his chagrin, on the instructions of the inspector. Likewise on the final part of the long 1-in-80 ascent to Haslemere the inspector required the regulator to be eased back, otherwise a rather more spirited attack on that climb would have been recorded.

Despite the dampening effects of the inspector's instructions Petersfield was passed early and an average slightly in excess of 60 m.p.h. was returned for the 20·4 miles from Godalming. A very severe signal check was encountered at Buriton siding and an exact observance of the restriction at Rowlands Castle fulfilled the demands of the inspector. A succession of 'yellows' in the Havant area stopped any time being regained there and the agitation of the inspector at the approach to Fareham (he seemed to anticipate the sharp curve at the entry to the station by about two miles) prevented the arrival being less than one minute late. The net time could fairly be said to be 87 minutes, although had driver Edwards worked the engine as he wished, the time would have come down to about 84 minutes net. Equivalent figures to Portsmouth might be 82½ and 80 minutes.

Another run in which the locomotive was not extended appears in Table 95. In this instance No. 34006 had a moderate load on the up *Atlantic Coast Express* schedule of 70 minutes from Sidmouth Junction to passing Wilton (the intermediate timings were unusually indicated in this particular case, it being customary to give nothing more than 37 minutes to pass Yeovil Junction in the case of the *A.C.E.*), and was worked very lightly to attain a net time of $75\frac{1}{4}$ minutes, just in excess of 60 m.p.h. for the start-to-stop journey. It will be observed that figures for cut-off have not been given because of the doubtful accuracy associated with the reverser indicator on the original locomotives. As likely as not the reverser was placed in one position and all adjustments were on the regulator. The rate of coaling for this run was not heavy. The strongest work was done on 160 p.s.i. in the steamchest on the climb to Honiton; notable was the rise to Hewish summit undertaken with 125 p.s.i. and also 120 p.s.i. on all other climbs. With such a large amount of steam in reserve, an attempt to regain the time lost by the check at Axminster, due to the tardy closing of level crossing gates, really should have been made. At no time was the locomotive shy for steam as the readings of 220/230/240 p.s.i. of boiler pressure show.

Next there is tabulated (96) a run in which the engine was opened up rather more than was usually the case. By 6.20 p.m. the London rush-hour had tailed off and consequently running before time out of town could be indulged in without a crop of signal checks. No. 34025 on the Ramsgate semi-fast got away exceptionally briskly through London Bridge and there was a constant gain on schedule. The climb to the North Downs at Knockholt was made on three-quarters to full regulator except when passing through Chislehurst, where easing took place to regain water-level. This vigorous working resulted in a $4\frac{1}{2}$-minute early arrival at Sevenoaks. The restart was marred by the necessity to set back but no time was lost and steaming was never a problem, despite the demands on the boiler.

Occasionally, however, steaming difficulties would arise both with original and modified types. Some drivers would try to use as little steam as possible, whilst others would take the opposite course and open the engine up. More often than not the latter policy paid off by giving a sharper exhaust and livening up the fire: on one occasion a relieving crew was warned by the men on the first leg that the engine had to be worked hard or it would 'die on them'. In the event great tenderness was lavished on the engine and the inevitable occurred. On a further occasion, an original *West Country* class member was on a down express from Salisbury and doing poorly; the fireman was flogging away filling the firebox to give a vast black fire and the driver muttered from time to time about conditions. At Seaton Junction boiler pressure was 160 p.s.i. and 120 p.s.i. was being used in the steamchest; Honiton was looming ahead and the driver obviously could not overcome his awe of the incline and so he advanced the regulator. By milepost $157\frac{1}{2}$ boiler pressure rose to 190 p.s.i. (185 p.s.i. in steamchest) and in the next mile rose further to 210 p.s.i. (205 p.s.i. in steamchest)! Immediately the regulator was eased back boiler pressure fell, owing to lack of blast on the fire. This over-firing also was characteristic of runs on routes where the locomotives were handled by crews not accustomed to the class.

One of the easiest of runs from the point of view of stoking was that under detail B of Table 89. Fireman Munns of Salisbury shed had not previously travelled over the GW route from Westbury to Exeter and so did not know what to expect. Because of this, he built up a big fire, rather on the lines of those to be seen on the *Kings* at Paddington on westbound trains; pressure was right up to blowing-off point and the white feather was showing almost continuously throughout the run, which was accomplished on steamchest pressures of about 100 p.s.i. For Brewham summit the figure rose to 120 p.s.i. and for the assault on Whiteball it was 160 p.s.i. at Wellington and 140 p.s.i. into the tunnel (in both cases boiler pressure was 240 p.s.i.). Cut-off was unchanged for the whole of the run at 25 per cent and only *one* spell of firing took place—between Taunton and Norton Fitzwarren. As Munns remarked '. . . you can free-wheel on this road—I thought it was supposed to have some heavy banks'.

Finally, in Table 97, is a fully detailed record of how a re-built *Merchant Navy* was worked up to a three-figure speed. This was a railtour special for which an unprecedented timing of 78 minutes from Waterloo to Salisbury had been laid down on the understanding that the load was not to exceed eight vehicles. On the day it was found two very severe relaying restrictions were in force at points where high speed would normally be enjoyed, and to get matters off to a good start driver Hooker and his mate had the coal hopper at Nine Elms shed prematurely discharge its load as their locomotive moved into position. Consequently, coal had to be cleared from around the cab and firebox before the depot could be left and the arrival at Waterloo was about five minutes before the train was due away. Inspector and observer boarded No. 35023 and a quick explanation followed with the fireman making mention of it being a 'special run'. To this last remark, Hooker assured the fireman, who was not his regular mate, that he wouldn't go down to Salisbury any quicker than on that particular day!

The start was not very brisk (a characteristic of this driver), being due in some measure to a general sorting out of themselves on the part of the four occupants of the cab. In the suburban area cut-off was 20 per cent; after Hampton Court Junction the regulator was advanced and 85 m.p.h. was attained before the long speed restriction at West Byfleet, to which exemplary attention was paid. After this slowing the cut-off became 25 per cent and acceleration followed all the way up to milepost 31, passed at 74 m.p.h. It would not have been difficult to have reached 80 m.p.h. by this point and doubtless this would have occurred if there had been no relaying hindrance. Just after the check at Hook, injector trouble was apparent but was cured by Basingstoke. From here Hooker opened out to three-quarter regulator and as the speed built up eased back: the increase in speed was gradual, so much so that some passengers, although recording the passage of the train, were surprised to find that they were about to note 100 m.p.h. The climax of 102 m.p.h. was achieved on about half regulator (140–150 p.s.i. in the steamchest) on the by now standard 25 per cent cut-off on a rocklike steadiness of 240 p.s.i. boiler pressure. No pushing the engine here and she rode magnificently—and quietly.

Speed did not fall below 80 m.p.h. on the climb to Grateley, more steam being taken for the final length to the summit. Then at Allington the engine was eased and again at Porton but speed still climbed (the signalman at Porton was reported to have spoken to Salisbury to the effect that he had never seen a train go by so fast!) to reach 98 m.p.h. on the descent to Tunnel Junction. A record of this run has appeared in print claiming a second 'hundred' at Porton but, pleasant as it might be to think a Southern express returned a couple of centuries in the same run, the weight of evidence fails to support this. A slow entry into the island platform at Salisbury was necessary because driver Hooker had never previously run into that road and also had to draw up abreast of the water column. Net time was $71\frac{1}{4}$ minutes.

With such ease did a *Merchant Navy* demonstrate the way to reach 100 m.p.h. and, if a partisan note is excusable at this juncture, the comment of a passenger may not be irrelevant (even if considered by supporters of other camps as irreverent!); contrasting the foregoing trip with a special which ran elsewhere with specially picked and prepared engines but failed—unluckily—to reach a three-figure speed, he said, 'The Southern just did it quietly with an ordinary engine'. Indeed they did— if one terms Bulleid Pacifics ordinary engines!

Chapter 13

TECHNICAL ASSESSMENT OF BULLEID PACIFIC PERFORMANCE

J. N. C. Law, B.Sc.(Lond.), C.Eng., F.I.Mech.E.

For their size the Bulleid Pacifics have an excellent claim to be among the most powerful ever built in the British Isles and, without any question, they were also among the fastest. Maximum speeds were never specifically investigated because no occasion ever arose to do so, although if any special attempt down from Roundwood to Eastleigh had ever been made, speeds over 110 m.p.h. should have been reached without undue difficulty and, with a light enough train, 120 m.p.h. might even have been a practical possibility.

In assessing the relevant capabilities of locomotive classes the simplest approach is to calculate the equivalent drawbar horsepower (e.d.h.p.) over a measured distance in a measured elapsed period. Speeds downhill, although spectacular, are not generally of great interest because much of the energy is contributed by gravity and power output is not exceptional. Nonetheless a run such as by No. 34002 in detail B of Table 25 would call for something in the region of 765 e.d.h.p. down from Worting Junction to Farnborough; this represents a total of about 1485 I.H.P. in normal weather.

The best conditions, therefore, are provided by a long ascent, such as from Eastleigh to Roundwood, where the majority of the work is against gravity, concerning the exact magnitude of which there can be no doubt. The term e.d.h.p. includes the energy expended in lifting the locomotive's own weight (after allowance has been made for expenditure of water and fuel) but excludes the factor of speed which so greatly affects the amount of power expended by the engine in moving itself. Comparisons of performance on an e.d.h.p. basis are valid at similar speeds; where, however, the band of performance is wide—as in a high-power high-speed machine such as the Bulleid engines—it is important to be able to estimate the total power developed at any point in a range of, say, 45–90 m.p.h.

It is possible, by using data provided in the Test Bulletins on the *Merchant Navy* locomotives, to estimate the power absorbed by an engine in overcoming its own internal and external tractive resistance, including that of the tender. After allowance for weight difference, the same data may be used for the smaller Pacifics.

In normal daily service these engines regularly developed high power but even so there were large reserves which were seldom tapped. Probably the most outstanding case is that of rebuilt No. 35012 with the up *Bournemouth Belle* (Table 66). The train of ten Pullman cars and a van weighed 429 tons tare (445 tons gross); speed was 69 m.p.h. at Winchester and yet No. 35012 accelerated this heavy train steadily up the 1-in-252 gradient to 76 m.p.h. at Roundwood, thereby joining the exclusive group of British steam locomotives known to have reached an estimated level of 3000 I.H.P. which, calculation indicates, was just attained at the top of the climb (the others are the LMS *Duchess of Abercorn*, several LNER A4s and one BR(ER) A1). That the exceptional effort of No. 35012 is not entirely isolated is shown by the adjoining detail in the same Table 66, although at a slightly lower performance level.

The smaller engines had similar reserves of power over day-to-day requirements. For example, in Table 64 (detail B) rebuilt No. 34001 with an eleven-coach train of 374 tons tare (400 tons gross) accelerated from 66 m.p.h. at Winchester Junction to 69 at Micheldever, which represents 1670 e.d.h.p. and some 2245 I.H.P. Again, in Table 67 detail D, with ten coaches (337/352 tons) another rebuilt engine—No. 34044—went from 58 m.p.h. at Wallers Ash to 71 m.p.h. at Roundwood to yield a calculated 1825 e.d.h.p. and about 2410 I.H.P., which would appear to represent the high-water mark of power output for a small rebuilt engine in normal service over a period of about five minutes.

All the foregoing runs came in the last years of the classes when keen crews really tried to find out the maximum that could be got from their engines, and the available records for the original designs were not made in such testing conditions but are still of great interest.

It has proved difficult to obtain details of any run in which the original *Merchant Navy* was fully extended. In the 1948 Interchanges both Bulleid Pacific classes took part with distinction but it was the smaller engines which provided all the sparkle. An excellent example of this is the climb from Exeter to Whiteball by No. 34006 with 449/475 tons during which a calculated 1610 e.d.h.p. was sustained between Silverton and Burlescombe. At 64 m.p.h. this corresponds to about 2100 I.H.P. This run is, in fact, slightly higher in quality than that by rebuilt engine No. 34044, which is an interesting point. As a counterpart, the run by No. 35017 climbing Shap from the north with 503/525 tons in 1948 represents the original larger engine (1935 I.H.P.). While a number of spot readings of high e.d.h.p. outputs were obtained in the 1948 Locomotive Interchanges, care should be taken not to regard such figures as being a direct measurement of the relative capacity of each engine class. Nevertheless the figures are of interest as demonstrating the capability of an engine to 'pull out of the bag' a short burst of very high power, as indeed Nos. 34004 and 34006 did on more than one occasion.

In order to place the Bulleid engines in perspective a table of selected runs made by these engines and their contemporaries has been prepared. These runs are not necessarily the best runs an engine of the class concerned may have made but are merely the best of those of which suitable logs are available.

COMPARATIVE SHORT-TERM POWER OUTPUTS OF BULLEID PACIFICS AND THEIR CONTEMPORARIES

	Type and No.	Weight (tons)	Load	Duration min	Duration sec	Av. Speed m.p.h.	Location	Height Difference or gradient	E.d.h.p.	I.H.P.	Grading
LMS	*Duchess* 6234	106¼	20/604/610	8	46	56·1	Wreay/Plumpton	196 ft	2645	3035	23·8
SR/BR	*M.N.* 35012(R)	98	11/429/445P	7	06	72·25	Winchester J./Litchfield	1-in-252	2035	2775	22·8
LNER	A4 60022	103	11/390/415	8	35	80·5	Essendine/Stoke S. B.	228 ft	2060	2800	22·5
SR	*W.C.* 34006	86	14/449/475	11	16	63·9	Silverton/Burlescombe	223 ft	1610	2100	21·2
BR/ER	A1 60128	104	14/462/463	7	06	64·9	Milepost 103/95	12 ft F	2205	2735	21·2
LMS	*Royal Scot* 4615¼(R)	83	15/482/515	9	58	52·6	Axminster/Mp 133¼ (Mp 142)	226 ft	1745	2045	21·0
SR/BR	*W.C.* 34044(R)	90	10/337/352	4	59	67·3	Wallers Ash/Roundwood	1-in-252	1825	2410	20·8
BR	*Britannia* 70014	94	8/282/300	7	05	86·6	Bedford N.J./Milepost 59¾	205 ft	1375	2185	18·7
SR	*M.N.* 35017	94¾	16/503/525	12	34	43·0	Clifton/Shap Summit	341 ft	1660	1935	18·0
GWR	*King* 6013	91	12/393/420	12	16	62·25	Silverton/Whiteball	256 ft	1375	1860	18·0

(R) = Rebuilt   P = includes 10 Pullman cars   F = Falling

E.d.h.p. figures are obtained using published data for locomotives and rolling stock. No allowance has been made for wind and where this was favourable estimates may tend to be high. Power absorbed by locomotive resistance calculated from published data has been added to obtain cylinder horsepower (I.H.P.). Grading is based on I.H.P. per ton of engine weight (without tender) against duration.

PERFORMANCE TABLES

Throughout the tables of the performance section a uniform presentation has been attempted. Some points may conveniently be mentioned here in amplification: names of locomotives have been omitted to save space and avoid the possibility of attributing a name to a locomotive either before it was affixed or after it was removed (reference to the chronology section will serve as a ready method of obtaining the name); the distinction between original and rebuilt locomotives is indicated by the placing of (R) immediately after the number (all locomotives in the tables may be taken as being in original condition unless followed by this indication); where known, the sheds to which the drivers were attached is given (sometimes in abbreviated form), usually following the name of the driver; schedules are always in minutes and fractions thereof; permanent restrictions are given against the point at or near which the restriction is operative and is indicated by (*20), the figures being the maximum permitted speed in miles per hour; mileages are given to one place of decimals and have been completely re-assessed from the relevant working timetables (consideration was given to quoting miles and chains which is more precise—and no more space-wasting— than two places of decimals but comparative unfamiliarity amongst recorders rules this out); temporary and signal restrictions are indicated by 'p.w.s.' and 'sigs' respectively in the elapsed time column, the speed entered on the same line being the actual, rather than the restriction, speed; the speed is in miles per hour to the lower whole number in all cases.

On the vexed question of estimated net time a statement of the position adopted may prove useful. One school of thought (in which those with engineering experience often find themselves) maintains that such estimation serves no useful purpose and should not be attempted, whilst the opposite faction will purport to produce a net time of 69 minutes from Southampton to Waterloo from an elapsed figure of 114 minutes, when continuing delays have occurred throughout the journey.

In selecting details for inclusion in the tables preference has been given, so far as reasonably possible, to unchecked runs, followed by those having a minimum of checks. In the above quoted example (which is not exactly but certainly very similar

to some received) the run would be included if there had been a
dead stand for nearly 45 minutes outside Waterloo—or even
Eastleigh—but not, as was the case, because of engineering
delays, signal stops and delays from other trains. The principal
factor in assessing estimated net times is the ability of the boiler
to produce steam at the rate required for the assumed performance; with a dead stand or delays at either end of a run there is
little problem to overcome as steam demands are not great but a
delay after a big effort enables the boiler to be rallied—even if
only for five minutes—and here the statement of a net time is
questionable.

Another point of view which has been expressed may be
mentioned. It is that a delay early in the run may give rise to a
performance that would otherwise not have occurred. This is
undoubtedly true, as happened with driver Sibley on the penultimate run of the down *Atlantic Coast Express*, but it is not
entirely valid. To take this particular case: there was a signal
stop between Vauxhall and Nine Elms and (as a result?)
Salisbury was reached in 78 minutes from Waterloo. The net
time was estimated at $74\frac{1}{2}$ minutes, which was deduced from
passing Clapham Junction $3\frac{1}{2}$ minutes later than would be expected on an unchecked run. It is granted that the driver might
have been content to reach Salisbury in 78 minutes had no
check occurred and this was the incentive for the performance.
The locomotive, however, demonstrated its ability to run from
Clapham Junction to Salisbury in $67\frac{1}{2}$ minutes and there is no
reason to suppose that the scheduled seven minutes from
Waterloo could not have been achieved in the circumstances—
indeed the safety valves were blowing-off as the train was
halted—and upon such grounds this particular figure, as well as
the others that appear in the performance tables, is considered
to be reasonable.

A rather more questionable practice, which has been indulged in for many years in some quarters, is that of aggregating
the best point-to-point times of two or more runs on the same
route to produce a theoretical net time. This has been avoided
in the present instance because it not only overlooks the question
of boiler output being sustained but also recorders' varying
timing points. To illustrate this the following hypothetical case
has been drawn up:

	Run 1		Run 2		Run 3	
	min.	sec.	min.	sec.	min.	sec.
Timing point L pass	32	01	35	08	33	31
Timing point M pass	35	17	38	25	36	43
Timing point N pass	38	20	41	27	39	50

Between stations L and N all three recorders agree the time to be 6 min 19 sec, yet the aggregate of the best point-to-point times works out as:

L to M			3	12
M to N	3	02		

Total: 6 min 14 sec

This may be accounted for by one recorder taking his time at the near platform ramp, another the far platform ramp (such habits *are* known to exist!), whilst the third has his own points for each particular station such as the footbridge, or an over-bridge at one end of a station, which may be indentified easily in the dark. Each recorder will produce a perfectly good end-to-end log of a run but to use these on an aggregated basis can but lead to unjustified assumptions. It may be less objectionable with different runs made by the same recorder although it still lacks a scientific approach to the matter.

Commentary on the tabulated runs has concentrated on giving information not available from the tables rather than describing each run in detail. In most instances the recordings speak for themselves and it has been necessary to do no more than fill in with additional detail and provide background information.

Finally, it has been thought advisable to include here a note concerning the mileposts on the West of England main line. It is common knowledge that these are not sited with precision in every case. East of Basingstoke there are isolated instances of this; west of Basingstoke the errors are more significant. Table 1 gives the apparent mileages of various stations and mileposts together with the corrected figures. It is understood the error commences at milepost $53\frac{1}{2}$, being four chains further away from Waterloo than it indicates, and by Salisbury increases to ten chains, although where the increase occurs is not plain. The ten-chain error is constant as far as Tisbury; then it widens considerably—so much so that Pinhoe is 30 chains (or 0·4 miles) further away from London than the mileposts suggest. From Crediton to Ilfracombe the error remains constant, as it does on the Okehampton route, at 12 chains. Most recorders on the West of England route preferred to ascertain speeds by the rail-joint method and thereby overcame the problem of these discrepancies which might occasion some confusion to the casual observer.

TABLE 1

MILEAGE DISCREPANCIES BASINGSTOKE TO ILFRACOMBE

Apparent mileage		Location	Correct mileage	
Miles	Chains		Miles	Chains
53	40	Milepost 53½	53	44
83	46	Salisbury	83	56
86	07	Wilton	86	17
96	13	Tisbury	96	23
105	18	Gillingham	105	29
112	02	Templecombe	112	15
118	04	Sherborne	118	22
122	47	Yeovil Junction	122	69
131	32	Crewkerne	131	53
139	31	Chard Junction	139	58
144	42	Axminster	144	66
147	63	Seaton Junction	148	08
153	40	Milepost 153½	153	65
154	56	Honiton	155	01
167	20	Milepost 167¼	167	49
168	39	Pinhoe	168	69
170	21	Exmouth Junction	170	49
171	30	Exeter Central	171	60
172	12	Exeter St David's	172	41
173	50	Cowley Bridge Junction	173	60
179	20	Crediton	179	32
226	19	Ilfracombe	226	31

TABLE 2

BROMLEY SOUTH TO CHATHAM

Detail		A		B		C		D		E	
Date		18 Jan 1955		17 May 1955		26 Oct 1954		19 Oct 1954		1 June 1948	
Train (ex. Victoria)		8.35 a.m.		8.35 a.m.		8.35 a.m.		8.35 a.m.		10.35 a.m.	
Locomotive no.		34066		34017		34065		34065		21C135	
Vehicles		9		10		10		10		13	
Tare load (tons)		300		332		333		335		359	
Gross load (tons)		320		350		355		355		385	
Driver		Gingell		George		Gingell		Banton		—	
		(BAT)		(BAT)		(BAT)		(BAT)			
Recorder		A. J. Baker		A. J. Baker		A. J. Baker		A. J. Baker		A. J. Baker	
Mls.	**Sch.**	**M. S.**	**Speed**	**M. S.**	**Speed**	**M. S.**	**Speed**	**M. S.**	**Speed**	**M. S.**	**Speed**
0·0 BROMLEY SOUTH	0	0 00		0 00		0 00		0 00		0 00	
1·1 Bickley		3 22		8 38		3 29		3 55		4 27	28
1·7 *Bickley Junction S.B.*	5	4 35	38/51	9 59	31	4 45	33/48	5 20	30/46	6 02	
2·3 *St Mary Cray Jnc.*	6	5 30	50	10 58	48/46	5 42	46	6 21	45	7 10	42/41
3·8 St Mary Cray		7 04	71/61	12 42	70/63	7 17	71/66	8 02	65/58	8 58	65/58
		sigs									
6·5 Swanley	11	9 48	40	15 06	64	9 36	64	10 31	57	11 32	58
9·6 Farningham Road		13 02	80/69	17 33	90/77	11 59	88/76	13 15	78/64	14 11	81/68
12·5 Fawkham		15 24	76/64	19 39	81/66	14 04	81/68	15 43	71/56	16 31	70/53
15·1 Meopham		17 41	72	21 45	76	16 06	74/64	18 10	67	19 05	60
16·0 Sole Street	21	18 35	66	22 35	71	16 58	68	19 06	63	20 06	56/70
20·2 *Cuxton Road S.B.*	26	21 37	83	25 50	80	20 04	82	22 22	80	24 46	28/55
		sigs		sigs.		sigs				sigs	
22·1 *Rochester Bridge Jnc.*	29½	25 07	15	29 02	24	24 01	15	25 10	30	27 26	35
(*30)				sigs							
22·9 Rochester		26 33	48	30 43		25 36	41	26 24	45	28 34	45
				sigs		sig. stop					
23·4 CHATHAM	32	27 48		32 31		28 26		27 37		30 01	
Estimated net time (mins)		25¼		31		25¼		27½		28¾	

BULLEID'S PACIFICS

TABLE 3

CHATHAM TO BROMLEY SOUTH

Detail		A	B	C	D	E
Date		5 Mar 1952	6 May 1953	15 Oct 1957	12 Apr 1956	9 Sept 1952
Train (ex. Chatham)		2.53 p.m.	3.16 p.m.	2.53 p.m.	2.53 p.m.	2.53 p.m.
Locomotive no.		34102	34092	34102	34070	34091
Vehicles		8	10	10	10	11
Tare load (tons)		268	333	333	333	365
Gross load (tons)		285	350	355	360	390
Driver (BAT)		Whiting	Webb	Hill	Gingell	Philpott
Recorder		A. J. Baker	A. J. Baker	A. J. Baker	A. J. Baker	A. J. Baker

Mls.	Sch.	M. S. Speed	M. S. Speed	M. S. Speed	M. S. Speed	M. S. Speed
0·0 CHATHAM	0	0 00	0 00	0 00	0 00	0 00
				sigs 20		
0·6 Rochester		1 42 47	1 56 46	2 27 38	1 53 41	2 15 42
1·3 *Rochester Bridge Jnc.*	2½	2 45 44/51	3 00 43/51	3 57 36/44	3 11 35/42	3 27 39/45
(*30)						
3·2 *Cuxton Road S.B.*		5 36 40/43	5 44 44/48	7 13 41/45	6 35 38/43	6 30 40/43
7·4 Sole Street	16	11 45 36	11 36 36	13 12 38	12 40 39	13 32 31
						p.w.s. 20
8·3 Meopham		13 02 57/55	12 56 57/53	14 25 62/59	13 45 60/57	16 00
10·9 Fawkham		15 26 80/78	15 28 76/72	16 47 76/66	16 18 80/77	19 18 70/67
13·8 Farningham Road		17 35 86	17 47 83	19 16 81	18 24 90/76	21 38 82
		sigs 56			sigs	
16·9 Swanley	26	20 27 51	20 23 65	22 01 67	22 07 25	24 21 65/72
19·6 St Mary Cray		23 08 63	22 49 70	24 14 82/66	25 05 68/58	26 37 74/61
21·1 *St Mary Cray Jnc.*	31	25 05	24 35	25 32 72	26 29 67	27 56 65
21·7 *Bickley Junction S.B.*	32	26 03	25 31	26 09	27 10 62	28 36 61
22·3 Bickley		27 07	26 33	26 52 66	27 53 65	29 16 66
		sigs 40		p.w.s. 30		
23·4 BROMLEY SOUTH	35	29 17	28 16	28 29	29 17	30 52
Estimated net tme (mins)		28¼	28¼	27½	27½	29

TABLE 4
CANNON STREET TO WHITSTABLE

Detail	A	B	C
Date	17 Sept. 1947	12 June 1959	5 Aug 1957
Train (ex. Cannon Street)	4.45 p.m.	5.14 pm.	4.46 p.m. (see text)
Locomotive no.	21C163	34013(R)	34081
Vehicles	10	11	9
Tare load (tons)	330	368	298
Gross load (tons)	352	395	325
Driver	—	L. Moody (RAM)	S. Gingell
Conditions	—	Fine	Heavy rain
Recorder	Rev. R. S. Haines	S. C. Nash	J. R. Skinner

Mls.		A Sch.	A M.	A S.	A Speed	B Sch.	B M.	B S.	B Speed	C Sch.	C M.	C S.	C Speed
0·0	CANNON STREET	0	0	00		0	0	00					
0·7	LONDON BRIDGE (*20)		2	23		3	3	15		0	0	00	
3·7	New Cross (*45)		6	46	50	7½	7	47	47/27 sigs	5	5	23	43 sig. stop
6·0	Hither Green	12	10	13		11	11	50	35	8½	13	43	32
7·8	Grove Park			p.w.s.			14	44	35		16	48	38
9·1	Elmstead Woods		16	56	—/43		16	55	33 sigs		18	45	43 sigs
10·1	*Chislehurst Junction* (*20)		18	36		17	18	55	42/28	15	20	30	34
11·0	*St Mary Cray Junction*		—	p.w.s.		19	20	15	34		22	39	21
12·5	St Mary Cray		22	23			22	27	54 p.w.s.		24	37	64/66
15·1	Swanley	24	25	21	63	25	25	46	35	22	27	17	62/36
18·3	Farningham Road		28	09	73		29	26	70		30	43	84
20·4	*Fawkham Junction*			—			31	28	61		—		71
21·1	Fawkham		30	46			32	11	57/51		33	04	74/63 sigs
23·7	Meopham		33	35			35	01	57		36	51	8
24·6	Sole Street	33½	34	38	58	35	36	01	60	32	39	29	40
28·8	*Cuxton Road S.B.*			—		39½	39	30	77	37	43	32	80
30·8	*Rochester Bridge Junction* (*30)			sigs			42	20	29		48	13	28
32·0	CHATHAM (*30)	43½	43	36		45	44	46	34	42	51	26	19 sig. stop
33·7	Gillingham		45	52		48	47	35	36		57	53	
36·7	Rainham		49	14	72		51	23	62		61	33	60/63
39·3	Newington (*65)		51	39			53	56	65/61		63	59	76/70
42·5	Sittingbourne	56	54	28		59	56	49	81	56	66	29	76/87
45·7	Teynham		57	22			59	24	77/66 sigs		68	44	92/84
49·7	FAVERSHAM (*30)	65	62	27		67	63	43	27	65	73	45	
52·6	*Graveney Siding*			—			67	43	65				
56·8	WHITSTABLE	10	9	31		76	72	28					
Estimated net time (mins)			59¾+9¼				71				56		

TABLE 5

VICTORIA TO DOVER MARINE

Detail	A	B
Date	31 May 1951	13 April 1950
Train (ex. Victoria)	10.0 a.m.	9.0 a.m.
Locomotive no.	35028	34091
Vehicles	14	14
Tare load	418	427
Gross load	445	455
Driver (Stewarts Lane)	Brown	Norman
Recorder	A. J. Baker	A. J. Baker

Mls	Sch.	M. S.	Speed	Sch.	M. S.	Speed
0·0 VICTORIA	0	0 00		0	0 00	
3·2 Brixton (*25)	7	7 40	29	7	8 28	28
4·0 Herne Hill (*45)	8½	8 52	39	8½	9 48	37
5·7 Sydenham Hill		11 53	33		13 37	24
		p.w.s.	28			
8·7 Beckenham Junction	16½	16 32	50	17	17 58	58
10·9 Bromley South		19 12	57		20 31	57
12·6 *Bickley Junction S.B.* (*40)	22	21 32	32	23	23 00	30
		sigs	38			
14·9 ORPINGTON	27	25 19	33	28	27 13	42
16·4 Chelsfield		27 56	37		29 28	
17·6 Knockholt		30 05	34		31 38	32
21·7 Dunton Green		34 29	71		36 25	66
23·2 SEVENOAKS (*60)	37½	35 49		39	37 52	
23·8 *Sevenoaks Tunnel North*		36 20	60		38 27	54
28·1 Hildenborough (*75)		40 20	71		42 27	78
30·6 TONBRIDGE (*50)	45½	43 02	40/49	47	45 13	33
					p.w.s.	35
35·9 Paddock Wood	51½	48 35		53½	52 24	
40·5 Marden		52 35	73		56 25	71
43·0 Staplehurst		54 51	63		58 34	66
46·3 Headcorn		57 44	72/62		61 15	76/67
51·5 Pluckley		62 25	68		65 40	73
55·1 *Milepost 54*		65 35	64		68 44	66
57·2 ASHFORD (*70)	72	67 25	73	75	70 32	74
		p.w.s.				
61·5 Smeeth		71 07	48		74 27	60/63
65·3 Westenhanger		75 26	54		78 16	54
66·5 Sandling Junction	81½	76 47	67	85	79 36	
70·4 Shorncliffe		80 17			83 21	64
71·0 Folkestone Central (*60)		80 58			84 03	60/61
72·0 Folkestone Junction (*60)	87	81 59	56/58	91	85 03	60/65
		sigs				
77·5 *Archcliffe Junction* (*10)		90 09			91 27	
78·0 DOVER MARINE	95	91 45		100	93 10	
Estimated net time (mins)		86½			92¼	

TABLE 6

CHARING CROSS–WATERLOO–ASHFORD–FOLKESTONE CENTRAL

Detail	A	B	C	D
Date	17 Apr 1954	5 Sept 1955	9 May 1960	19 Sept 1957
Train (ex. Charing Cross)	12.55 p.m.	4.15 p.m.	1.10 p.m.	1.8 p.m.
Locomotive no.	34079	34075	34022(R)	34076
Vehicles	10	10	10	11
Tare load (tons)	332	335	338	371
Gross load (tons)	350	360	355	395
Driver	Croucher (DOV)	—	Thomas (RAM)	Shelvey (RAM)
Recorder	A. J. Baker	A. J. Baker	A. J. Baker	A. J. Baker

Mls.		A			B			C			D	
	Sch	M. S.	Speed	Sch	M. S.	Speed	Sch	M. S.	Speed	Sch	M. S.	Speed
0·0 CHARING CROSS	0	0 00										
0·8 WATERLOO		3 08		0	0 00		0	0 00		0	0 00	
		sigs	12		sigs	20						
1·9 London Bridge (*20)	5	6 36		3	3 35		3	3 18		3	3 22	
								sigs	35			
4·9 New Cross (*45)	9	10 39	57	7	7 48	58	7	7 46		7	7 15	61
		sigs	50									
7·2 Hither Green	12½	13 25	54	10	10 21		10	10 55	47		9 56	56/61
9·0 Grove Park		15 35			12 33			13 23			11 51	
10·3 Elmstead Woods		17 18	44		14 19	43		15 16	41		13 31	45
11·2 Chislehurst	18	18 31	52	15½	15 36	50	16½	16 35	49	16½	14 49	50
											p.w.s.	
13·8 Orpington	21	21 24	62	18½	18 35	60	19½	19 49	54	21½	19 40	18
15·3 Chelsfield		22 53			20 09			21 35			22 24	37/34
16·6 Knockholt		24 18	53		21 36	51		23 18	41		24 41	36
20·6 Dunton Green		28 02	77		25 24	76		27 36	66		29 19	70
22·1 SEVENOAKS (*60)	31	29 21		28	26 42		29½	29 13		31½	30 46	
22·7 Sevenoaks Tunnel North		29 53	63		27 13	66		29 52	50		31 23	53
27·0 Hildenborough (*75)		34 30	70		31 07	63/77		34 29	71		35 21	82
		sigs	32					p.w.s.	56		sigs	35
29·5 TONBRIDGE (*50)	39	38 09	48	35½	33 35	48	37½	37 10	52	39½	38 18	42
34·8 Paddock Wood	45	43 30	72/69	41	38 47		43½	42 15	82	45½	44 36	72/69
39·4 Marden		47 24	73/65		42 31	78/70		46 05			48 32	74
41·9 Staplehurst		49 37	73		44 38	74		48 18	65		50 47	64
					p.w.s.	58						
45·3 Headcorn		52 28	67/70		47 42	61		51 11	77		53 31	75
50·5 Pluckley		57 18	60/66		52 47	68		55 53	64/72		58 00	67/78
54·0 Milepost 54		60 41	60		55 59	65/70		59 02	64		61 10	66/73
						10		p.w.s.	48		sigs	40
56·1 ASHFORD (*70)	65	62 37	70/61	60½	60 14		65½	62 03		67½	64 49	
60·4 Smeeth		66 35	65		65 06	61/67						
64·2 Westenhanger		70 15	61		68 40	62		7 00	61		6 56	62
65·4 Sandling Junction		71 30			69 54			10 48	59		10 44	60
69·3 SHORNCLIFFE		75 01	70		73 14	77		12 04	65/72		11 59	74
					sigs	20	17	16 19		17	16 02	
70·0 FOLKESTONE CENTRAL	80	76 18		76½	75 09					2	2 33	
Estimated net time (mins)		73			69½			61½ (to Ashford)			59½ (to Ashford)	

TABLE 7
TONBRIDGE TO ASHFORD

Detail		A	B	C	D	E
Date		22 Feb 1958	24 Apr 1958	6 Aug 1959	13 Apr 1960	2 June 1960
Train (ex. Charing Cross)		9.8 a.m.	9.8 a.m.	9.10 a.m.	9.10 a.m.	9.10 a.m.
Locomotive no.		34098	34078	34005(R)	34005(R)	34037(R)
Vehicles		10	11	11	11	11
Tare load (tons)		331	364	364	365	364
Gross load (tons)		355	390	395	390	385
Driver (Bricklayers Arms)		—	Todd	Kennett	Nebbs	Longhurst
Recorder		C. R. Richardson	A. J. Baker	A. J. Baker	A. J. Baker	A. J. Baker

Mls.	Sch.	M. S.	M. S. Speed	M. S. Speed	M. S. Speed	M. S. Speed
0·0 TONBRIDGE	0	0 00	0 00	0 00	0 00	0 00
			45	39	40	39
5·3 Paddock Wood	8	6 57	7 11 81/77	7 35 78	7 34 78	7 41 81
9·9 Marden		10 25	10 57 82/69	11 17 76	11 17 71	11 18 74
12·4 Staplehurst		12 14	13 02 85	13 13 84	13 17	13 15 81
15·7 Headcorn		14 38	15 39 72	15 41 87/78	15 49 85/76	15 43 84/75
20·9 Pluckley		18 25	19 54 82	19 30 86	19 55 82	19 40 81/76
24·4 *Milepost 54*		—	22 49 77/81	22 09 83	22 43 79	22 22 81
				sig.stop	p.w.s. 42	p.w.s. 50
26·6 ASHFORD	30	24 21	25 19	28 11	25 24	25 10
Estimated net time (mins)		24¼	25¼	24¾	25¼	25

TABLE 8
ASHFORD TO TONBRIDGE

Date	10 March 1960		
Train	2.32 p.m. ex. Ashford		
Locomotive no.	34001(R)		
Vehicles	9		
Tare load (tons)	302		
Gross load (tons)	320		
Driver (Bricklayers Arms)	Longhurst		
Recorder	A. J. Baker		

Mls.	Sch.	M. S.	Speed
0·0 ASHFORD	0	0 00	
		p.w.s.	33
2·1 *Milepost 54*		4 31	51
5·7 Pluckley		7 52	78/76
10·9 Headcorn		11 39	91
14·2 Staplehurst		13 56	
16·7 Marden		15 45	80/85
21·3 Paddock Wood	22	19 03	82/85
26·6 TONBRIDGE (*50)	27 pass	23 45 pass	48
Estimated net time to passing Tonbridge (mins.)		23½	

TABLE 9
ASHFORD TO WATERLOO

Detail	A	B	C	D	E
Date	9 Feb 1956	3 May 1956	6 Aug 1959	11 May 1960	21 July 1955
Train (ex. Ashford)	5.11 p.m.	5.11 p.m.	2.36 p.m.	5.11 p.m.	5.11 p.m.
Locomotive no.	34078	34099	34026(R)	34003(R)	34087
Vehicles	10	10	10	10	11
Tare load (tons)	336	336	337	338	366
Gross load (tons)	355	360	360	365	395
Driver	Dann (RAM)	Gifford (RAM)	Kennett (BA)	Hurst (RAM)	Card (RAM)
Recorder	A. J. Baker	A. J. Baker	A. J. Baker	A. J. Baker	A. J. Baker

Mls.	A			B		C			D			E	
	Sch.	M. S.	Speed	M. S.	Speed	Sch.	M. S.	Speed	Sch.	M. S.	Speed	M. S.	Speed
0·0 ASHFORD	0	0 00		0 00		0	0 00		0	0 00		0 00	
										p.w.s.	33		
2·1 *Milepost 54*		3 55	53	4 21	47		4 55	49		4 17	53/72	4 33	45
										sigs			
5·7 Pluckley		7 20	73/70	7 58	71/68		8 28	73/67		8 33	34	8 15	72/69
				p.w.s.									
10·9 Headcorn		11 34	81/78	12 51	40		12 49	79		13 52	83	12 27	83
14·2 Staplehurst		14 12	81	16 28	68		15 30			16 25	81	14 57	
										p.w.s.	63		
16·7 Marden		16 18	67	18 45	65		17 39	68		18 40	74	16 53	77
										sigs			
21·3 Paddock Wood	22	20 03	77	22 28	80/68	22	21 25	74/63	22	22 47	51/59	20 20	83/70
		p.w.s.	32										
26·6 TONBRIDGE(*50)	27	27 00	48/50	26 52	55/61	27	26 23	50/56	27	28 37	40/48	24 36	48/60
										p.w.s.			
29·1 Hildenborough		30 25		29 35	54		29 27			33 01	26	27 33	
31·4 *Sevenoaks Tunnel South*		33 55	42	32 29	47		32 28	45		36 22	50	30 30	48
33·4 *Sevenoaks Tunnel North*		36 30	47	35 10	44		35 00	47		38 53	48	33 01	47
34·0 SEVENOAKS(*60)	39	37 10		35 54		39	35 40		39	39 34		33 41	
35·6 Dunton Green		38 35	72	37 28	65		37 09	67		41 02	74	35 07	73
39·6 Knockholt		42 27	56	41 57	48		41 34	46		44 56	54	38 52	57
				p.w.s.									
40·8 Chelsfield		43 35	71	43 44	38		42 47			46 05		39 59	
42·3 Orpington	49	44 48	77	45 19	65	48½	44 02	76/72	48½	47 19	76	41 09	81/78
44·9 Chislehurst	51½	46 58	73	47 49	60	52	46 10	78	51½	49 43	60/67	43 08	80/77
		sigs	16	sigs	20					sigs	30		
47·2 Grove Park		50 10		51 27	35		48 03	79		52 22		44 56	81
48·9 Hither Green	55	52 13	64	54 03		56	49 47		55½	54 31	57	46 21	
										sigs	30	sigs	48
50·5 St Johns (*45)		53 57		55 55	45		51 45	48		57 08	42	48 17	55
		sigs	40										
51·3 New Cross	58	55 00	54	56 56		59	52 42	52	58½	58 11	46	49 05	50/64
		sigs	20	sigs	22		sigs	44		sigs	5		
54·3 London Bridge (*20)	62½	59 42	32	61 12		63½	56 41		63	64 38	26	52 25	
		sigs	18		41		sigs	25			41	sigs	20
55·3 WATERLOO	65	62 12		63 45		66½	59 16		67	67 16		55 04	
Estimated net time (mins)		56¾		57¾			58¾			58		54¼	

TABLE 10
DOVER MARINE TO VICTORIA

Detail	A	B	C
Date	10 July 1960	31 Jan 1952	16 Aug 1951
Train (ex. Dover Marine)	6.13 p.m.	5.15 p.m.	6.10 p.m.
Locomotive no.	34088(R)	35026	34091
Vehicles	12	14	14
Tare load (tons)	394	420	436
Gross load (tons)	420	445	470
Driver (Stewart's Lane)	—	Brown	Triggs
Recorder	DWW	A. J. Baker	A. J. Baker

Mls.		Sch.	M. S.	Speed	Sch.	M. S.	Speed	Sch.	M. S.	Speed
0·0	DOVER MARINE	0	0 00		0	0 00		0	0 00	
6·0	Folkestone Junction	12	11 07	40		12 04		12	12 52	
7·0	Folkestone Central		12 31			13 17			14 28	
			p.w.s.							
7·6	Shorncliffe		13 48	30		14 04	54		15 33	41
11·5	Sandling Junction		19 53	46	18	18 07		19	20 49	
12·7	Westenhanger		21 24	54		19 24	60		22 24	48
16·5	Smeeth		25 03	68		22 33	83/80		25 59	69/66
20·8	ASHFORD (*70)	31½	28 53	40	27	25 45	82	29	29 25	80
			p.w.s.							
22·9	*Milepost 54*		31 38			27 21	76/84		31 05	73/80
26·5	Pluckley		35 03	66		30 03			33 51	74
						p.w.s. 22				
31·7	Headcorn		39 21	74		36 54	63		37 37	88
			sigs							
35·0	Staplehurst		42 21	54		39 51	72/70		39 58	—/78
37·5	Marden		45 02	58/65		41 59			41 49	
									p.w.s.	13
42·1	Paddock Wood	49½	49 18	62	46	45 36	81/61	50	49 56	57/54
			sigs							
47·4	TONBRIDGE (*50)	54½	55 43	35	51	50 25	42/50	55	55 36	48/52
49·9	Hildenborough		59 17	42		53 54			58 46	
52·2	*Sevenoaks Tunnel South*		—	43		57 23	42		62 30	37
54·2	*Sevenoaks Tunnel North*		65 22	42		60 46			65 53	34
54·8	SEVENOAKS (*60)	65½	66 08		63	61 39	32	67	66 39	
56·3	Dunton Green		67 40	62		63 38	50		68 14	65
						sigs 34				
58·2	*Polhill Tunnel South*		—			66 36	41		70 01	
60·4	Knockholt		72 11	45		70 30	31		72 26	49
61·6	Chelsfield		—			71 54			73 40	68
									sigs	28
63·1	ORPINGTON		74 50	67		73 13	73	76½	76 00	45
65·4	*Bickley Junction S.B.* (*40)	77½	77 34		75½	76 06	30	80	79 26	40
67·1	Bromley South		79 39	55		79 13	34		81 50	49
69·3	Beckenham Junction	83	82 11		81	82 35	51	85	84 44	
			sigs. sev.						sigs	
74·0	Herne Hill (*45)	90	88 31		88	88 31	60	93	96 36	
74·8	Brixton (*50)		90 57		89	89 35	46/52	94	98 01	
			sigs						sigs	
78·0	VICTORIA	97	95 58		95	95 01		100	105 02	
Estimated net time (mins)			91			90			89½	

TABLE 11
WATERLOO TO SALISBURY

Detail	A	B	C	D	E
Date	23 June 1964	3 Apr 1964	13 June 1956	23 Apr 1962	4 Sept 1964
Train (ex. Waterloo)	11.0 a.m.	7.0 p.m.	11.0 a.m.	11.0 a.m.	11.0 a.m.
Locomotive no.	34095(R)	34086	35011	35024(R)	35022(R)
Vehicles	11	11	13	13	13
Tare load (tons)	366	371	430	430	441
Gross load (tons)	385	410	460	460	470
Driver	—	—	Letchford (9E)	Roberts (9E)	Sibley (SALS)
Recorder	J. G. McEwan	D. J. Maidment	D. A. Lock	A. P. Swinburne	DWW

Mls.		A Sch	M. S.	Speed	B Sch	M. S.	Speed	C Sch	M. S.	Speed	D Sch	M. S.	Speed	E Sch	M. S.	Speed
0·0	WATERLOO	0	0 00		0	0 00		0	0 00		0	0 00		0	0 00	
1·3	Vauxhall (*40)		—	—/54		3 35	—/56		—	32		3 27	34/51 sigs		sig. stop	
3·9	Clapham Jnc. (*40)	7	7 15	40	7	7 06	46 sigs	7	7 20	49	7	7 22	25	7	10 26	40
7·2	Wimbledon		11 13	58		11 34	35		11 30	56		11 30	60		14 28	56
9·8	New Malden		13 49	61		14 35	62		sig. stop			13 55	68		16 57	65
12·0	Surbiton		15 51	66		16 41	70		—			15 50	70		18 57	70
13·3	Hampton Court Junction	18	16 59	71	18	17 52	75 sigs 40	18	20 33		18	16 56	71	18	20 02	72
17·1	Walton-on-Thames		20 01	74		22 32	64		—			19 58	77		23 05	73
19·1	Weybridge		21 44	72		sig. stop			27 30	64		21 32	78/81		24 46	74
21·7	West Byfleet		23 46	76		—			p.w.s.	15		23 27	77		26 47	78
24·3	WOKING	27†	25 53	72	28†	34 25	62 sigs 50	28†	34 47		27†	25 30	76	27†	28 56	74/70
28·0	Brookwood		29 07	69		38 06	58		39 38	51		28 28	74		32 01	71
31·0	Milepost 31		31 56	65		41 03	67		—	55		31 00	71		34 35	70
33·2	Farnborough		33 52	69		42 57	72		45 14	67		32 50	75		36 26	74
36·5	Fleet		36 34	73/75		45 40	80		—			35 20	78		39 03	76
39·8	Winchfield		39 15	73		48 15	83 p.w.s.		—			37 55	77		41 37	78
42·2	Hook		41 10	74/76		51 58	28		53 22	69/74		39 37	81/84		43 29	76/81
47·8	BASINGSTOKE (*65)		45 52	65		57 30	65		58 11	68		44 05	65		47 52	68
50·3	Worting Jnc.	50	48 16	64	53	59 55	69	51	60 29	65	50	46 27	63	50	50 11	65
52·4	Oakley		50 19	62		61 52	72		—			48 15	72		52 01	72
55·6	Overton		52 55	72		64 38	80		—			50 47	78		54 31	80
59·2	Whitchurch North		56 00	80		67 26	84		68 10	78		53 27	82		57 12	80
61·1	Hurstbourne		57 23	83/78		68 50	86/90		69 34	89/82		54 50	84/79		58 38	86/78
66·4	ANDOVER JUNCTION		61 19	82		72 50	83		73 14	95		58 40	86		62 31	84
67·8	Red Post Jnc.		—			—	81		—			59 42	80		63 35	76¦81
72·7	Grateley		66 20	71/67		77 13	72		78 12	61		63 38	67		67 33	71
75·6	Allington S.B.		68 50	72		—			—			65 55	82		69 57	79
78·2	Porton		70 47	85		82 00	85/90 sigs		—	86		67 48	86/90		71 53	84/86
82·6	Tunnel Jnc. (*50)		74 30		82½	86 42	20	80½	86 22			71 35	45		75 25	
83·7	SALISBURY	80	77 03		85	89 37		83	88 47		80	74 03		80	78 07	
	Estimated net time (mins)		77			76			77¾			73½			74½	

†At *Woking Junction*

TABLE 12

WATERLOO TO SALISBURY

Detail		A			B			C		
Date			27 May 1966			18 Apr 1959			26 Mar 1959	
Train (ex. Waterloo)			4.54 p.m.			3 p.m.			1 p.m.	
Locomotive no.			34060(R)			34064			35007(R)	
Vehicles			11			12			13	
Tare load (tons)			336¾			395			438	
Gross load (tons)			360			410			470	
Recorder			DWW			J. L. Lean			J. L. Lean	
Mls		Sch.	M. S.	Speed	Sch.	M. S.	Speed	Sch.	M. S.	Speed
0·0	WATERLOO	0	0 00		0	0 00		0	0 00	
3·9	Clapham Junction (*40)	7	7 02	44	7	7 01	45	7	6 52	47
7·2	Wimbledon		10 55	58		12 11			11 09	53
						p.w.s.	27			
12·0	Surbiton		15 16	70		17 27	48		15 57	60
						sigs				
13·3	*Hampton Court Junction*		16 24		18	19 02	47	18	17 13	62
			p.w.s.							
19·1	Weybridge		24 48	68		25 57	60		24 04	63
21·7	West Byfleet		26 58	74		—	69		—	
24·3	WOKING	30	29 51		28	29 38	64	29	28 33	
						sigs.				
3·7	Brookwood		6 08	60		33 35	54		8 17	47
6·7	*Milepost 31*		9 03	62		36 53	55		—	
12·2	Fleet		13 33			42 04	65		17 20	72
15·5	Winchfield		16 03	75		45 00	66		20 04	73
17·9	Hook		17 57	77		47 09	65/72		22 04	70/72
23·5	BASINGSTOKE (*65)	27	23 13		55	52 48			27 03	56
2·5	*Worting Junction*		4 48	52	5½	5 16	39	29	29 57	50
4·6	Oakley		7 01	64		7 47	56		32 28	49
7·8	Overton		9 44	75		10 48	67		35 42	58
11·4	Whitchurch		12 25	84		—			—	
13·3	Hurstbourne		13 47	84		15 18	78		—	77
18·6	ANDOVER JUNCTION	21	18 22		21	20 12		45	45 22	
1·4	*Red Post Junction*		3 53	41/63		3 42	38/59		3 35	35
6·4	Grateley		9 00	60/59		9 15	55		9 09	55/54
9·3	*Allington S.B.*		11 47	69		—			—	
			p.w.s.							
11·9	Porton		14 54	25/70		14 01	81/88		14 08	72/83
16·2	*Tunnel Junction* (*50)		20 01		18½	17 18		18½	17 32	54
17·3	SALISBURY	22	22 58		21	19 35		21	20 00	
Estimated net times (mins)										
Waterloo–Woking			26¼			—			28½	
Waterloo–Basingstoke			—			49¼			—	
Woking–Basingstoke			23¼			—			—	
Woking–Andover Junction			—			—			45¼	
Basingstoke–Andover Junction			18¼			20¼			—	
Andover–Salisbury			20			19½			20	
Total			87¾ (3 stops)			89 (2 stops)			93¾ (2 stops)	

18. Except for a modified tender No. 34015 *Exmouth*, pictured hauling an up train near Bere Alston in the spring of 1961, had by then received the more noticeable modifications including modified cab, long smoke deflector wings, removal of sheeting between front buffer beam and cylinder, battens for *Devon Belle* plates, speedometer and A.W.S. gear.

19. No. 34064 *Fighter Command* had received the Giesl ejector and modified tender by April 1965, when it was heading the Plymouth–Brighton train east of Salisbury.

20. First of the rebuilds, No. 35018 *British India Line,* made its *début* at Waterloo on 14 February 1956 when bowler-hatted inspector Dan Knight took the opportunity to make a close examination.

21. No. 35020 *Bibby Line* accelerating towards Wilton on 18 June 1956 with the controlled road testing train which was operated between Salisbury and Exeter (see Chapter 5).

22. One of the smaller Pacifics in modified form. No. 34059 *Sir Archibald Sinclair* climbs out of Alresford with an up diverted Bournemouth train on 15 May 1966.

23. No 34019 *Bideford* climbing Upton Scudamore bank with a Westbury–
Poole cement train in August 1965.

24. It was in Devonshire however that these engines were most often seen on
freight turns. No. 34024 *Tamar Valley* with an up train near Bere Ferrers in
May 1961.

TABLE 13
SALISBURY TO EXETER CENTRAL

Detail		A			B			C			D			E	
Date		26 July 1954			7 Sept 1959			26 Aug 1957			23 June 1964			26 Oct 1963	
Train (ex. Waterloo)		11.5 a.m.			11.0 a.m.			11.0 a.m.			11.0 a.m.			11.0 a.m.	
Locomotive no.		34023			35012(R)			35005			34095(R)			34005(R)	
Vehicles		10/7§			10/8§			11			11			11	
Tare load (tons)		328/227			336/272			360			366			369	
Gross load (tons)		350/240			360/290			380			385			390	
Driver		—			—			—			—			Davey (EXJ)	
Recorder		D. A. Lock			Rev. J. E. T. Phillips			D. A. Lock			J. G. McEwan			P. M. Widgery	
Mls.	Sch.	M. S.	Speed	Sch.	M. S.	Speed	Sch.	M. S.	Speed	Sch.	M. S.	Speed	Sch.	M. S.	Speed
0·0 SALISBURY	0	0 00		0	0 00		0	0 00		0	0 00		0	0 00	
2·5 Wilton (*40)		—			6 02	45		6 40	40	6	6 06	45	6	6 20	46/66
8·3 Dinton		—			11 47	69		—			12 24	63/61		12 31	64/66
														p.w.s.	
12·6 Tisbury		15 17	68/69		15 18	75		18 22	54/57		16 39	64		16 53	10/49
17·6 Semley		20 05	56		19 23	69		23 47	50/78		21 40	56		25 48	47
								p.w.s.							
21·7 Gillingham		23 42	73		22 19	90		27 25	58		25 05	81		29 26	78
					p.w.s.										
23·9 *Milepost 107½*		—	—/77		25 18	20		29 44	56/80		27 00	65/82		31 22	62/82
					p.w.s.										
28·5 TEMPLECOMBE		29 47			30 45	69		33 25			30 37			34 59	69
30·0 Milepost 113½		—	52		32 11	62		—	57		32 15	55		36 23	60
30·9 Milborne Port		—			32 59	72		35 49			33 08	60		37 12	70
34·6 Sherborne		35 44	79		35 39	93		38 37	91		36 10	83		40 05	85/76
39·2 YEOVIL JNC.	41	39 30		41	38 43	86	41	41 53	82	39	39 56	70/72	39	43 30	79
41·4 Sutton Bingham		—			40 27	76		43 47			41 49	71		45 21	68
42·8 *Milepost 126½*		—	52		41 38	68/87		—	64		43 10	63		46 38	63/81
48·0 Crewkerne		—	70/47		45 31	76		49 07	82		47 32	75		50 45	69
49·8 *Milepost 133½*		51 23†			47 13	61		51 40†	57		49 45	47		52 34	53
56·0 Chard Junction		—	75		51 47	92		55 37	85		55 52	65/63		57 42	79/84
61·1 AXMINSTER		60 12	82		54 59	100		59 15	90	60	60 36	78/80		61 26	78/82
64·4 Seaton Junction		62 45	65		57 04	90		61 35	74		63 14	70		63 55	72
69·1 *Milepost 152½*		—			61 18	54		—			69 38	33		69 36	34
70·1 *Milepost 153½*		70 53‡	32		62 27	52		68 00‡	37		71 22	34		71 31	30
71·3 Honiton		72 38	65		63 32	71/90		69 30	86		72 40	84		73 04	54/76
75·9 SIDMOUTH		p.w.s.													
JUNCTION	79	79 18		79	67 30		79	74 00		73	76 46		73	77 29	
3·8 Whimple		5 08			4 54	74		6 13	71		5 35	71		6 00	69/78
7·4 Broad Clyst		8 00	84		7 28	90		8 59	81		8 17	89		8 56	75
9·3 Pinhoe		—			8 52	75		—			9 40	73		10 28	64
11·1 *Exmouth Jnc.*	11	11 17		11	10 34		11	12 11		11	11 20		11	12 13	
					sigs										
12·1 EXETER CENTRAL	14	13 17		14	13 00		14	14 12		14	13 25		14	14 39	
Estimated net time (mins)															
Salisbury–Sidmouth Junction		76¾			64			73¾			76¾			74¼	
Sidmouth Junction–Exeter Central		13¼			12½			14¼			13½			14¾	

† At Hewish Gates ‡ West portal of tunnel § Reduced at Sidmouth Junction

TABLE 14
SALISBURY TO EXETER CENTRAL

Detail	A			B			C		
Date	31 Mar 1959			23 Sept 1961			7 Apr 1961		
Train (ex. Waterloo)	11.0 a.m.			11.0 a.m.			11.0 a.m.		
Locomotive no.	35012(R)			35028(R)			35028(R)		
Vehicles	11			12/8†			12/10†		
Tare load (tons)	367			393/263			399/335		
Gross load (tons)	390			425/285			430/360		
Driver (EXJ)	—			Burridge			Whitfield		
Recorder	Rev. J. E. T. Phillips			DWW			Rev. J. E. T. Phillips		
Mls.	Sch	M. S.	Speed	Sch	M. S.	Speed	Sch	M. S.	Speed
0·0 SALISBURY	0	0 00		0	0 00		0	0 00	
1·4 *Milepost 85*		3 28			—			3 17	
2·5 Wilton (*40)		5 00	56		6 13	48/68		4 53	53
8·3 Dinton		10 18	73		12 25			10 26	68/66
					p.w.s. 20				
12·6 Tisbury		13 43	77		18 36	55		14 15	69
17·6 Semley		17 45	70		23 36	60		18 53	58
21·7 Gillingham		20 42	90		26 51	86		22 14	82
		p.w.s.						p.w.s.	
23·9 *Milepost 107½*		23 23	15		—			24 39	20
		p.w.s.						p.w.s.	
28·5 TEMPLECOMBE		29 38	68		31 40	78		30 34	66
30·0 *Milepost 113½*		31 17	52		32 56	65		32 17	50
30·9 *Milborne Port*		32 10	62		—			33 15	59
34·6 Sherborne		35 00	90		36 17	94		36 17	90
39·2 YEOVIL JUNCTION	41	38 22	80	40	39 17		41	39 30	86
41·4 Sutton Bingham		40 05	75		40 52			41 10	75
42·8 *Milepost 126¼*		41 17	69/86		—	73		42 22	69/82
48·0 Crewkerne		45 07	72		45 37	80		46 21	75
49·8 *Milepost 133¼*		46 49	62/82		47 12	65		48 03	60
56·0 Chard Junction		51 29	76		51 43	91		52 47	87
61·1 AXMINSTER		55 20	90		54 52	104		56 06	98
64·4 Seaton Junction		57 40	80		56 55	90		58 12	88
67·6 *Milepost 151*		60 31	57		—			60 58	56
68·1 *Milepost 151½*		—			60 00	60		—	
69·1 *Milepost 152½*		62 15	50		61 03	59		62 45	48
70·1 *Milepost 153½*		63 28	49		62 17	eased		64 08	47
71·3 Honiton		64 37	69/90		63 32	62		65 23	64/81
75·9 SIDMOUTH JUNCTION	79	68 35		75	68 18		79	69 50	
3·8 Whimple		5 17	70		4 58	71		4 56	
7·4 Broad Clyst		8 12	79		7 37	84		7 35	90
9·3 Pinhoe		9 50	62		8 58	82		8 56	
11·1 *Exmouth Junction*	11	11 43		11	10 30		11	10 30	
12·1 EXETER CENTRAL	14	13 45		14	12 37		14	12 37	
Estimated net time (mins)									
Salisbury–Sidmouth Junction	64½			65			66¾		
Sidmouth Jnc.–Exeter Central	13¾			12½			12½		

† Reduced at Sidmouth Junction.

TABLE 15
SALISBURY TO EXETER CENTRAL

Detail	A	B	C
Date	16 Sept 1961	19 Apr 1947	13 Aug 1949
Train (ex. Waterloo)	11.0 a.m.	10.50 a.m.	12 noon
Locomotive no.	35029(R)	21C2	35008
Vehicles	13/9‡	15	14
Tare load (tons)	432/303	500 (est.)	543
Gross load (tons)	475/330	535 (est.)	575
Driver	Bennett (EXJ)	—	—
Recorder	S. C. Nash	J. M. B. Edwards	A. J. Baker

Mls.		A Sch.	A M. S.	A Speed	B Sch.	B M. S.	B Speed	C Sch.	C M. S.	C Speed
0·0	SALISBURY	0	0 00		0	0 00				
1·7	*Milepost 85¼*		—			4 54	30			
2·5	Wilton (*40)		5 32	52		6 24	40	0	0 00	
8·3	Dinton		11 25	70		13 01	60		10 07	58/50
12·6	Tisbury		15 19	67		17 15	62		15 02	54/58
17·6	Semley		20 00	61		22 15	51		20 35	46
21·7	Gillingham		23 20	85		25 49	79		24 15	79
23·9	*Milepost 107½*		25 04†	78/90		27 42	66/76		26 15	57/78
28·5	TEMPLECOMBE		28 17	71		31 34	60	27	30 08	
30·0	*Milepost 113½*		—			33 18	48		—	47
30·9	Milborne Port		30 22	68		34 20	56		32 53	—
34·6	Sherborne		33 07	93		37 33	77		36 05	83/68
39·2	YEOVIL JUNCTION	40	36 26	78		41 20	71	40	39 45	73
41·4	Sutton Bingham		38 18	62		43 29	57		41 45	54/64
42·8	*Milepost 126¼*		—			45 08	50/63		—	
									p.w.s.	26
48·0	Crewkerne		44 02	75		50 07	57		50 13	60
49·8	*Milepost 133¼*		—	50		52 29	41		53 32	31
56·0	Chard Junction		51 18	81		58 16	75		59 15	74
61·1	AXMINSTER		55 00	88		62 30	74		63 08	—/87
64·4	Seaton Junction		57 26	75		65 21	54		65 36	73
						p.w.s.				
68·1	*Milepost 152½*		63 43§	28		—	26		71 49	30
69·1	*Milepost 153½*		65 20§	30		—			73 38	34
71·3	Honiton		67 13	78		78 33	60/72		75 15	—/80
75·9	SIDMOUTH JUNCTION	75	72 12		92	83 17		83	80 10	
3·8	Whimple		5 13	78		5 27	65		6 01	38
7·4	Broad Clyst		7 59	88		8 26	75/77		9 00	80
9·3	Pinhoe		9 25	70		10 01	60		10 31	
11·1	*Exmouth Junction*	11	11 17			11 50	58	13	12 20	
			sigs							
12·1	EXETER CENTRAL	14	14 16		18	14 12		16	14 46	

Estimated net time (mins)	A	B	C
Salisbury–Sidmouth Junction	72¼	79¼	77½
Sidmouth Junc.–Exeter Central	14	14¼	14¾

† At Buckhorn Weston Tunnel East End ‡ Reduced at Sidmouth Junction
§ At Honiton Tunnel East or West Portals

TABLE 16
SALISBURY TO EXETER CENTRAL

Detail	A				B				C			
Date	1 Sept 1961				11 May 1962				26 June 1959			
Train (ex. Salisbury)	8.32 p.m.				8.32 p.m.				8.29 p.m.			
Locomotive no.	35026(R)				34015				34002			
Vehicles	8				9				10			
Tare load (tons)	256				283				325			
Gross load (tons)	276				305				354			
Driver (EXJ)	Whitfield				Clements				Clements			
Recorder	DWW				DWW				J. R. Skinner			

Mls.	Sch.	M.	S.	Speed	Sch.	M.	S.	Speed	Sch.	M.	S.	Speed
0·0 SALISBURY	0	0	00			0	00		0	0	00	
2·5 Wilton (*40)		5	06			5	20	48		5	37	49
8·3 Dinton		10	40	73		11	37	70		11	18	75/72
12·6 Tisbury		14	08	76		15	20	72		14	53	78
17·6 Semley		18	09	68		19	59	56		19	01	69
21·7 Gillingham		21	24	82/86		23	27	76/58		22	06	86/57
28·5 Templecombe		26	34	72		29	30	78/62	31	28	03	74/59
30·9 Milborne Port		28	36	72		32	07	66		30	26	64
34·6 Sherborne		31	25	84		35	10	81		33	16	83
			sig. stop									
39·2 YEOVIL JUNCTION	42	39	52			39	43		43	37	37	
2·2 Sutton Bingham		—				5	00	42/76		4	52	
8·8 Crewkerne		—				11	31	58		11	32	69/47
16·9 Chard Junction		—				19	30	66		18	45	83/90
							sigs					
22·0 AXMINSTER	25	38	01			26	28		27	22	57	
3·3 Seaton Junction		4	34	62		5	03	54		5	23	52
7·0 *Milepost 151½*		—				10	25	33		—		
8·0 *Milepost 152½*		9	42	50		12	10	37		13	23†	39
10·2 Honiton		12	04	74/82		15	09	61/80		14	53	61
14·8 Sidmouth Junction (*70)		15	36	73		18	59	71		18	22	85/69
18·6 Whimple		18	39	76		21	55	84		21	31	79
22·2 Broad Clyst		21	21	84		24	31			24	05	88
24·0 Pinhoe		22	47	74		25	54	75		25	27	74
25·8 *Exmouth Junction*	31	24	34			27	33		31	27	46	40
			sigs								sigs	
26·9 EXETER CENTRAL	34	27	42			29	56		34	31	45	

Estimated net times (mins)			
Salisbury–Yeovil Junction	35¾	39¼	37½
Yeovil Junction–Axminster	Delayed	24	23
Axminster–Exeter Central	27½	30	29½

† At *Milepost 153½*

TABLE 17

SALISBURY TO EXETER CENTRAL

Detail		A			B	
Date		4 Mar 1964			1 Oct 1961	
Train (ex. Salisbury)		8.32 p.m.			5.47 p.m.	
Locomotive no.		35003(R)			34048(R)	
Vehicles		8			10	
Tare load (tons)		272			330	
Gross load (tons)		295			350	
Recorder		D. J. Maidment			Lt. Commander Harwood	
Mls.	Sch.	M. S.	Speed		M. S.	Speed
0·0 SALISBURY	0	0 00			0 00	
2·5 Wilton (*40)	6	5 21	48		6 05	—/65
8·3 Dinton		10 58	73/71		12 36	18
					p.w.s.	
12·6 Tisbury		14 38	75		19 13	61
17·6 Semley		19 10	67		24 18	56
21·7 Gillingham		22 25	80/86		27 35	83
23·9 Milepost 107½		—	69/90		29 26	68
28·5 TEMPLECOMBE		27 45	78		33 00	82
30·0 Milepost 113½		—			34 33	55
30·9 Milborne Port		30 00	68		35 25	78
34·6 SHERBORNE		32 48	85		39 02	
39·2 YEOVIL JUNCTION	42	37 32			7 03	
2·2 Sutton Bingham		4 31	40		5 00	
3·9 Milepost 126½		—	50/75		7 02	41
8·8 CREWKERNE	12	11 33			11 40	77/52
8·1 Chard Junction		10 26	83		18 47	78
13·2 AXMINSTER	16	15 28			23 40	
3·3 SEATON JUNCTION		4 38	64		6 24	
7·0 Milepost 151½		—	50/46		11 10	41
10·2 HONITON	19	13 49			13 20	
4·6 SIDMOUTH JUNC. (*70)		5 25	82/68		6 15	
8·4 Whimple		8 39	80		5 27	
12·0 Broad Clyst		11 37	77		8 15	83
13·9 Pinhoe		13 08	84		9 48	
15·7 Exmouth Junction	15	15 02			11 33	
16·7 EXETER CENTRAL	18	17 24			13 46	

TABLE 18

SALISBURY TO AXMINSTER

Detail	A	B
Date	25 Sept 1965	3 Aug 1964
Train (ex. Salisbury)	11.51 a.m.	12.32 p.m.
Locomotive no.	34024(R)	35014(R)
Vehicles	9	12
Tare load (tons)	298	405
Gross load (tons)	320	430
Driver	Tox (SAL)	—
Recorder	DWW	P. M. Widgery

Mls.	Sch.	M. S.	Speed	Sch.	M. S.	Speed
0·0 SALISBURY	0	0 00		0	0 00	
1·7 *Milepost 85¼*		4 30			4 20†	27
2·5 Wilton (*40)	5½	5 49	44/66	6	6 17	45
8·3 Dinton		11 49	62		12 13	68/65
12·6 Tisbury		15 50	66		16 05	67
					p.w.s.	
17·6 Semley		20 39	54		20 50	37
21·7 Gillingham		24 08	77		25 18	69
23·9 *Milepost 107½*		26 06	63		27 24	56
26·2 *Milepost 109¾*		28 00	78		—	79
28·5 TEMPLECOMBE	27½	29 49	67		31 15	64
30·0 *Milepost 113½*		31 30	50		32 45	55
30·9 Milborne Port		32 32	56		33 38	63
34·6 Sherborne		35 39	84		36 41	81/67
39·2 YEOVIL JUNCTION	36	39 37	72	40	40 26	72
41·4 Sutton Bingham		41 40	62		42 23	63
42·8 *Milepost 126¼*		43 04	56/78		43 45	58/75
48·0 Crewkerne		47 25	65		48 10	64
49·8 *Milepost 133¼*		49 23	50		50 10	48
56·0 Chard Junction		54 20	80		55 37	74
61·1 AXMINSTER	54	59 14		62	60 41	
Estimated net time (mins)		59¼			59¾	

† At *Milepost 85*

TABLE 19
YEOVIL JUNCTION TO EXETER CENTRAL

Detail	A	B	C
Date	22 Jan 1948	23 May 1958	26 Mar 1959
Train (ex. Yeovil Junction)	3.45 p.m.	3.45 p.m.	3.45 p.m.
Locomotive no.	21C1	34053	35007(R)
Vehicles	10	13	13
Tare load (tons)	320 (estd.)	436	438
Gross load (tons)	345 (estd.)	460	465
Recorder	J. M. B. Edwards	J. L. Lean	J. L. Lean

Mls.		Sch.	M.	S.	Speed	Sch.	M.	S.	Speed	Sch.	M.	S.	Speed
0·0	YEOVIL JUNCTION	0	0	00		0	0	00		0	0	00	
2·2	Sutton Bingham		4	57	38/43		5	20	33		5	28	32
8·8	Crewkerne		11	55	67		12	54	66		12	56	66
10·7	*Milepost 133¼*		14	18	46		15	18	40		15	16	41
16·9	Chard Junction		20	17	62		21	08	67		20	55	72
22·0	Axminster		24	57	68/73		25	45	62/73		25	05	72/76
25·2	Seaton Junction		27	54	59		28	37	60		27	43	
30·0	*Milepost 152½*		33	52	43		37	27	22/21		34	30	31
32·2	Honiton		36	27	64/78		41	36	50/76		37	51	58/78
36·8	Sidmouth Junction (*70)		40	20	68		45	40	69		41	37	71
40·5	Whimple		43	37	73		49	12	53		44	55	62
44·2	Broad Clyst		46	31	78		52	08	77		47	47	77
46·1	Pinhoe		48	03	66		—				—		
47·8	*Exmouth Junction*	57	49	52	58	52	55	31	53		51	03	55
48·9	EXETER CENTRAL	60	52	03		55	57	47			53	19	

TABLE 20

EXETER CENTRAL TO SALISBURY

Detail		A			B		C		D		E	
Date		4 Sept 1956			9 Apr 1964		10 Apr 1964		30 Sept 1961		11 Apr 1964	
Train (ex. Exeter Central)		12.30 p.m.			12.30 p.m.		12.30 p.m.		12.30 p.m.		12.30 p.m.	
Locomotive no.		35023			34002		35013(R)		35029(R)		35025(R)	
Vehicles		11			11		11		11		11	
Tare load (tons)		357			368		378		367		368	
Gross load (tons)		380			385		390		390		390	
Driver		—			Davey (EXJ)		F. Turner (EXJ)		—		Gidley (EXJ)	
Recorder		A. G. S. Davies			DWW		DWW		R. N. Clements		DWW	
Mls.	Sch.	M. S.	Speed	Sch.	M. S.	Speed	M. S.	Speed	M. S.	Speed	M. S.	Speed
0·0 EXETER CENTRAL	0	0 00		0	0 00		0 00		0 00		0 00	
1·1 *Exmouth Junction*		4 08			3 40		3 47		4 19		4 08	
2·8 Pinhoe		6 41			6 14	50	6 13	52	7 03	67	6 49	50
4·7 Broad Clyst		8 23	70		7 53	75	7 51	74	8 39	75	8 28	74
8·4 Whimple		11 54	55		11 36	52	11 17	56	11 43	64	11 56	48
9·2 *Milepost 161¼*		—	45		13 58	40	13 15	49	13 26	59	14 07	44
12·1 SIDMOUTH JUNCTION	18	16 53		17	16 52		15 49		15 38		16 55	
1·3 *Milepost 158*		—	50		3 02	48	2 46	48	—	54	3 07	45
4·6 Honiton		7 35	43		7 36	40	6 55	44	6 49	47	7 40	41
5·8 *Milepost 153½*		9 35†	40		9 23	40	8 33	42	8 24†	44	9 27	39
6·8 *Milepost 152½*		—			10 47	50/82	9 48	52/80	—	—/82	10 49	50/77
11·5 Seaton Junction (*60)		15 00	70		14 50	72	13 53	67	13 23	72	14 51	76
13·1 *Milepost 146¼*		—	73		16 07	80	15 13	80	—	87	16 08	90
14·8 AXMINSTER		17 48	64		17 26	76	16 28	78	15 59	78	17 16	80
19·9 Chard Junction		22 53			21 37	74	20 43	70	20 12	72	21 22	74
		p.w.s.	15									
26·1 *Milepost 133¼*		—			27 06	64	26 32	62	25 43	63	26 51	68
28·0 Crewkerne		34 30	74		28 47	73	28 09	80	27 14	80	28 25	76
29·1 *Milepost 130¼*		—	87		29 41		29 01	86	—	84	29 15	91
33·1 *Milepost 126¼*		—			33 02	60	32 02	66	31 19	65	32 10	76
34·5 Sutton Bingham		39 26	79		34 20		33 11	75	32 33	74	33 15	
36·8 YEOVIL JUNCTION	39	41 10	75	37	36 10	78	34 48	85	34 22	72	34 51	82
41·3 Sherborne		44 50	66/52		40 18	68/46	38 22	77/58	38 11	75/56	38 25	78
45·0 Milborne Port		48 33	59		44 22	51	41 53	60	41 34	64	41 40	62
46·0 *Milepost 113½*		—			45 22	40	42 49	58	—		42 29	64
47·4 TEMPLECOMBE		50 44	70/90		46 47	68/85	44 10	75/84	43 38	82/94	43 44	78/87
52·0 *Milepost 107½*		—			50 37	56	47 36	68	46 53	72	47 05	
54·2 Gillingham		55 59	70		52 45	70	49 25	80	48 37	84	48 51	83
58·3 Semley		60 54	39		57 12	48	53 07	58	52 08	60/77	52 12	70
63·3 Tisbury (*75)		65 33	77/80		61 47	78/80	57 20	80	55 59	74/72	56 02	86
67·6 Dinton		68 50	86		65 04	82/84	60 38	84	59 44	76/80	59 12	80/84
73·4 Wilton South (*40)		73 10		70	69 45		65 12		64 29		63 50	
									sigs		sigs	
75·9 SALISBURY	79	76 22		74	74 13		69 35		70 48		68 18	
Estimated net time (min)												
Exeter Central–Sidmouth J.		16¾			16¾		15¾		15¾		17	
Sidmouth J.–Salisbury		72			74¼		69½		68¾		68	

† At Honiton Tunnel West portal

TABLE 21

EXETER CENTRAL TO SALISBURY

Detail	A	B
Date	17 July 1963	3 Oct 1965
Train (ex. Exeter Central)	12.30 p.m.	5. 20 p.m.
Locomotive no.	34062(R)	35022(R)
Vehicles	12	8
Tare load (tons)	399	268
Gross load (tons)	425	285
Driver	Welling (EXJ)	G. Hooper(9E)
Recorder	P. M. Widgery	S. C. Nash

Mls.		Sch.	M. S.	Speed	Sch.	M. S.	Speed
0·0	EXETER CENTRAL	0	0 00		0	0 00	
1·1	*Exmouth Junction*		4 06	20	3	3 37	
2·8	Pinhoe		6 55	57		5 55	70
4·7	Broad Clyst		8 39	72		7 30	74
8·4	Whimple		12 06	54		10 46	62
9·2	*Milepost 161¼*		14 28‡	47/60		12 34	56
						sigs	
12·1	SIDMOUTH JUNCTION	17	16 48		21	15 26	27
13·4	*Milepost 158*		3 06	48		—	
16·7	Honiton		7 44	40/42		20 40	60
17·9	*Milepost 153½*		9 30	39		22 06†	55
18·9	*Milepost 152½*		10 53	52/80		22 52†	63
23·7	Seaton Junction (*60)		15 01	77		26 46	87/72
26·9	AXMINSTER		17 43	74/65	38	29 09	80
32·0	Chard Junction		22 08	67/63		33 04	75
38·2	*Milepost 133¼*		27 58	58		38 00	73
40·1	Crewkerne		29 34	77		39 18	88
41·2	*Milepost 130¼*		30 25	85		—	
45·2	*Milepost 126¼*		33 32	71		43 06	75
46·7	Sutton Bingham		34 40	80		44 09	86
48·9	YEOVIL JUNCTION	37	36 20	82	59	45 44	82
53·5	Sherborne		39 50	78		49 12	81
57·2	Milborne Port		43 16	62		52 18	67
58·1	*Milepost 113½*		44 05	62		—	
59·6	TEMPLECOMBE		45 24	75/86	70	54 15	88
64·1	*Milepost 107½*		48 54	64		—	—/76
66·4	Gillingham		50 47	80		59 18	88
70·5	Semley		54 28	56		62 29	69
75·5	Tisbury (*75)		58 47	75		66 19	82
79·8	Dinton		62 13	75/78		69 44	78
85·5	Wilton South (*40)		67 18	39/54	95	74 26	43/50
88·1	SALISBURY	74	71 33		100	78 56	pass
Estimated net time (mins)			16¾ + 71½			77½ (to stop)	

† At Honiton Tunnel West or East Portals   ‡ At *Milepost 161*

TABLE 22
EXETER CENTRAL TO SALISBURY

Detail	A	B	C	D	E
Date	5 Aug 1962	7 June 1959	14 Aug 1958	1 Aug 1959	1 Aug 1958
Train (ex. Exeter Central)	1.0 p.m.	12.2 p.m.	4.30 p.m.	4.30 p.m.	4.30 p.m.
Locomotive no.	34067	35009(R)	35017(R)	35030(R)	34006
Vehicles	10	14	12	12	12
Tare load (tons)	345	465	398 (est.)	398	397
Gross load (tons)	370	495	430 (est.)	430	420
Driver	—	—	—	Heard (EXJ)	—
Recorder	S. C. Nash	S. C. Nash	Rev. R. S. Haines	S. C. Nash	Rev. J. E. T. Phillips

Mls.		A Sch	M. S.	Speed	B Sch	M. S.	Speed	C Sch	M. S.	D Sch	M. S.	Speed	E Sch	M. S.	Speed
0·0	EXETER CENTRAL				0	0 00		0	0 00	0	0 00		0	0 00	
1·1	*Exmouth Jnc.*					4 00			3 31		4 06	36		3 45	
2·8	Pinhoe					—			5 54		6 26	70		6 13	59
4·7	Broad Clyst					7 59	72		7 36		8 07	71		7 43	80
8·4	Whimple					11 02	54		11 05		11 37	58		10 55	61
9·2	*Milepost 161½*					—			13 19		—			12 51	49
12·1	Sidmouth Jnc.					15 45 p.w.s.	45/60		15 52		15 37	53/72		14 58	57/69
16·7	Honiton					22 17	27/40		21 12		19 59	58		19 42	50
17·9	*Milepost 153½*					24 22†	38		23 05		21 33†	50		21 14	45
18·9	*Milepost 152½*					—			—		—			22 32	58
23·7	Seaton Jnc. (*60)					29 24	83		28 39		26 09	86/76		26 15	90
26·9	AXMINSTER	0	0 00		34	32 43			30 59		28 40	74		28 32	82
5·1	Chard Junction		8 20	60/64		8 08	56		35 18		33 05	69		32 46	67
11·3	*Milepost 133½*		14 37	55		14 31	56		41 22		38 40	64		38 33	60
13·2	Crewkerne		16 23	78		16 12	80		43 03		40 13	92		40 12	81
18·3	*Milepost 126¼*		21 05	55		—	70		46 52		44 00	66		44 02	74
19·7	Sutton Bingham		22 31	65		21 40	75		48 01		45 12	80		45 10	76
22·0	YEOVIL JNC.	27	25 38		27	24 32		54	51 10	54	47 40		54	47 50	
4·6	Sherborne		7 35	61					p.w.s. 7 10						
8·3	Milborne Port		11 39	54					12 10						
10·7	TEMPLECOMBE		13 57	86/64				15	sigs 16 11						
17·5	Gillingham		19 27	77					p.w.s. 7 54						
21·6	Semley		23 27	52					11 38						
26·6	Tisbury (*75)		27 54	78					15 47						
30·9	Dinton		31 19	78/80					18 56						
36·7	Wilton South (*40)	39	36 10	46/50					23 18						
39·2	SALISBURY	43	39 54					32	27 45						

† At Honiton Tunnel West Portal

TABLE 23

AXMINSTER TO SALISBURY

Detail	A			B			C			D		
Date	9 Aug 1962			21 Aug 1965			21 Aug 1965			7 Aug 1965		
Train (ex. Axminster)	6.38 p.m.			3.32 p.m.			12.27 p.m.			12.27 p.m.		
Locomotive no.	35009(R)			34077(R)			34026(R)			34015		
Vehicles	7			9			10			10		
Tare load (tons)	235½			300			322½			325½		
Gross load (tons)	255			320			345			350		
Driver	—			Hoare (SAL)			Jury (EXJ)			Vince (EXJ)		
Recorder	D. A. Foale			DWW			DWW			DWW		

Mls.	Sch.	M. S.	Speed	Sch.	M. S.	Speed	Sch.	M. S.	Speed		M. S.	Speed
0·0 AXMINSTER	0	0 00		0	0 00		0	0 00			0 00	
5·1 Chard Junction		6 47	70/67		7 58	54/64		7 42	59/66		7 31	60/66
11·3 *Milepost 133¼*		12 06	68		14 09	57		13 36	58		13 32	58
13·2 Crewkerne		13 36	79/82		15 47	72/87		15 16	73/80		15 11	76/84
18·3 *Milepost 126¼*		17 38	71		19 41	72		19 33	62		19 33	64
19·7 Sutton Bingham		18 45	81/83		20 56	70		20 46			20 47	
								sigs				
22·0 YEOVIL JUNCTION	27	21 32		25	22 42	70/75	29	22 48	55		22 36	73/66
								sigs				
4·6 Sherborne		6 56	61		26 31	72/56		29 18	32		26 30	75/50
		p.w.s.	18									
8·3 Milborne Port		13 03	49		29 54	61		35 07			30 13	56
9·2 *Milepost 113¼*		14 05	53		30 45	62		36 10	48		31 09	58
					sigs							
10·7 TEMPLECOMBE	16	16 13		34½	33 27		39½	37 37	61/68		32 29	72/86
4·5 *Milepost 107½*		5 25	59		5 44	50		41 55	48		36 02	60
6·8 Gillingham		7 21	82		7 52	67		44 10	66		38 00	74
					sigs							
10·9 Semley		10 49	62		12 31	25		48 40	46		42 05	52
15·9 Tisbury (*75)		14 47	82/80		18 15	72/76		53 23	61		46 32	74
					sigs							
20·2 Dinton		17 57	82/85		22 50			57 23	70		50 13	68/70
26·0 Wilton South (*40)		22 37	38/50	28	29 10		64½	62 45			55 51	
28·5 SALISBURY	33	26 50		32½	33 13		69	67 45			60 21	

Estimated net times (min)			
Axminster–Yeovil Junction	21½	—	—	—
Axminster–Templecombe	—	33	—	—
Axminster–Salisbury	—	—	64	60½
Yeovil Junc.–Templecombe	13½	—	—	—
Templecombe–Salisbury	26¾	29½	—	—

TABLE 24

TEMPLECOMBE TO SALISBURY

Detail	A	B	C
Date	27 June 1959	11 June 1960	29 July 1962
Train (ex. Templecombe)	5.43 p.m.	5.43 p.m.	5.41 p.m.
Locomotive no.	35016(R)	34013(R)	35028(R)
Vehicles	13	13	13
Tare load (tons)	420	434	427½
Gross load (tons)	430	470	460
Driver	—	—	Hoare (SALS)
Recorder	J. L. Lean	J. L. Lean	DWW

Mls.	Sch.	M. S. Speed	Sch.	M. S. Speed	Sch.	M. S. Speed
0·0 TEMPLECOMBE	0	0 00	0	0 00	0	0 00
2·3 *Milepost 109¾*		—		—		3 41 56
4·5 *Milepost 107½*		5 58 60		6 09 64		— 41
		p.w.s. 41		p.w.s.		
6·8 Gillingham		8 26 —/68		8 37 50/72		9 11 66
10·9 Semley		12 50 48		12 41 48		13 28 48
15·9 Tisbury (*75)		17 07 75		16 58 80		17 47 78
20·2 Dinton		20 26 79/86		20 11 80/82		21 11 76
26·0 Wilton South (*40)		24 51 49/53		24 40 42		25 43
28·5 SALISBURY	32	28 45	32	28 50	33	29 07

Estimated net time (mins)	28¼	28¼	29

TABLE 25

SALISBURY TO WATERLOO

Detail	A	B	C	D
Date	31 July 1963	9 April 1964	18 Dec 1956	19 July 1962
Train (ex. Salisbury)	2.9 p.m.	2.13 p.m.	2.15 p.m.	1.59 p.m.
Locomotive no.	34062(R)	34002	35023	35020(R)
Vehicles	9	11	12	12
Tare load (tons)	301	368	395	399
Gross load (tons)	320	395	425	430
Driver	Hoare(SALS)	Hoare(SALS)	Letchford(9E)	—
Recorder	DWW	DWW	D. A. Lock	Rev. J. E. T. Phillips

Mls.	Sch.	M. S.	Speed	Sch.	M. S.	Speed	Sch.	M. S.	Speed	Sch.	M. S.	Speed
0·0 SALISBURY	0	0 00		0	0 00		0	0 00		0	0 00	
1·1 *Tunnel Junction* (*50)		3 44	33		3 41	33		—			3 11	
5·5 Porton		9 53	45		9 43	42		8 10	54/52		8 13	55
8·1 *Allington S.B.*		13 10	52		12 56	52		—			11 03	60
11·0 Grateley		16 09	63		15 56	62		13 42	65		13 42	70/94
15·9 *Red Post Junction*		20 02	80		19 47	84		—				
17·3 ANDOVER JUNCTION		21 05	80		20 49	81/86		18 23	90		18 00	94
21·1 *Milepost 62¼*		24 15	66		23 42 p.w.s.	73		—			—	81
22·6 Hurstbourne		25 34	72		25 21	15		22 24	71		21 35	88
24·5 Whitchurch North		27 10	70		29 02	45		—			22 57	81
28·1 Overton		30 10	74		33 04	62		—			25 36	82
31·3 Oakley		32 51	71		36 04	67		29 46	69		27 56	81
33·4 *Worting Junction*	34	34 37	72	34	37 50	74	36	31 28	80	34	29 24	86
35·9 BASINGSTOKE		36 39	76		39 46	80/86		33 18	85		31 02	93/100
41·5 Hook		41 08	70		43 51	80		37 08	88		34 23	97
43·9 Winchfield		43 07	76		45 37	82		—			35 55	92
47·2 Fleet		45 33	82		48 00	82		41 08	85		38 07 p.w.s.	82 30
50·5 Farnborough		48 02	80		50 26	80		43 25	89/87		40 58	30
52·7 *Milepost 31*		49 44	78/84		52 06 sig.stop	79		—			44 32	45
55·7 Brookwood		51 58	83/74		60 09			47 03	90		47 25	75
59·4 WOKING	54	54 52	81	54	63 32	78	58	49 25	96	54	50 03	90
62·0 West Byfleet		56 47 sigs	84		65 36	80		—			51 50	92
64·6 Weybridge		59 22	48		67 36	78		52 49	89		53 28	90
66·6 Walton-on-Thames		61 39	65		69 12	78		—			54 53	90
70·4 *Hampton Court Junc.*		64 54	73		72 08	76		56 50	84	65	57 27	86
71·7 Surbiton		65 57	76		73 11	75		—	eased		58 20	82
73·9 New Malden		67 49	72		75 02			—			60 02 sigs	82
76·5 Wimbledon		70 04 sigs	64		77 12			61 42			62 10	50
79·8 Clapham Junction (*40)	73	73 52		73	80 39		78	66 36		75	66 23	
82·4 Vauxhall (*40)		sigs			sigs			71 08			69 45 sigs	10
83·7 WATERLOO	80	80 37		80	88 07		85	74 18		82	73 43	
Estimated net time (mins)		78½			76¼			71¾			68½	

Note: All schedule passing times at Woking are for *Woking Junction*

TABLE 26
SALISBURY TO WATERLOO

Detail	A			B		
Date	13 June 1956			10 May 1963		
Train (ex. Salisbury)	2.15 p.m.			2.9 p.m.		
Locomotive no.	35002			35009(R)		
Vehicles	13			13		
Tare load (tons)	430			430		
Gross load (tons)	460			460		
Driver	Letchford (9E)			Hoare (SALS)		
Recorder	D. A. Lock			S. C. Nash		
Mls.	Sch.	M. S.	Speed	Sch.	M. S.	Speed
0·0 SALISBURY	0	0 00		0	0 00	
1·1 Tunnel Junction (*50)		—			3 09	40
5·5 Porton		8 48	49/51		8 37	50
8·1 *Allington S.B.*		—			11 40	56
11·0 Grateley		14 50	69		14 32	60
15·9 *Red Post Junction*		—	84		18 20	85
17·3 ANDOVER JUNCTION		19 39	73/79		19 23	81
		p.w.s.				
22·6 Hurstbourne		25 23			23 21	79/80
24·5 Whitchurch North		—			24 52	76
38·1 Overton		—	70		27 42	77
31·3 Oakley		—			30 10	78
33·4 *Worting Junction*	36	36 18	78	34	31 47	80
35·9 BASINGSTOKE		38 12	86/91		33 40	83
41·5 Hook		42 07	84		37 40	86
43·9 Winchfield		—			39 25	82
47·2 Fleet		46 10	87		41 46	85
50·5 Farnborough		48 32	82		44 08	83
52·7 *Milepost 31*		—			45 48	81/84
					p.w.s.	
55·7 Brookwood		52 22	87		48 36	32
59·4 WOKING	58†	54 59	86	54†	52 35	70
62·0 West Byfleet		—			54 36	84
64·6 Weybridge		59 03	81		56 29	80
66·6 Walton-on-Thames		—			58 00	80
70·4 *Hampton Court Junction*		63 36	79		60 51	79
71·7 Surbiton		—			61 50	79
73·9 New Malden		—			63 37	77
76·5 Wimbledon		68 28	75		65 42	69
79·8 Clapham Junction (*40)	78	71 39		73	68 52	40/50
82·4 Vauxhall (*40)		74 59			72 15	
83·7 WATERLOO	85	78 44		80	75 32	
Estimated net time (mins)		75			73½	

† At *Woking Junction*

TABLE 27

SALISBURY TO WATERLOO

Detail	A			B			C		
Date	10 June 1967			17 May 1958			25 Jan 1964		
Train (ex. Salisbury)	12.35 p.m.			6.22 p.m.			9.59 a.m.		
Locomotive no.	34108(R)			34056			35025(R)		
Vehicles	10			12			10		
Tare load (tons)	334½			396			340		
Gross load (tons)	365			415			360		
Driver	Fordrey(9E)			Hopkins (9E)			—		
Recorder	DWW			J. L. Lean			J. G. McEwan		
Mls.	Sch.	M. S.	Speed	Sch.	M. S.	Speed	Sch.	M. S.	Speed
0·0 SALISBURY	0	0 00		0	0 00				
1·1 *Tunnel Junction* (*50)		3 46	45/56		3 20	33			
5·5 Porton		8 36	59		9 00	47			
8·1 *Allington S.B.*		11 15	62/69		12 48	41			
11·0 Grateley		13 51	73/87		15 57	59/77			
15·9 *Red Post Junction*		17 31	80		—	69			
17·3 ANDOVER JUNCTION	22	19 10		24	22 16		0	0 00	
3·8 *Milepost 62½*		6 02	52		5 48	53		—	
5·3 Hurstbourne		7 28	68		—			8 20	60
7·2 Whitchurch North		9 07	72		9 01	67/64		10 09	63
10·8 Overton		12 06	75		12 14	69		13 23	70
14·0 Oakley		14 40	76		14 49	74		16 04	73
16·1 *Worting Junction*	17½	16 25	69	20	16 32	75	19	17 43	75
18·6 BASINGSTOKE	20½	19 16		24	19 07			19 40	80/82
5·6 Hook		6 30	81		6 52	65		23 56	76
8·0 Winchfield		8 16	82		8 47	75		25 46	78
11·3 Fleet		10 34	88		11 17	83		28 12	83
14·6 Farnborough		12 54	80/47 p.w.s.		13 36	85		30 40	
16·8 *Milepost 31*		15 13	53		—	80		—	77
19·8 Brookwood		17 53	82 sigs		17 26	84		34 40	85
23·5 WOKING	26½	21 42		24†	20 17	76	42†	37 26	77
2·7 West Byfleet		4 17	65/71		—	72		39 26	81
5·2 Weybridge		6 27	72		23 32	76		41 22	80
7·3 Walton-on-Thames		8 05	76/77		26 13	73		43 02	76
11·0 *Hampton Court Junction*	14	11 02	75	34	29 12	76 sigs		45 56	77
12·3 Surbiton		12 06	72		31 04	16		47 00	76
14·6 New Malden		14 00	68		33 44	48		48 53	74
17·1 Wimbledon		16 26	63		37 56	56 sigs		51 07	69
20·4 Clapham Junction (*40)	26	20 05		44	42 40	37/51	61	54 33	40
24·3 WATERLOO	33	26 04		51	49 10		68	61 20	

† At *Woking Junction*

TABLE 28
SALISBURY TO ANDOVER

Detail	A		B	
Date	5 July 1967		20 Dec 1966	
Train (ex. Salisbury)	6.38 p.m.		6.38 p.m.	
Locomotive no.	35008(R)		34001(R)	
Vehicles	6		9	
Tare load (tons)	196½		253½	
Gross load (tons)	205		260	
Driver	De'Ath (BAS)		De'Ath (BAS)	
Recorder	R. M. Grainger		D. A. Foale	
Mls.	M. S.	Speed	M. S.	Speed
0·0 SALISBURY	0 00		0 00	
1·1 *Tunnel Junction* (*50)	3 16	48/60	4 02	40
	p.w.s.			
5·5 Porton	10 33	52	8 48	61/60
8·1 *Allington S.B.*	13 17	67	11 20	65
11·0 Grateley	15 35	80	13 48	77
14·6 *Milepost 69*	17 54	102	—	92
15·9 *Red Post Junction*	18 50	82	17 24	52
			sigs	
17·3 ANDOVER	20 53		19 47	
Estimated net time (mins)	18¼		19½	

TABLE 29
ANDOVER JUNCTION TO BASINGSTOKE

Detail	A		B		C			D		
Date	5 July 1967		20 Dec 1966		31 July 1965			19 Apr 1947		
Train (ex. Salisbury)	6.38 p.m.		6.38 p.m.		1.46 p.m.			8.15 p.m.		
Locomotive no.	35008(R)		34001(R)		34063			21C152		
Vehicles	6		9		10			11		
Tare load (tons)	196½		253½		333			350 (est.)		
Gross load (tons)	205		260		365			370 (est.)		
Driver	De'Ath(BAS)		De'Ath(BAS)		Twyman(9E)			—		
Recorder	R.M. Grainger		D. A. Foale		A. Wild			J. M. B. Edwards		
Mls.	M. S.	Speed	M. S.	Speed	Sch.	M. S.	Speed	Sch.	M. S.	Speed
0·0 ANDOVER JUNCTION	0 00		0 00		0	0 00		0	0 00	
						p.w.s. 16				
3·8 *Milepost 62½*	—		5 37	60		7 51	44		6 00	43
5·3 Hurstbourne	6 18	74/71	6 52	74		9 32	60		8 39	56
7·2 Whitchurch North	7 53	74	8 24	72		11 24	59		10 28	66/70
10·8 Overton	10 40	83	11 16	79/77		14 41	67		13 39	66
14·0 Oakley	13 00	79	13 42	80		17 28	72		16 41	62
16·1 *Worting Junction*	14 46	65	15 28	71	18½	19 16	71	21	18 45	63
			sigs			sigs			sigs	
18·6 BASINGSTOKE	18 05		19 46		22	22 58		26	22 30	
Estimated net time (mins)	18		18½			20½			22	

TABLE 30

ANDOVER JUNCTION TO WOKING

Detail		A		B		C		D
Date		7 May 1962		12 Mar 1960		3 Aug 1964		Aug 1952
Train (ex. Andover Junction)		5.17 p.m.		5.17 p.m.		5.16 p.m.		5.16 p.m.
Locomotive no.		34059(R)		35007(R)		34032(R)		35003
Vehicles		10		10		12		12
Tare load (tons)		325(est)		324		400		410
Gross load (tons)		340(est)		330		440		445
Recorder		DWW		J. L. Lean		R. L. Sewell		J. L. Lean
Mls.	Sch.	M. S.	Speed	M. S.	Speed	M. S.	Speed	M. S.
0·0 ANDOVER JUNCTION	0	0 00		0 00		0 00		0 00
3·8 *Milepost 62½*		6 31	44	—	50	6 47	42	—
5·3 Hurstbourne		8 12	58	7 22	64	8 33	56	8 55
7·2 Whitchurch North		10 07	60	9 07	64	10 38	54	11 07
10·8 Overton		13 23	68	12 18	70	14 15	62	14 57
14·0 Oakley		16 07	72	15 00	69/71	17 15	68	18 02
16·1 *Worting Junction*	19	17 52	71	17 02	60	19 10	64	20 02
18·6 BASINGSTOKE		19 53	76/81	19 20	61	21 35	62	22 08
24·2 Hook		24 17	70	23 43	76	26 43	67	26 45
26·5 Winchfield		26 25	70	25 34	76	28 45	73	28 40
		p.w.s.						
29·9 Fleet		31 11	58	28 02	82	31 25	76	31 45
33·1 Farnborough		34 23	70	30 30	79	34 15	63	—
35·4 *Milepost 31*		36 18	68	—		36 17	66	—
				sigs	56			
38·4 Brookwood		38 43	76/79	35 44	54	38 52	72	38 15
		sigs		sigs				
42·0 WOKING	44	43 07		40 46		42 40		42 10
Estimated net time (mins)		40		38¾		42¾		42¼

TABLE 31

EXETER ST DAVID'S TO DEVONPORT KING'S ROAD

Date	18 September 1954
Train	4.10 p.m. ex. Exeter Central
Locomotive no.	34057
Vehicles	10
Tare load (tons)	335
Gross load (tons)	350
Recorder	J. L. Lean

Mls.		Sch.	M. S.	Speed
0·0	EXETER ST DAVID'S	0	0 00	
1·2	*Cowley Bridge Junction* (*25)	3	3 40	28
4·3	Newton St Cyres		7 45	50
6·9	Crediton (*45)		10 44	54/45
10·6	Yeoford		15 17	50
11·5	*Coleford Junction* (*40)	17	16 31	44/35
15·3	Bow		22 04	50/55
18·5	North Tawton		25 45	45/65
21·3	Sampford Courtenay		28 55	44/50
25·0	OKEHAMPTON	38	34 25	
2·1	*Meldon Quarry* (*20)		5 51	26
3·4	*Milepost 200¾*		8 53	28
6·7	Bridestowe		12 34	63/64
9·9	Lydford		15 49	57
11·2	Brentor		—	44/67
16·3	TAVISTOCK NORTH	25	23 31	
4·1	*Milepost 217¾*		6 34	43/58
6·5	BERE ALSTON	10½	9 35	
2·8	Bere Ferrers		5 14	46
4·7	Tamerton Foliot		7 22	61/62
7·0	St Budeaux		9 41	61
8·5	Ford		11 30	44
9·5	DEVONPORT KING'S ROAD	16½	13 24	

TABLE 32

OKEHAMPTON TO EXETER ST DAVID'S

Detail	A		B	C	D
Date	7 June 1954		25 Apr 1952	22 Mar 1950	1 Aug 1960
Train (ex. Devonport)	11.16 a.m.		4.6 p.m.	4.6 p.m.	4.6 p.m.
Locomotive no.	34059		34031	34011	34109
Vehicles	10		5	6	7
Tare load (tons)	333		165	177	236
Gross load (tons)	350		175	190	250
Recorder	J. L. Lean		J. L. Lean	A. J. Baker	J. L. Lean

Mls.	Sch.	M. S. Speed	Sch.	M. S. Speed	M. S. Speed	M. S. Speed
0·0 OKEHAMPTON	0	0 00	0	0 00	0 00	0 00
3·7 Sampford Courtenay		5 12 64		5 15 62	4 49 64/60	5 04 65
6·5 North Tawton		7 32 78/67		7 31 82/74	7 17 75/61	7 37 70
9·6 Bow		10 03 75		10 08 76	10 08 68/65	10 41 61/64
13·4 *Colejord Junction* (*40)	16	13 40 41	16	13 44 35	14 09 58/66	14 46 41
					sigs 38	
14·4 YEOFORD		14 53 –/69	18	15 39	16 19	16 17
				B/1		
18·1 Crediton (*45)		18 21 51		4 48 43	5 26 44	
20·7 Newton St Cyres		20 55 66/71		7 27 72	8 11 70	
				sigs 10		
23·7 *Cowley Bridge Junction* (*25)	28	24 00	12	11 41	11 17 40	
		sigs				
25·0 EXETER ST DAVID'S	32	26 44	15	14 23	13 52	
Estimated net time (mins.)		26½		B/1–13½	16+13¾	

Detail B/1—No. 34043 with 5 coaches (165/180 tons) recorded by A. J. Baker

TABLE 33

PADSTOW TO HALWILL

Date	5 August 1961
Train	11.0 a.m. ex. Padstow
Locomotive no.	34035
Vehicles	10
Tare load (tons)	339
Gross load (tons)	355
Conditions	Rain at start then fine
Recorder	A. G. S. Davies

Mls.	Sch.	M. S.	Speed
0·0 PADSTOW	0	0 00	53
		sigs	
5·7 WADEBRIDGE	9	10 54	
4·1 St Kew Highway		7 53	39/28
7·8 PORT ISAAC ROAD	15	13 21	31
4·1 DELABOLE	11	10 00	29
		sig. stop (4½ mins)	
2·4 CAMELFORD	6	12 40	
4·5 OTTERHAM	10	9 13	23/38
4·9 Tresmeer		6 34	
8·5 Egloskerry		10 56	61
12·9 LAUNCESTON	20	16 31	
5·0 Tower Hill		7 23	31/44
8·6 Ashwater		13 14	26/52
13·7 HALWILL	24	21 10	

TABLE 34

EXETER ST DAVID'S TO BARNSTAPLE JUNCTION

Detail	A			B			C	
Date	18 June 1954			1 Aug 1948			21 Aug 1948	
Train (ex. Waterloo)	4.40 p.m.			12 noon			12 noon	
Locomotive no.	34024			34018			34018	
Vehicles	6			9			10	
Tare load (tons)	231			354			387	
Gross load (tons)	240			385			415	
Recorder	G. F. Bloxam			P. W. B. Semmens			A. J. Baker	
Mls.	Sch.	M. S.	Speed	Sch.	M. S.	Speed	M. S.	Speed
0·0 EXETER ST DAVID'S	0	0 00		0	0 00		0 00	
							sigs	10
1·2 *Cowley Bridge Junction*								
(*25)	3	3 25		3	3 43		4 39	
4·3 Newton St Cyres		6 45			7 26	52/55	8 51	
6·9 Crediton (*45)		9 10	—/64		11 30		12 03	48
10·6 Yeoford		12 30			21 31	46	16 18	57
11·5 *Coleford Junction*	17	13 35		17	22 50	45	17 25	44
13·5 Copplestone	20	16 10		20	25 36		19 52	32/46
15·1 Morchard Road	23	19 00		23	28 13		22 28	28/54
		p.w.s.	15					
17·5 Lapford	26	23 50		26	31 46	—/60	26 10	27/58
21·3 Eggesford	32	29 00		32	37 08	—/57	31 18	30/62
25·3 South Molton Road†	38	34 10		37½	42 04		36 15	30/57
28·1 Portsmouth Arms	43	39 40		42	46 17	—/55	40 03	32/58
		sigs						
32·3 Umberleigh	48	45 00		47	51 32		45 14	35
34·7 Chapelton		47 40	76		54 23	60/66	48 11	70
39·0 BARNSTAPLE JUNC-								
TION	57	52 03		56	59 13		52 59	
Estimated net time (mins)	50			52¾			52	

Speed restrictions: Coleford Junction–Umberleigh   Not to exceed 55 m.p.h.
Umberleigh–Barnstaple Junction   Not to exceed 60 m.p.h.
† Renamed King's Nympton by time of run in detail A.

TABLE 35

BARNSTAPLE JUNCTION TO EXETER ST DAVID'S

Detail	A			B		
Train	10.0 a.m. ex. Mortehoe			*Devon Belle*		
Date	31 Aug 1959			5 Sept 1948		
Locomotive no.	34034			34020		
Vehicles	7			10		
Tare load (tons)	236			387		
Gross load (tons)	265			415		
Recorder	N. Beeching			A. J. Baker		
Mls.	Sch.	M. S.	Speed	Sch.	M. S.	Speed
0·0 BARNSTAPLE JUNCTION	0	0 00		0	0 00	
4·3 Chapelton		5 34	65		6 39	62
6·7 Umberleigh	10	8 25	68	10	9 10	47/60
10·8 Portsmouth Arms	15	13 41	62	15	14 03	40/54
13·7 King's Nympton†	20	17 50	54	20	17 50	33/52
17·6 Eggesford	25	23 18	60	25	23 15	28/57
21·5 Lapford	30	28 23	60	30	28 32	25/46
23·8 Morchard Road	33	31 54	52	33	32 13	30/43
25·5 Copplestone	36	34 35	47	36	34 59	32
27·4 *Coleford Junction*	38	36 51	69	38	37 27	
28·4 Yeoford		37 44	73/80		38 33	77
32·1 Crediton (*45)		41 00	41		41 49	42
					p.w.s.	15
34·7 Newton St Cyres		43 31	74		45 38	42
					sigs	
37·7 *Cowley Bridge Junction* (*25)	52	46 32	27/38	50	52 21	18
39·0 EXETER ST DAVID'S	55	49 19		53	55 05	
Estimated net time (mins)	49¼			50¼		

Speed restrictions: Barnstaple Junction–Umberleigh　Not to exceed 60 m.p.h.
Umberleigh–Coleford Junction　Not to exceed 55 m.p.h.
† Named South Molton Road at time of run in detail B.

TABLE 36

WATERLOO TO SOUTHAMPTON CENTRAL

Detail	A	B	C	D	E
Date	21 Mar 1967	12 Feb 1959	4 June 1965	25 Nov 1947	3 Apr 1965
Train	10.30 a.m.	10.30 a.m.	8.30 a.m.	12.30 p.m.	10.30 a.m.
Locomotive no.	35028(R)	35030(R)	35005(R)	21C20	35012(R)
Vehicles	10	11	11	10	12
Tare load (tons)	333½	366	368	397	400
Gross load (tons)	360	390	392	417	430
Driver	Hooper (9E)	Letchford (9E)	—	—	King (9E)
Conditions	—	Drizzle	Fine	—	—
Recorder	P. Widgery	DWW	M. D. Barrett	J. G. Webber	R. O. Havery

Mls.		A Sch.	M.S.	Speed	B Sch.	M.S.	Speed	C Sch.	M.S.	Speed	D Sch.	M.S.	Speed	E Sch.	M.S.	Speed
0·0	WATERLOO	0	0 00		0	0 00		0	0 00		0	0 00		0	0 00	
												sigs				
3·9	Clapham Junction (*40)	7	6 59	42/56	7	6 53	41	7	6 20	41	7	8 38	20	7	8 19	40
			p.w.s.													
7·2	Wimbledon		12 43	29		11 12	54		10 08	60		13 50	51		12 26	56
9·8	New Malden		15 55	61		13 39	68		12 33	64		16 30	63		—	
12·0	Surbiton		18 03	67		15 34	72		14 30	73		18 36	66		16 58	68
13·3	*Hampton Court Junction*	18	19 10	71	18	16 37	74	18	15 40	77		19 45	70	18	18 07	70
17·1	Walton-on-Thames		22 11	76		19 27	78		18 20	82/80		22 57	66			
19·1	Weybridge		23 47	77/80		20 58	81		—			24 45	66/80		22 53	75
21·7	West Byfleet		25 44	77		22 52	83		21 42	83		26 52	78		—	
												sigs				
24·3	WOKING	28†	27 50	75	28†	24 54	76	28†	23 40	78/77	28†	29 10	67	28†	27 06	70
28·0	Brookwood		30 52	69		27 44	77		26 31	79/75		—			—	
31·0	Milepost 31		33 32	66		30 03	75		28 52	76		35 22	65		33 00	66
33·2	Farnborough		35 23	74/75		31 49	76		30 31	80/79		37 24	67		34 54	75
36·5	Fleet		38 00	74/75		34 17	80		32 53	84/88		40 15	71		37 31	77/80
												sigs				
39·8	Winchfield		40 41	72/71		36 49	75		35 13	85		44 00	47		40 02	76
42·2	Hook		42 39	72/74		38 44	73		36 56	84		46 42	57/68		41 54	77
			sigs						sigs							
47·8	BASING-STOKE (*65)		48 08	48		43 09	74		41 48	36		51 53	65		46 17	66
			p.w.s.						sigs							
50·3	*Worting Junction* (*65)	60	51 37	22	52	45 25	65	52	47 15	35	53	54 20	54	52	48 39	62
52·5	Wootton S.B.		55 36	42		sig.stops(2)			49 49	46		—			50 48	
56·2	Roundwood S.B.		59 37	57/65		sigs			—			60 30	61		—	
			sigs									sigs				
58·1	Micheldever		61 25	41		66 03	34		55 01	73/75		62 35	30		55 34	
60·3	Weston S.B.		64 22	53		69 02	62		—			65 23			57 06	84
61·8	*Wallers Ash S.B.*		65 51	65		—			p.w.s.	25		66 45	68		58 11	85
64·5	*Winchester Junction*	76	68 09	74	66	72 39	79	66½	—		68½	69 09	70	66	59 56	90

† At *Woking Junction*

Table 36—Waterloo to Southampton Central (contd)

Detail	A			B			C			D			E		
Mls.	Sch.	M. S.	Speed	Sch.	M. S.	Speed	Sch.	M. S.	Speed	Sch.	M. S.	Speed	Sch.	M. S.	Speed
66·6 WINCHESTER CITY		69 49	78		74 10	82		67 17	75/82		70 57	71		61 23	87
69·0 *Shawford Junction*		—			—	86		sigs	69		sigs	22		—	
69·7 Shawford		72 11 p.w.s.	81/82		76 20	92		sigs	75		75 15			63 36	86
73·6 EASTLEIGH	84½	77 19	25	73	78 55	86	74	72 49 sigs	60	77	78 48	70	73	66 34	69
75·8 Swaythling		80 37	51/54		—			75 36	47		80 45	70		68 33 sigs	
77·3 St. Denys		82 13	48		81 30			77 48	42		81 55	69		71 23	29
78·2 *Northam Junction* (*15)	90	83 38 sig.stop	17	78	82 37		79	sig.stop		82	83 00	17	78	—	
79·2 SOUTHAMPTON CENTRAL	93½	89 06		81	85 30		82	91 43		85	86 00		81	78 08	
Estimated net time (mins)	73¾			70½			71¼			77¼			74½		

TABLE 37

WATERLOO TO SOUTHAMPTON CENTRAL

Detail	A	B	C	D	E
Date	5 June 1958	15 July 1957	12 May 1959	25 Jan 1966	14 May 1959
Train	6.30 p.m.	6.30 p.m.	10.30 a.m.	8.30 a.m.	6.30 p.m.
Locomotive no.	34040	35021	34095	35008(R)	34048(R)
Vehicles	12	12	12	13	13
Tare load (tons)	400	401	403	415	420
Gross load (tons)	430	425	430	445	455
Driver	R. W. Purchase (BM)	Horne	Pragnell (9E)	Hooper (9E)	Frampton (BM)
Conditions	Fine	Cloudy	Fine	—	Fine
Recorder	J. G. Webber	M. Hedges	J. G. Webber	R. M. Grainger	J. G. Webber

Mls.	Sch.†	M. S.	Speed	M. S.	Speed	M. S.	Speed	M. S.	Speed	M. S.	Speed
		A		B		C		D		E	
0·0 WATERLOO	0	0 00		0 00		0 00		0 00		0 00	
3·9 Clapham Junction (*40)	7	7 52 sigs		6 45	47 p.w.s.	7 21		7 15	41	6 40	
7·2 Wimbledon		12 35	46	11 07	22	11 30	54	11 27	53	10 35	55
9·8 New Malden		15 22	56	15 05		14 04	64	14 00	59	13 10	63
12·0 Surbiton		17 35	60	17 30	61	16 10	63	16 08	64	15 19	65
13·3 *Hampton Court Junction*	18	18 46	66	18 43	64	17 21 sigs	68	17 16	69	16 28	69/73

Table 37—Waterloo to Southampton Central (contd)

Detail	Sch.	A M. S. Speed	B M. S. Speed	C M. S. Speed	D M. S. Speed	E M. S. Speed
Mls.						
17·1 Walton-on-Thames		21 57 73/70	22 07 66	22 00 sigs	20 20 73	19 42 69
19·1 Weybridge		—	24 01 63	24 47 24	22 01 73	21 30 67/73
21·7 West Byfleet		25 42 76	26 15 70	29 42 57 sigs	24 02 77	23 36 71
24·3 WOKING	28‡	27 55 73	28 42 63	32 36 58/51	26 15 70	25 58 70
28·0 Brookwood		31 07 70	32 20 58	36 38 57	29 27 67	29 17 63
31·0 Milepost 31		33 58 62	35 29 57	39 47 57	32 12 64 p.w.s.	32 18 59
33·2 Farnborough		36 01 65	37 46	41 58 65	34 38 39	34 24 65
36·5 Fleet		38 48 71	40 52 65	44 48 70	39 45 39	37 16 70/73
39·8 Winchfield		41 31 75/69	43 51	47 40 70/69	45 33 16	40 07 70
42·2 Hook		43 30 70/73	46 00	49 48 70/67	50 01 50/65 sigs	42 09 69/73
47·8 BASINGSTOKE (*65)		48 11 71 sigs	50 57 67/70	54 43 60	58 18 23	46 52 71
50·3 Worting Junction (*65)	52	50 55 28	53 27 53	57 20 50	62 30 41	49 10 64
52·5 Wootton S.B.		—	55 59 52	—	65 45 15 p.w.s.	—
56·2 Roundwood S.B.		59 03 61	—	63 35 66	—	55 14 59
58·1 Micheldever		60 43 68	61 14 72	65 07 76	75 24 69	56 56 70
60·3 Weston S.B.		—	62 56 76	66 43 83	77 08 78	58 40 75
61·8 Wallers Ash S.B.		—	64 06 80	67 45 85	78 15 83	59 52 75 sigs
64·5 Winchester Junction	66	—	66 04 83	69 40 85	80 10 85	63 02 25 sigs
66·6 WINCHESTER CITY		67 31 78	67 37 82	71 07 88	81 38 87	66 05 50/34
69·0 Shawford Junction		—	—	—	91	—
69·7 Shawford		—	81	69 55 84/86	73 17 90/82 sig.stop	83 45 89 sig.stop	70 03 65
73·6 EASTLEIGH	73	73 05 61	72 39 81	78 25	88 47 27	74 53 73
75·8 Swaythling		p.w.s. 13	74 18 83	82 20 51	92 08 56	76 47 77 sigs
77·3 St. Denys		79 25 35	75 22 sigs	—	93 32 65	77 56 15
78·2 Northam Junction (*15)	78	81 05 25	77 07 10 sigs	85 05	95 02 15	80 15
79·2 SOUTHAMPTON CENTRAL	81	84 11	80 40	88 00	98 15	83 20
Estimated net time (mins)		78½	77½	76¼	74½	76½

† Not applicable to detail D

‡ At Woking Junction

TABLE 38

WATERLOO TO SOUTHAMPTON CENTRAL

Detail	A	B	C	D	E
Date	4 Apr 1965	2 July 1955	9 May 1959	25 Oct 1963	28 Dec 1946
Train	12.30 p.m.	6.30 p.m.	10.30 a.m.	12.30 p.m.	12.30 p.m.
Locomotive no.	35007(R)	34109	34010(R)	35005(R)	21C18
Vehicles	12	13	13	12	12
Tare load (tons)	428½	430	435	472	495
Gross load (tons)	445	465	460	500	520
Driver	Harman (BM)	—	Letchford (9E)	Rabbetts (BM)	—
Conditions	Drizzle	Fine	Fine	—	—
Recorder	P. Widgery	M. Hedges	J. G. McEwen	J. G. Webber	J. F. Clay

Mls.	Sch.	M. S.	Speed	Sch.	M. S.	Speed	Sch.	M. S.	Speed	Sch.	M. S.	Speed	Sch.	M. S.	Speed
0·0 WATERLOO	0	0 00	sigs	0	0 00		0	0 00		0	0 00	p.w.s.	0	0 00	
3·9 Clapham Junction (*40)	7	8 52	45	7	8 01	45	7	7 21	38	7	9 17	45	7	8 20	
								p.w.s.	15						
7·2 Wimbledon		13 00	55		12 12			12 27	39		13 35	52		11 10	
9·8 New Malden		15 28	69		14 50	61/66		15 23	56		16 10	62		—	
					p.w.s.										
12·0 Surbiton		17 25	71		17 05	22		17 38	61		18 16	67		16 40	65
13·3 Hampton Court Junction	18	18 29	74	18	19 35		18	18 46	64	18	19 25	68/74			
17·1 Walton-on-Thames		21 29	72		23 55	60		22 03	69		22 37	70/67		sigs	
19·1 Weybridge		23 09	71/76		25 55	60/74		23 51	66		24 21	68/75		24 45 sigs	
21·7 West Byfleet		25 12	73		28 07	69		25 59	71		26 27	73		37 20 sigs	
					sigs	5									
24·3 WOKING	28†	27 23	71	30†	31 35	11	28†	28 17	70	28†	28 43	69	28†	46 00	10
28·0 Brookwood		30 33	68		—			31 27	67		32 05	63		51 05	45
31·0 Milepost 31		33 16	65		41 37	47		34 07	66		—	59		55 35	55
32·2 Farnborough		35 10	75		43 57			36 07	70		37 08	67		—	
36·5 Fleet		37 42	79/82		46 57	68		38 51	71		40 01	70/72		60 25	73
39·8 Winchfield		40 12	79/77		49 49	70		41 38	71		42 47	70/69		—	
42·2 Hook		42 00	79/82		51 55	66/72		43 39	69		44 50	70/74		65 00	79
47·8 BASINGSTOKE (*65)		46 16	65		56 36	68		48 18	74		49 32	68/70		69 10	60
		sigs.													
50·3 Worting Junction (*65)	52	50 22	25	56	58 57	54	52	50 28	62	52	51 54	53/55	53	72 02	55
		sig.stop													
52·5 Wootton S.B.		75 37			61 22	55		—			54 17	57		74 50	60
56·2 Roundwood S.B.		82 22	45		—			—			57 53	63		—	
58·1 Micheldever		85 47	Stop		66 27	73		57 25	74		59 30	76		81 10	75
60·3 Weston S.B.		—			68 09	75		—			—			—	
61·8 Wallers Ash S.B.		91 21	72		69 17	78		—			62 15	72		—	
64·5 Winchester Junction	66	93 25	82	74½	71 18	80	66	—		66	64 10	86	68½	—	

† At *Woking Junction*

Table 38—Waterloo to Southampton Central (contd)

Detail	A			B			C			D			E		
Mls.	Sch.	M. S.	Speed	Sch.	M. S.	Speed	Sch.	M. S.	Speed	Sch.	M. S.	Speed	Sch.	M. S.	Speed
66·6 WINCHESTER CITY		94 56	84/85		73 02	76/78		64 00	78		65 38	87		86 50	80
69·7 Shawford		97 10	82		75 26 p.w.s.	—/88		66 22 sigs	81/82		67 50	85		—	
73·6 EASTLEIGH	73	100 13	70	83	80 50		73	69 50 sigs	48	73	70 34 sigs	81	77	91 45	86
75·8 Swaythling		102 05	74		83 39	56		72 52 sigs	45		72 53 sigs	15		—	
77·3 St. Denys		103 17			85 05	62		75 12	35		75 48	18		94 35	76
78·2 *Northam Junction* (*15)	78	104 51	20	88	86 30	24	78	—		78	78 56		82	95 40 sig.stop	
79·2 SOUTHAMPTON CENTRAL	81	107 40		91	89 16		81	81 08		81	81 18		85	100 03	
Estimated net time (mins)		73¾			77¼			76			75¾			78	

TABLE 39
WATERLOO TO WINCHESTER CITY

Detail	A	B	C	D	E
Date	26 May 1967	27 Aug 1966	5 July 1957	17 June 1967	30 Apr 1964
Train (ex. Waterloo)	4.22 p.m.	6.30 p.m.	3.20 p.m.	8.30 a.m.	6.30 p.m.
Locomotive no.	34034(R)	34108(R)	34007	35007(R)	35029(R)
Vehicles	8	11	11	11	12
Tare load (tons)	262	365	371	371	402
Gross load (tons)	280	395	415	400	430
Driver	Fordrey (9E)	Lovell (BM)	Hill (BM)	Evans (9E)	Rabbetts (BM)
Conditions	Light wind	Fine; W. wind	—	—	Fine
Recorder	R. M. Grainger	M. C. Thompson	P. G. Barlow	A. C. Rawlings	J. G. Webber

Mls.	Sch.	M. S.	Speed	Sch.	M. S.	Speed	Sch.	M. S.	Speed	Sch.	M. S.	Speed	Sch.	M. S.	Speed
0·0 WATERLOO	0	0 00		0	0 00		0	0 00		0	0 00		0	0 00	
3·9 Clapham Junction (*40)	7	6 24	43	7	7 20	39	7	7 14	37	7	7 41	40	7	6 46	40
7·2 Wimbledon		10 08	63		11 28	53		11 24	58		11 41	60		10 49	57
9·8 New Malden		12 24	73/71		13 59	63/67		13 52	66		14 04	68		13 13	69
12·0 Surbiton		14 15 sigs	76/79		16 07 p.w.s.			—			16 01	71		15 07	72
13·3 *Hampton Court Junction*	18	15 18 sigs	61	18	17 51	43	18	17 07	64	18	17 05	73	18	16 10	76

Table 39—Waterloo to Winchester City (contd)

Detail	A			B			C			D			E		
Mls.	Sch.	M. S.	Speed	Sch.	M. S.	Speed	Sch.	M. S.	Speed	Sch.	M. S.	Speed	Sch.	M. S.	Speed
17·1 Walton-on-Thames		19 20	32		22 00	63/61		20 29	67		20 10	72		19 03	78
19·1 Weybridge		22 30 p.w.s.	41/16		23 55	67		22 20 p.w.s.	64/67 15		21 56	67/72		20 40	75/81
21·7 West Byfleet		27 58 sigs	44/51		26 06	72		26 41	42		24 10	71		22 34	80
24·3 WOKING	30‡	31 06	58	28‡	28 23	69	28‡	29 56	55	30‡	26 26	68	28‡	24 40	77
28·0 Brookwood		34 26	71		31 36	67		33 42	60/63		29 36	70		27 38 sigs	73
31·0 *Milepost 31*		36 54	75/79		34 25	64		36 38	61		32 14	69		30 15	52
33·2 Farnborough		38 41	73		36 25	68/72		38 40	67		34 02	75		32 46	55
36·5 Fleet		41 12	82/86		39 14	71/73		41 33	70/68		36 36	80/83		35 46	71/77
39·8 Winchfield		43 33	84/83		42 00	70		44 24	71/66		30 03 p.w.s.	80		38 26	75
42·2 Hook		45 14	86/90		44 04	72/73		46 30	67/71		41 29 sigs	27/62		40 17	77/81
47·8 BASINGSTOKE (*65)		49 09	72		48 49	65		52 21 p.w.s.	68 15		48 41 sigs	38/44		44 36	76
50·3 *Worting Junction* (*65)	63	51 21	64	60	51 24	57	54	56 38	42	67½	52 53	34	52	46 57	62
52·5 *Wootton S.B.*		53 24	68		53 52	54		59 56	39		56 10	50		49 07	62
56·2 *Roundwood S.B.*		56 03†	78/83		57 36	61		—			59 43	68		52 20	71
58·1 Micheldever		57 42	80		59 17	70		65 50	67		61 13	80		53 47	81
60·3 *Weston S.B.*		59 12	88		61 10 p.w.s.	66		—			62 43	87		55 16	87
61·8 *Wallers Ash S.B.*		60 09	94/97		62 53	41		—			63 43	91/95		56 16 sigs	92/93
64·5 *Winchester Junction*	83	61 52	87	75½	66 28	41	71	70 50	81	83½	65 28		66	58 22 sig.stop	63
66·6 WINCHESTER CITY	86	64 07		78½	70 05		74	73 09		85½	67 50		69	62 55	
Estimated net time (mins)		56			66			66			61			58½	

‡ At *Woking Junction*   † At *Litchfield Tunnel*

TABLE 40
WATERLOO TO WINCHESTER CITY

Detail	A			B			C			D			E		
Date	1 Apr 1964			8 June 1964			21 Aug 1959			24 Oct 1952			30 May 1958		
Train (ex. Waterloo)	6.30 p.m.			3.30 p.m.			6.30 p.m.			4.35 p.m.			4.34 p.m.		
Locomotive no.	35030(R)			35021(R)			35025(R)			34110			34107		
Vehicles	12			12			13			13			13		
Tare load (tons)	400			408			431			432			441		
Gross load (tons)	430			440			465			465			470		
Driver	Rabbetts (BM)			Woods (BM)			Jones (BM)			Gould			Pragnell (9E)		
Conditions	—			Fine			Fine			—			—		
Recorder	J. G. Webber			DWW			J. G. Webber			J. G. Webber			A. J. Baker		
Mls.	Sch.	M. S.	Speed	Sch.	M. S.	Speed	Sch.	M. S.	Speed	Sch.	M. S.	Speed	Sch.	M. S.	Speed
0·0 WATERLOO	0	0 00		0	0 00		0	0 00		0	0 00		0	0 00	
											sigs				
3·9 Clapham Jnc. (*40)	7	6 55	39	7	6 54	50/61	7	6 53		7	8 59	42	7	7 10	48/53
														p.w.s.	24
7·2 Wimbledon		11 04	56		10 24	64		11 09	51		13 26	50		12 34	
9·8 New Malden		13 32	67		12 37	72		13 44	64		16 15	60		16 05	66
12·0 Surbiton		15 29	72		14 24	74		15 48	67		18 25	62		18 23	64
13·3 Hampton Court Junction	18	16 33	74	18	15 24	79/84	18	16 55	70	18	19 39	63/74	18	19 34	74
17·1 Walton-on-Thames		19 27	75		18 09	80		19 59	73		22 58	66		22 52	—/65
19·1 Weybridge		21 06	74/80		19 38	81/86		—	70/76		24 51	61/72		24 46	
21·7 West Byfleet		23 03	78		21 31	80		23 47	73		27 05	67		26 57	76
		sigs	32												
24·3 WOKING	28†	26 13		28†	23 32	77	28†	26 03	70	28†	29 32	64	28†	29 22	66
28·0 Brookwood		30 43	57		26 32	73		29 15	66		33 00	63		32 49	
31·0 Milepost 31		33 52	58		29 09	66		32 05	63		36 02	58		35 49	58
		sigs	41												
33·2 Farnborough		36 42	47		31 03	70		34 05	69/70		38 10	66		37 56	73/66
								sigs							
36·5 Fleet		39 57	68		33 40	78		37 49	43		41 06	66		40 50	73/69
39·8 Winchfield		42 50	70		36 12	77/74		42 54	47		44 08	66		43 45	74/67
42·2 Hook		44 49	71/77		38 04	76/80		44 29	60/64		46 25	60/68		45 51	68/76
								sigs							
47·8 BASINGSTOKE (*65)		49 21	71		42 20	76		50 10	36		51 39	64		50 49	
					sigs. sev. 5										
50·3 Worting Jnc. (*65)	52	51 38	65	52	46 00		52	53 47	33	55	54 24	50	54	53 43	43
52·5 Wootton S.B.		53 43	65		50 14	54		—			—			56 53	
					sig. stop										
56·2 Roundwood S.B.		56 53	71		59 07			61 10	59		61 08	58		61 01	61
					sigs										
58·1 Micheldever		58 22	80		62 12	30		62 46	73/84		62 55	67		62 42	73
60·3 Weston S.B.		59 58	83		65 16	55		—			64 34			—	81
					p.w.s.									sigs	
61·8 Wallers Ash S.B.		61 00	86		67 26			—			65 40	88		66 19	32/51
														sigs	47
64·5 Winchester Jnc.	66	62 49	98	66	71 02	58		—		71	67 41	80	69½	70 11	66
		sigs													
66·6 WINCHESTER CITY	69	65 10		69	73 50		69	69 45		74	70 14		72½	73 13	
Estimated net time (mins)	60¾			58			62¾			69¼			68¼		

† At Woking Junction

Bulleid's Pacifics

TABLE 41

WATERLOO TO BASINGSTOKE

Detail	A	B	C	D	E
Date	20 Nov 1965	15 May 1965	30 May 1960	23 Sept 1965	21 Sept 1966
Train (ex. Waterloo)	5.30 p.m.	9.20 p.m.	5. 30 p.m.	5.30 p.m.	5.30 p.m.
Locomotive no.	34090(R)	35005(R)	34006	35029(R)	34102
Vehicles	10	10	10	11	11
Tare load (tons)	345	330	338	372	373
Gross load (tons)	365	350	365	395	395
Driver	Saunders (9E)	Hooper (9E)	—	Gaffney (9E)	Wilton (9E)
Conditions	NE wind	Fine	Fine	Dry; calm	—
Recorder	M. C. Thompson	R. M. Grainger	M. H. Cobb	A. Wild	D. W. Tuck

Mls.	M. S. Speed	M. S. Speed	M. S. Speed	M. S. Speed	M. S. Speed
0·0 WATERLOO	0 00	0 00	0 00	0 00	0 00
3·9 Clapham Junction (*40)	6 25 47	6 53 40	7 02 43	7 12 42/53	7 59 37
7·2 Wimbledon	10 08 67	10 47 48/33 p.w.s.	11 10 56/20 p.w.s.	11 06 60	12 29 52
9·8 New Malden	12 26 70	14 57 53	15 00 20	13 27 66	15 10 60/63
12·0 Surbiton	14 18 75	17 03 71	19 21	15 26 72	17 20 61
13·3 Hampton Court Junction	15 10 77	18 06 75	20 53 65	16 28 75/80	18 36 63/70
17·1 Walton-on-Thames	18 06 80	20 55 82	24 22 62	19 19 79/75	21 54 70
19·1 Weybridge	19 38 82/84	22 26 78/88	26 26 70	20 56 78/82	23 42 64/61
21·7 West Byfleet	21 30 82	24 12 86	28 44	22 50 79	26 18 52 p.w.s.
24·3 WOKING	23 31 80	26 05 83	31 09 64	24 52 75	31 40 29
28·0 Brookwood	26 18 75	28 48 81	34 45 60	28 34 26	36 36 55
31·0 Milepost 31	p.w.s.	31 05 75	37 58 55	32 46 55	39 45 59
33·2 Farnborough	32 54 25	32 44 80	40 11 61	35 58 25	41 53 64
36·5 Fleet	36 25 56/62	35 05 85/88	43 25 60/62	40 14 62/73	44 45 73/79
39·8 Winchfield	40 34 28	37 23 83	46 40 60/61	43 04 71	47 20 77/76
42·2 Hook	43 58 56/64	39 04 85/90	49 04 59/65	45 00 75/83 sigs	49 12 79/82
47·8 BASINGSTOKE	50 59	43 48	54 53	51 34	54 42
Estimated net time (mins)	43	41½	50¾	43	51

TABLE 42

WATERLOO TO BASINGSTOKE

Detail	A	B	C	D
Date	9 June 1965	31 May 1966	7 June 1965	7 June 1962
Train (ex. Waterloo)	5.30 p.m.	5.30 p.m.	5.30 p.m.	6.0 p.m.
Locomotive no.	35017(R)	34077(R)	35005(R)	35025(R)
Vehicles	11	12	12	13
Tare load (tons)	373	400	405	437
Gross load (tons)	400	425	430	470
Driver	Saunders(9E)	Dente (9E)	Saunders(9E)	—
Conditions	Fine; calm	Fine; lt. NE wind	Dry; calm	Fine
Recorder	A. Wild	A. Wild	D. W. Tuck	M. H. Cobb

Mls.	M. S.	Speed	M. S.	Speed	M. S.	Speed	M. S.	Speed
0·0 WATERLOO	0 00		0 00		0 00		0 00	
3·9 Clapham Junction (*40)	6 31	43/59	7 15	42/50	6 36	45	8 20	46
7·2 Wimbledon	10 11	61	11 23	55	10 18	62	12 19	61
9·8 New Malden	12 37	66	13 57	62	12 30	75	14 55	65
12·0 Surbiton	14 35	74	16 05	67	14 19	79	17 02	63
13·3 *Hampton Court Junction*	15 35	77/82	17 15	56	15 18	80/81	18 11	72
				p.w.s.	sig. stop			
17·1 Walton-on-Thames	18 20	81/80	23 40	51	22 55	53	21 22	67
19·1 Weybridge	19 50	83/85	25 57	60	25 00	64	23 09	72
21·7 West Byfleet	21 38	81	28 17	68	27 05	75	25 19	
	sigs		sigs					
24·3 WOKING	23 45	72	30 41	65	29 12	77	27 40	67
	sigs							
28·0 Brookwood	26 58	56	34 02	65	32 00	79	31 03	62
	sigs							
31·0 *Milepost 31*	30 19	50	36 52	63	34 22	75	34 00	61
33·2 Farnborough	32 27	70	38 52	68/71	36 06	79	36 02	69/73
36·5 Fleet	35 04	80/84	41 43	69/72	38 34	82	38 50	76
39·8 Winchfield	37 28	82/81	44 30	68/67	41 00	80/81	41 36	70/71
42·2 Hook	39 10	83/86	46 34	69/72	42 49	80	43 37	70/73
	sigs				sigs			
47·8 BASINGSTOKE	44 20		52 24		48 47		48 59	
Estimated net time (mins)	41¼		48½		41¾		48	

TABLE 43
WATERLOO TO WOKING

Detail	A			B			C			D			E		
Date	19 Mar 1966			10 July 1961			10 July 1959			13 July 1962			27 July 1964		
Train (ex. Waterloo)	2.45 a.m.			5.39 p.m.			5.0 p.m.			5.0 p.m.			5.0 p.m.		
Locomotive no.	34077(R)			34082(R)			35023(R)			34018(R)			34002		
Vehicles	12			11			11			11			12		
Tare load (tons)	290			366			368			374			398		
Gross load (tons)	320			400			390			405			435		
Driver	Hendicott (9E)			Robinson(9E)			—			—			—		
Conditions	Fine; NE wind			Fine			—			Fine			Dry		
Recorder	A. Wild			D. J. Maidment			D. J. Maidment			M. H. Cobb			C. R. Richardson		

Mls.	Sch.	M. S.	Speed	Sch.	M. S.	Speed	Sch.	M. S.	Speed	M. S.	Speed	M. S.
0·0 WATERLOO	0	0 00		0	0 00		0	0 00		0 00		0 00
3·9 Clapham Junction (*40)	7	7 36	50/59 sigs	7	7 20	43	7	6 41	40	6 48	51	7 50
7·2 Wimbledon		12 53	15		11 29	59		11 00	56	10 22		12 00
9·8 New Malden		15 58	64		14 02	65		13 35	61	12 48	65	14 37
12·0 Surbiton		17 58	70		16 06	69		15 44	64	14 50	69	17 00
13·3 *Hampton Court Junction*	18	19 04	71/77	18½	17 18	75/80	18	—	68/75	15 57	70	18 10
17·1 Walton-on-Thames		22 04	74/73		20 10	79		20 11	73	19 09	65	21 19
19·1 Weybridge		23 43	75		21 44	79/86		22 02	69	20 59	73	23 00
21·7 West Byfleet		25 40	79		23 37	84		24 12	73	23 11	68	25 27
24·3 WOKING	32	29 33		31	26 17		30	27 24		26 28		28 40
Estimated net time (mins)	26			26¼			27½			26¼		28¾

TABLE 44
SURBITON TO WOKING

Detail	A			B		C		D	
Date	4 Feb 1967			7 Jan 1967		5 July 1967		28 Oct 1966	
Train (ex. Waterloo)	8.35 a.m.			8.35 a.m.		8.35 a.m.		8.35 a.m.	
Locomotive no.	35023(R)			34036(R)		35007(R)		34036(R)	
Vehicles	8			8		10		10	
Tare load (tons)	260			264		312		328	
Gross load (tons)	280			285		326		345	
Recorder	M. D. Barrett			M. D. Barrett		M. D. Barrett		M. D. Barrett	

Mls.	Sch.	M. S.	Speed	M. S.	Speed	M. S.	Speed	M. S.	Speed
0·0 SURBITON	0	0 00		0 00		0 00		0 00	
1·3 *Hampton Court Jnc.*	3	2 48	48	2 48	48	2 59	46	2 52	46
5·1 Walton-on-Thames		6 22	70	6 41	62	6 35	69	6 33	67/66
7·1 Weybridge		8 16	73/79	8 49	66/72	8 29	75/77	8 28	71/74
9·6 West Byfleet		10 11	79	10 58	68	10 28	73/74	p.w.s.	20
12·3 WOKING	15½	13 02		13 55		13 40		16 47	
Estimated net time (mins)	13			14		13¾		13¼	

TABLE 45
WOKING TO BASINGSTOKE

Detail	A		B		C		D		E	
Date	13 June 1967		4 July 1967		8 July 1967		22 May 1967		5 July 1967	
Train (ex. Waterloo)	2.30 a.m.		2.45 a.m.		2.45 a.m.		8.35 a.m.		8.35 a.m.	
Locomotive no.	35007(R)		34001(R)		34095(R)		35003(R)		35007(R)	
Vehicles	5		7		8		9		10	
Tare load (tons)	147		170		190½		295		312	
Gross load (tons)	160		185		205		305		326	
Driver (Nine Elms)	Hendicott		Porter		Porter		—		—	
Recorder	D. A. Foale		M. Smith		M. D. Barrett		M. D. Barrett		M. D. Barrett	

Mls.	M. S.	Speed	M. S.	Speed	M. S.	Speed	M. S.	Speed	M. S.	Speed
0·0 WOKING	0 00		0 00		0 00		0 00		0 00	
	sigs									
3·7 Brookwood	5 13	77/84	5 00	75	6 05	65	5 28	63	6 14	62
6·7 *Milepost 31*	7 29	82	7 18	83/90	8 37	74	8 13	67/61	8 58	69/74
8·9 Farnborough	9 14	63	8 50	86	10 18	82/85	10 24	62	10 53	71
12·2 Fleet	11 53	88/90	11 05	94	12 37	84/87	13 14	75/82	13 34	76/77
15·5 Winchfield	14 23	81	13 19	89	14 53	82	15 43	77/79	16 12	71
17·9 Hook	16 05	85	14 55	87	16 33	86	17 36	78/82	18 20	68/71
	sigs		sigs	40	sigs		sigs	24	sig. stop	
23·5 BASINGSTOKE	22 41		20 49		22 17		24 13		28 05	
Estimated net time (mins)	20¾		20		22		22½		24	

TABLE 46
WOKING TO BASINGSTOKE

Detail	A		B		C		D		E	
Date	22 May 1965		1 Sept 1964		4 July 1966		6 July 1966		3 July 1967	
Train (ex. Waterloo)	2.45 a.m.		9.30 a.m.		8.35 a.m.		8.35 a.m.		8.55 a.m.	
Locomotive no.	34086		34051		34090(R)		34036(R)		35030(R)	
Vehicles	12		10		11		12		12	
Tare load (tons)	330		332		354½		357½		372	
Gross load (tons)	350		355		375		380		390	
Driver (Nine Elms)	Saunders		—		Porter		Porter		—	
Recorder	M. Smith		D. A. Foale		P. M. Widgery		P. M. Widgery		M. D. Barrett	

Mls.	Sch.	M. S.	Speed	Sch.	M. S.	Speed	Sch.	M. S.	Speed	M. S.	Speed	M. S.	Speed
0·0 WOKING	0	0 00		0	0 00		0	0 00		0 00		0 00	
3·7 Brookwood		6 16	50		6 59	53		6 13	57	5 49	60	6 22	53
6·7 *Milepost 31*		9 26	58		10 05	60		9 13	63	8 41	67	9 26	60/70
8·9 Farnborough		11 20	70		12 08	68		11 09	71/76	10 34	72/75	11 28	68 70
12·2 Fleet		14 05	80		14 52	77/80		13 48	74/78	13 14	73/75	14 14	70/65
15·5 Winchfield		16 41	78		17 23	77		16 23	75	15 56	70/69	17 00	67/71
17·9 Hook		18 34	78/82		19 12	78/80		18 16	78/81	17 59	70/72	19 12	67/72
										sig.stop			
23·5 BASINGSTOKE	28	23 45		29	24 36		37	23 16		30 19		24 44	
Estimated net time (mins)		23¾			24½			23¼		23¼		24¾	

TABLE 47
BASINGSTOKE TO SOUTHAMPTON

Detail	A			B		
Date	8 July 1967			29 June 1967		
Train (ex. Basingstoke)	4.5 a.m.			9.13 a.m.		
Locomotive no.	34095(R)			34087(R)		
Vehicles	7			12		
Tare load (tons)	177½			400½		
Gross load (tons)	195			425		
Driver (Nine Elms)	Porter			Hendicott		
Conditions	Damp			Dry; calm		
Recorder	DWW			A. Wild		
Mls.	Sch.	M. S.	Speed	Sch.	M. S.	Speed
0·0 BASINGSTOKE	0	0 00		0	0 00	
2·5 Worting Junction (*65)	7	4 49	52	5½	5 13	46
4·8 Wootton S.B.		7 06	63		7 52	53
8·5 Roundwood S.B.		10 12	78		10 54†	68
10·3 Micheldever		11 35	84		12 42	82
12·5 Weston S.B.		13 01	90		14 10	90
14·0 Wallers Ash S.B.		13 57	92/94		15 08	92/95
16·7 Winchester Junction	23½	15 47	78	21½	16 53	91
18·8 WINCHESTER CITY	26½	18 12			18 21	86
2·4 Shawford Junction		3 35			p.w.s.	39
3·1 Shawford		4 26	68/80		21 39	43/73
7·0 EASTLEIGH	11	9 12		29½	25 16	72
2·3 Swaythling		3 34	61/68		27 19	43
					sigs	
3·7 St Denys		4 46	64		30 52	30
					sigs	
4·6 Northam Junction (*15)	7½	6 00		35	32 52	15
					sigs	
5·7 SOUTHAMPTON	10½	8 11		38½	36 27	

† At Litchfield Tunnel

TABLE 48

BASINGSTOKE TO WINCHESTER CITY

Detail	A	B	C	D	E
Date	7 May 1967	7 Apr 1967	21 Aug 1964	11 Mar 1966	28 Apr 1964
Train (ex. Waterloo)	11.30 a.m.	8.35 a.m.	5.30 p.m.	5.30 p.m.	9.20 p.m.
Locomotive no.	34001(R)	35012(R)	35008(R)	35003(R)	35005(R)
Vehicles	8	10	11	11	11
Tare load (tons)	225½	315	370	373½	373
Gross load (tons)	240	330	395	390	395
Driver	Anderson (9E)	Parsons (9E)	—	Porter (9E)	Rabbetts (BM)
Conditions	Dry; calm	—	Fine; calm	—	Fine
Recorder	A. Wild	D. A. Foale	A. Wild	D. A. Foale	J. G. Webber

Mls.	Sch.	M. S.	Speed	Sch.	M. S.	Speed	Sch.	M. S.	Speed	Sch.	M. S.	Speed	Sch.	M. S.	Speed
0·0 BASINGSTOKE	0	0 00		0	0 00		0	0 00		0	0 00		0	0 00	
2·5 *Worting Jnc.* (*65)	5½	3 59	62	5½	4 50	52	5½	4 58	51	5½	4 52	52/60	5½	5 18	42
4·8 *Wootton S.B.*		6 02	68		7 06	65		7 23	56		7 14			8 13	53
6·2 *Steventon S.B.*		—	76		8 23 sigs	69/70		—			p.w.s.	16		—	
8·5 *Roundwood S.B.*		8 43†	74		11 28	25		10 21†	67		13 31	63		—	70
10·3 *Micheldever*		10 30	79		13 57	60		12 10	75		15 05	79		13 20	77
12·5 *Weston S.B.*		12 04	82		15 43	81		13 48	77		16 38	84		—	
14·0 *Wallers Ash S.B.*		13 11	81		16 47	88		14 56	72/75		17 42	88		15 51	91
16·7 *Winchester Jnc.*	22½	15 14	76	22½	18 35	94	21	17 03	73	21½	19 30	95	21	17 33	99/100 sigs
18·8 WINCHESTER CITY	25½	18 01		25½	21 00		24	19 29		25	21 49		24	20 15	
Estimated net time (mins)		18			18¾			19¼			18¾			19¾	

† At *Litchfield Tunnel*

TABLE 49

WINCHESTER CITY TO SOUTHAMPTON CENTRAL

Detail	A		B		C		D		E		F		G	
Date	1 Aug 1965		8 July 1967		5 July 1957		1 Apr 1964		30 Apr 1964		26 June 1963		30 May 1958	
Train (ex. Waterloo)	9.30 a.m.		8.30 a.m.		3.20 p.m.		6.30 p.m.		6.30 p.m.		6.30 p.m.		4.34 p.m.	
Locomotive no.	35003(R)		35023(R)		34007		35030(R)		35029(R)		34028(R)		34107	
Vehicles	11		11		11		12		12		12		13	
Tare load (tons)	363		368½		371		400		402		404		441	
Gross load (tons)	390		405		415		430		430		435		470	
Driver	Cummings		Hughes		Hill (BM)		Rabbetts (BM)		Rabbetts (BM)		—		Pragnell (9E)	
Conditions	—		Fine		—		—		Fine		Fine		—	
Recorder	D. W. Tuck		DWW		P. G. Barlow		J. G. Webber		J. G. Webber		M. H. Cobb		A. J. Baker	
Mls.	M. S.	Speed	M. S.	Speed	M. S.	Speed	M. S.	Speed	M. S.	Speed	M. S.	Speed	M. S.	Speed
0·0 WINCHESTER CITY	0 00		0 00		0 00		0 00		0 00		0 00		0 00	
			p.w.s.											
2·4 *Shawford Junction*	3 50	62	4 03		—		—		—		—		—	
3·1 Shawford	4 30	70/77	4 54	60	5 12	64	4 47	65	4 42	67	4 58		5 08	62
6·2 *Allbrook S.B.*	6 53	75		73	—	73	—	85	—	91	—	73	—	81
7·0 EASTLEIGH	7 32	75/77	8 11	75	8 28	60	7 46	80	7 38	84	8 12	69	8 33	70
9·2 Swaythling	9 26	71	10 00	74	10 37	68	9 27		9 16		—		10 35	73
10·7 St Denys	10 41	64	11 15	66	—		—		sigs		11 29		11 52	
11·6 *Northam Junction* (*15)	11 58		12 33		13 10	20	12 10	17	12 15		13 06		13 05	25
12·7 SOUTHAMPTON CENTRAL	14 50		15 22		15 42		15 13		15 25		16 03		16 19	
Estimated net time (mins)	14¼		15		15¾		15¼		15¼		16		16¼	

TABLE 50

WINCHESTER TO SOUTHAMPTON

Detail	A	B	C
Date	29 Jan 1967	4 Feb 1967	9 Oct 1965
Train (ex. Waterloo)	11.30 a.m.	8.35 a.m.	8.35 a.m.
Locomotive no.	34044(R)	35023(R)	34071(R)
Vehicles	7	8	9
Tare weight (tons)	233	266	293
Gross weight (tons)	245	290	320
Driver (Nine Elms)	Dente	—	Porter
Conditions	Fine	Fine	—
Recorder	D. W. Tuck	P. M. Widgery	P. M. Widgery

Mls.	M. S.	Speed	M. S.	Speed	M. S.	Speed
0·0 WINCHESTER	0 00		0 00		0 00	
1·2 St Cross S.B.	2 15	63	2 22	60	—	
2·4 Shawford Junction	3 11	75	—	73	—	
3·1 Shawford	3 47	80	3 57	80	4 05	78
5·2 Milepost 71¾	5 17	88	sigs	84	—	83
6·2 Allbrook S.B.	5 54	71	6 09	75/76	6 18	80
7·0 Eastleigh	6 36	73	6 51	75	6 56	78/80
8·4 SOUTHAMPTON AIRPORT	8 16		8 42		—	
9·2 Swaythling					8 38	78
10·7 St Denys					9 43	75
11·6 Northam Junction (*15)					10 55	25
12·7 SOUTHAMPTON CENTRAL					13 49	

TABLE 51

SOUTHAMPTON CENTRAL TO BOURNEMOUTH CENTRAL

Detail	A	B	C	D	E
Date	3 Aug 1959	21 Aug 1961	4 June 1965	17 June 1967	12 Feb 1959
Train (ex. Waterloo)	2.30 p.m.	2.30 p.m.	8.30 a.m.	8.30 a.m.	10.30 a.m.
Locomotive no.	34040	34029(R)	35005(R)	35007(R)	35030(R)
Vehicles	11	11	11	11	11
Tare load (tons)	369	363	368	373	368
Gross load (tons)	375	375	392	400	390
Driver	Sprague(BM)	—	—	Evans (9E)	Letchford (9E)
Conditions	Cloudy	Cloudy	—	Fine; lt. SW wind	Fine
Recorder	M. Hedges	M. Hedges	M. D. Barrett	A. Wild	G. F. Bloxam

Mls.	Sch.†	M. S.	Speed	M. S.	Speed	M. S.	Speed	M. S.	Speed	M. S.	Speed
0·0 SOUTHAMPTON CENTRAL	0	0 00		0 00		0 00		0 00		0 00	
				sigs. v. sev.				sigs. sli.			
2·6 Redbridge (*40)		5 08	52	6 42		4 50	43	5 10	53	5 29	45
6·2 Lyndhurst Road		8 48	59	10 46	55	8 38	60	8 51	63	9 21	61/69
8·8 Beaulieu Rd.(*75)		11 13	66/73	13 17	62/76	11 04	65/76	11 11	71/77	11 40	65/75
								sigs.			

Table 51—Southampton Central to Bournemouth Central (contd)

Detail		A	B	C	D	E
Mls.	Sch	M. S. Speed	M. S. Speed	M. S. Speed	M. S. Speed	M. S. Speed
13·6 Brockenhurst(*60)		15 18	17 12	14 58 66	15 05 67	15 23 82
14·5 *Lymington Jnc.*						
(*60)	17	16 13	18 00	15 57 61/60	15 57 66/63	16 05
16·3 Sway		18 06 56	19 42 62	17 42 63	17 35 70/74	17 30 70/75
19·3 New Milton		20 45 70	22 09 74	20 08 75	19 58 78/75	19 45 80/79
21·8 Hinton Admiral		22 53 77	24 07 83/86	22 05 80/86	21 53 86/88	21 38 86
25·1 Christchurch (*60)		25 32 71	26 27 82	24 32 68	24 21 65/67	23 55 85
27·1 Pokesdown		27 16 60	28 07 58	26 16 62	26 13 59	25 25 70
27·6 Boscombe		27 50 56	28 44 sigs	26 50 61	26 53 41 sig. stop	25 55 sig. stop
28·8 BOURNEMOUTH CENTRAL	34	29 43	31 01	29 07	32 44	29 53
Estimated net time (mins)		29¾	29¼	29	28½	28

† Not applicable to detail D

TABLE 52
SOUTHAMPTON CENTRAL TO BOURNEMOUTH CENTRAL

Detail		A		B	C	D
Date		26 June 1965		15 July 1957	4 Aug 1959	30 Apr 1964
Train (ex. Waterloo)		6.30 p.m.		6.30 p.m.	10.30 a.m.	6.30 p.m.
Locomotive no.		35028(R)		35021	35014(R)	35029(R)
Vehicles		12		12	12	12
Tare load (tons)		400		401	400	402
Gross load (tons)		425		425	430	430
Driver		Hutton (BM)		Horne	—	Rabbetts (BM)
Conditions		Fine; calm		Cloudy	Sunny	Fine
Recorder		A. Wild		M. Hedges	M. Hedges	J. G. Webber
Mls.	Sch.	M. S. Speed	Sch.	M. S. Speed	M. S. Speed	M. S. Speed
0·0 SOUTHAMPTON CENTRAL	0	0 00	0	0 00	0 00	0 00
2·6 Redbridge(*40)		5 08 51		5 00 51	5 56 50	5 04 48
6·2 Lyndhurst Road		9 00 57		8 53 56	9 48 56	9 11 60/61
						p.w.s.
8·8 Beaulieu Road (*75)		11 31 63/71		11 26 66/62	12 18 64/76	14 12 36
13·6 Brockenhurst(*60)		15 37 67		15 27	16 13	18 54 72
14·5 Lymington Junction (*60)	18½	16 31 63/58	17	16 17	17 03	19 45 68
16·3 Sway		18 18 61		18 01 61	18 48 60	21 22 71
19·3 New Milton		20 59 70/66		20 39 71	21 25 70	23 44 78
				sigs		
21·8 Hinton Admiral		23 06 78		23 28 20	23 28	25 34 91/93
				sigs. sev.		
25·1 Christchurch (*60)		25 45 69		29 05 17	25 56 83	27 57
27·1 Pokesdown		27 36 56		35 21	27 35	29 56 60
				sig. stop	sigs. v. sev.	
27·6 Boscombe		28 15 49		38 50	29 45	30 32 56
				sigs	sigs. v. sev.	
28·8 BOURNEMOUTH CENTRAL	38½	30 28	34	42 03	35 40	32 37
Estimated net time (mins)		30½		30	30	28¾

TABLE 53

SOUTHAMPTON CENTRAL TO BOURNEMOUTH CENTRAL

Detail		A	B	C	D	E
Date		4 Mar 1967	3 Dec 1966	13 June 1965	5 June 1965	29 Oct 1966
Train (ex. Waterloo)		12.30 p.m.	12.30 p.m.	12.30 p.m.	12.30 p.m.	12.30 p.m.
Locomotive no.		35007(R)	35013(R)	35017(R)	34101(R)	35007(R)
Vehicles		11	11	11	11	11
Tare load (tons)		421	419½	427½	428	438
Gross load (tons)		440	440	450	450	460
Driver		Elston (BM)	Hooper (9E)	Alexander (BM)	Cutting (9E)	—
Conditions		SW wind; fine	NW wind; fine	—	Fine; calm	Drizzle
Recorder		A. Wild	A. Wild	P. Widgery	A. Wild	D. J. Maidment

Mls.	Sch.†	M. S. Speed	M. S. Speed	M. S. Speed	M. S. Speed	M. S. Speed
0·0 SOUTHAMPTON CENTRAL	0	0 00	0 00 sigs 14	0 00	0 00	0 00
2·6 Redbridge (*40)		5 10 52	6 42 47	5 08 52 sigs 10	6 00 51	5 42 52
6·2 Lyndhurst Road		8 50 62	10 34 59	11 21 51/64	9 58 56	9 52 63
8·8 Beaulieu Road (*75)		11 16 67/74	13 02 67/74	13 58 62/76	12 32 64/69 sigs.sli	12 35 61/77
13·6 Brockenhurst (*60)		15 31 58	17 00 64	17 56 67	16 48 58	16 43 60
14·5 *Lymington Junction* (*60)	17	16 31 56/54	17 54 63/57	18 48 63/59	17 49 56/52	17 46
16·3 Sway		18 26 60/66	19 56 p.w.s.	20 32 62/72	19 47 59	20 32 57/15 sigs
19·3 New Milton		21 05 71/69	23 10 63	23 09 66/58	22 31 69/65	25 30 50/15 sigs
21·8 Hinton Admiral		23 09 79/80	25 17 77/81	25 36 60/69	24 40 78/80	29 04 65/79
25·1 Christchurch (*60)		25 51 57	27 57 61/64	28 41 66/69	27 20 65/66	31 55 64 sigs
27·1 Pokesdown		28 02 50	29 55 54	30 29 55	29 15 56	34 17 30
27·6 Boscombe		28 43 47 sig.stop	30 33 53 sig.stop	31 05 55	29 55 39 sig.stop	sigs
28·8 BOURNEMOUTH CENTRAL	34	33 51	37 21	33 17	35 53	38 00
Estimated net time (mins)		30¾	30	31	31¾	31

† Applicable to runs C and D

TABLE 54
SOUTHAMPTON CENTRAL TO BOURNEMOUTH CENTRAL

Detail		A		B		C		D		E	
Date		13 Mar 1964		4 July 1958		8 June 1965		10 June 1965		19 May 1948	
Train (ex. Waterloo)		*Pines Express*		6.30 p.m.		*Pines Express*		12.30 p.m.		12.30 p.m.	
Locomotive no.		34041		35022(R)		34044(R)		35011(R)		21C11	
Vehicles		12		13		13		12		12	
Tare load (tons)		420		434		459		468½		484	
Gross load (tons)		440		475		485		480		510	
Driver		—		—		Adams (BM)		Cooper (BM)		—	
Conditions		S. wind; dry		—		—		Fine		—	
Recorder		A. Wild		P. G. Barlow		A. Trickett		DWW		A. J. Baker	

Mls	Sch.	M. S.	Speed	M. S.	Speed	M. S.	Speed	M. S.	Speed	Sch.	M. S.	Speed
0·0 SOUTHAMPTON CENTRAL	0	0 00		0 00		0 00		0 00		0	0 00	
2·6 Redbridge(*40)	5†	5 38	43	—		5 45		6 19			5 47	
6·2 Lyndhurst Road		9 58	53/58	9 42	53/60	9 48		10 12	60		10 09	49/56
8·8 Beaulieu Road(*75)		12 36	63/71	12 28	57	12 27	—/76	12 47	70/76		13 05	50/61
13·6 Brockenhurst(*60)		16 48	61	16 40	73	16 30		16 54	66		17 40	57
14·5 *Lymington Jnc.*(*60)	17(18†)	17 48	54/50	—		17 31		17 55	60/56	19	18 36	—/51
16·3 Sway		19 50	58	19 19	58	19 28		19 48	58/68		20 35	—/64
19·3 New Milton		22 42	64	21 57	70/67	22 10	72	22 32	66		23 30	61
21·8 Hinton Admiral		24 56	74/76	24 00	78	24 11	—/82	24 37	80/82		25 44	75
25·1 Christchurch(*60)		27 45	60	26 37	62	26 55		27 16	74		28 24	70
27·1 Pokesdown		29 53		—		28 54		29 02	60		30 14	44
27·6 Boscombe		30 36		29 23	51	29 34		—			31 00	49
		sig. stop										
28·8 BOURNEMOUTH CENTRAL	34(36†)	39 12		32 01		31 38		31 24		36	33 02	
Estimated net time (mins)		32½		32		31¾		31½			33	

† Schedule for *Pines Express*

TABLE 55
SOUTHAMPTON CENTRAL TO BOURNEMOUTH CENTRAL

Detail		A		B		C		D		E	
Date		8 Nov 1957		11 Apr 1958		17 Oct 1958		17 May 1957		11 June 1965	
Train (ex. Waterloo)		7.30 p.m.		7.30 p.m.		7.30 p.m.		7.30 p.m.		3.30 p.m.	
Locomotive no.		34108		34105		35022(R)		34106		34024(R)	
Vehicles		6		6		7		8		13	
Tare load (tons)		204		204		236		269		423	
Gross load (tons)		215		210		250		280		450	
Driver		—		Rabbetts (BM)		—		Varney (BM)		Cooper (BM)	
Conditions		Fine		Fine		—		Damp		Dry	
Recorder		M. Hedges		M. Hedges		M. Hedges		M. Hedges		DWW	

Mls.	Sch.	M. S.	Speed	M. S.	Speed	M. S.	Speed	M. S.	Speed	M. S.	Speed
0·0 SOUTHAMPTON CENTRAL	0	0 00		0 00		0 00		0 00		0 00	
0·9 Millbrook		2 35		2 23	39	2 20		2 40	35	—	
2·6 Redbridge(*40)	5	4 46	50/47	4 37	52	4 33	53	5 00	49	6 14	
3·3 Totton		5 35	47	5 21	52	5 20	45	5 49	52	—	

Table 55—Southampton Central to Bournemouth Central (contd)

Detail	Sch.	A M. S. Speed	B M. S. Speed	C M. S. Speed	D M. S. Speed	E M. S. Speed
Mls.						
4·8 *Ashurst*		7 12 54	6 48 58	6 51 57	7 13 59	—
6·2 Lyndhurst Road		8 48 58	8 19 62	8 23 60	8 43 62	10 20 54
8·8 Beaulieu Road (*75)		11 19 67/74	10 35 72/77	10 44 71/80	11 02 71/77	13 07 60/66
13·6 BROCKENHURST	19	15 51	14 57	15 26	15 38	18 14
0·9 *Lymington Junction*	2½	2 30 35	3 06 30	2 53 33	2 50 32	5 05
2·8 Sway		4 55 40	5 47 36/51	5 25 38	5 32 35	8 29 48
5·7 New Milton		7 40 71/68	8 33 70/69	8 14 70/68	8 25 67/66	11 45 60
8·3 Hinton Admiral		9 42 72/83	10 33 74/85	10 16 72/80	10 29 80	14 06 72/78
				p.w.s.		
11·5 Christchurch (*60)		12 14 71	13 04 60	14 00 11	13 05 72	16 54 66
13·5 Pokesdown		14 11 51	15 13 44	19 00	14 50 56	18 48 62
14·0 Boscombe		14 53 51	16 02 46	20 00 40	15 32 50	—
15·2 BOURNEMOUTH CENTRAL	21	16 48	18 25	22 46	17 40	21 28

TABLE 56
SOUTHAMPTON CENTRAL TO BROCKENHURST

Detail	A	B	C	D	E
Date	19 Mar 1966	5 Feb 1967	1 May 1966	6 May 1966	10 May 1967
Train (ex. Waterloo)	2.45 a.m.	11.30 a.m.	11.30 a.m.	8.35 a.m.	†
Locomotive no.	34077(R)	35013(R)	34002	34036(R)	34104(R)
Vehicles	8	7	8	10	12
Tare load (tons)	187	230	266	328½	406½
Gross load (tons)	200	240	280	350	435
Driver	Hendicott (9E)	—	Enticknapp (9E)	Porter (9E)	Rowe (BM)
Conditions	Dry	—	—	—	Hot; dry
Recorder	A. Wild	M. D. Barrett	P. Widgery	P. Widgery	C. Bennett

Mls.	Sch.	A M. S. Speed	B M. S. Speed	Sch. C M. S. Speed	Sch. D M. S. Speed	Sch. E M. S. Speed
0·0 SOUTHAMPTON CENTRAL	0	0 00	0 00	0 0 00	0 0 00	0 0 00
0·9 Millbrook		2 13 46	— 35	2 37 37	2 29 38	2 23 38
2·6 Redbridge (*40)		4 10 58/50 sigs	4 23 51	5 4 49 56	5 4 43 53/51	5 4 35
3·3 Totton		5 16 22	5 09 54	5 30 59/63	5 27 54/61	5 14 57
4·8 *Ashurst*		8 00 48/59	6 42 61	—	—	6 38 59
6·2 Lyndhurst Road		9 36 63	8 08 68/77	8 17 62/68	8 22 63/72	8 10 59/62
8·8 Beaulieu Road		11 52 72	10 11 75/83	10 41 64	10 40 70/78	10 51 56/59
10·3 *Woodfidley* (*75)		13 11 77	11 16 77 sigs	12 06 72/68	11 58 75/80 sigs	12 33 p.w.s.
13·6 BROCKENHURST	20½	16 17	14 49	20½ 15 18	21½ 14 55	20 17 59
Estimated net time (mins)		14½	14½	15½	14¾	15½

† 8.30 a.m. ex. Newcastle

TABLE 57

SOUTHAMPTON CENTRAL TO BOURNEMOUTH CENTRAL

Detail	A	B	C	D	E
Date	8 July 1967	11 Dec 1965	7 Feb 1958	31 May 1954	11 June 1965
Train (ex. Waterloo)	2.45 a.m.	2.45 a.m.	5.30 p.m.	5.30 p.m.	5.30 p.m.
Locomotive no.	34095(R)	34098(R)	34064	34039	35008(R)
Vehicles	5	6	11	11	11
Tare load (tons)	148	186	362	369	368
Gross load (tons)	160	200	375	380	380
Driver	Porter (9E)	Hooper (9E)	—	Bailey	—
Conditions	Damp	NW wind	—	Dry	Dry
Recorder	M. D. Barrett	A. Wild	M. Hedges	M. Hedges	DWW

	A Sch.	A M. S.	A Speed	B M. S.	B Speed	C Sch.	C M. S.	C Speed	D Sch.	D M. S.	D Speed	E M. S.	E Speed
0·0 SOUTHAMPTON CENTRAL	0	0 00		0 00		0	0 00		0	0 00		0 00	
0·9 Millbrook		2 08	41	2 26	40		2 40	35		3 00		—	
2·6 Redbridge (*40)		4 22	52	4 30	56/46	5	5 03	48/46		5 23	49	5 00	57
3·3 Totton		4 53	58	5 17	51		5 49	50		6 05	53	—	
4·8 Ashurst		6 14	65/68	6 48	57		7 26	54		7 32	61	—	64
6·2 Lyndhurst Road		7 36	64	8 19	62		9 10	52		9 03	61	8 20	72
8·8 Beaulieu Road (*75)		9 43 sigs	80/83	10 36	72/80		11 52	62/71		11 30	67/74	10 36	80/84
13·6 BROCKENHURST	20½	13 58		15 02		19	16 34		19	16 12		14 48	
0·9 Lymington Junction		2 30	38	2 31	42/48	2½	2 54	32	2½	3 46	32	3 13	34
2·8 Sway		4 50	57/67	4 41	—/78		5 53	32/62		6 37	33/64	5 50	58/72
5·7 NEW MILTON	10½	7 57		7 58		11	9 21		10	9 54		8 53	
2·5 Hinton Admiral		3 18	81/93	3 50	65/69		4 10	—/69		4 16	65/69	4 50	66/74
5·8 CHRISTCHURCH	9	6 10		7 18		8	7 32		8	7 48		8 02	
2·0 Pokesdown		3 51 sig. stop	42	3 44 sig. stop	43/50	5	5 30		5	4 57		5 17	
3·7 BOURNEMOUTH CENTRAL	7½	10 55		9 00									

TABLE 58
BOURNEMOUTH CENTRAL TO SOUTHAMPTON CENTRAL

Detail	A			B			C			D			E		
Date	23 Aug 1964			19 Apr 1967			27 May 1958			19 July 1952			2 May 1954		
Train (ex. Bournemouth Central)	3.35 p.m.			6.33 p.m.			2.40 p.m.			8.40 a.m.			4.45 p.m.		
Locomotive no.	34006			34023			34044			34094			34109		
Vehicles	10			11			12			13			12		
Tare load (tons)	331½			358			401			430½			477		
Gross load (tons)	350			380			430			475			495		
Conditions	—			Clear			—			—			Rain; windy		
Driver	Kiff (Nine Elms)			Allen (Wey)			—			—			—		
Recorder	D. A. Foale			D. A. Foale			A. J. Baker			M. Hedges			M. Hedges		
Mls.	Sch.	M. S.	Speed	Sch.	M. S.	Speed	Sch.	M. S.	Speed	Sch.	M. S.	Speed	Sch.	M. S.	Speed
0·0 BOURNEMOUTH CENTRAL	0	0 00		0	0 00		0	0 00		0	0 00		0	0 00	
1·2 Boscombe		3 43	40		3 24	38		3 56			3 53	36		4 06	33
1·7 Pokesdown		4 25	51/70		4 11	52/65		4 44	—/71		4 43	45		5 00	44
3·7 Christchurch (*60)		6 17	64		6 05	64		6 42	64		6 38	69		7 02	66
7·0 Hinton Admiral		9 16	68/65		9 05	66/62		9 52	67/58		9 45	62/55		10 08	62/56
9·5 New Milton		11 29	71/75		11 24	67/74		12 21	65/62		12 19	60		12 45	
12·5 Sway		13 55	73		13 54	73		15 00	70		15 03	66		15 38	66
					sigs										
14·3 Lymington Junction (*60)	18	15 28	70		15 31	50		16 32	67		16 43	62	18	17 15	63
15·2 BROCKENHURST (*60)		16 13	71/76		16 37	58/67		17 17	77/80		17 33	70		18 08	70
20·0 Beaulieu Road (*75)		20 04	71/77		20 48	69/73		21 10	74/67		21 23	67/75		22 08	75/65
22·6 Lyndhurst Road		22 13	69		23 04	66/69		23 27	75/70		23 40	71		24 35	68
											sigs. v. sev.			pws	
25·5 Totton		25 04	47		25 42	59		25 53			27 48			28 18	
26·2 Redbridge (*40)	29	26 02	41/55		26 21	55/58		26 59	40/53	28	29 03	35/46		29 55	
		sigs						sigs							
28·8 SOUTHAMPTON CENTRAL	34	30 45		35	30 02		32	31 47		33	33 43		34	35 05	
Estimated net time (mins)	30			29½			31			31¼			32		

TABLE 59

BOURNEMOUTH CENTRAL TO SOUTHAMPTON CENTRAL

Detail	A	B	C	D	E
Date	31 Dec 1966	24 Jan 1965	2 May 1965	4 Aug 1963	19 May 1948
Train—Bournemouth Belle					
Locomotive no.	34047(R)	34041	35011(R)	35016(R)	21C11
Vehicles	11	11	11	12	12
Tare load (tons)	419	427½	428	474	484
Gross load (tons)	435	445	445	495	505
Conditions	Dry	Wet; calm	Dry; calm	Drizzle	—
Driver	Porter (Nine Elms)	Pope (Nine Elms)	Hendicott (Nine Elms)	Pope (Nine Elms)	—
Recorder	DWW	A. Wild	A. Wild	D. J. Coomber	A. J. Baker

Mls.	M. S.	Speed	Sch.	M. S.	Speed	Sch.	M. S.	Speed	Sch.	M. S.	Speed	Sch.	M. S.	Speed
0·0 BOURNEMOUTH CENTRAL	0 00		0	0 00		0	0 00		0	0 00		0	0 00	
1·2 Boscombe	—			3 13	40		3 23	42		—			3 43	
1·7 Pokesdown	4 06	46		3 58	54/65		4 08	53/64		4 04	55		4 30	—/66
3·7 Christchurch (*60)	6 02	63		5 54	63/61		6 03	62/61		5 59	65		6 29	58/62
7·0 Hinton Admiral	9 06	64/60		8 57	63/58		9 14	63/58		9 07	60/55		9 39	58/55
9·5 New Milton	11 34	61		11 34	61/69		11 40	62/71		11 41	58		12 17	65/61
12·5 Sway	14 11	69		14 15	67/62		14 15	70		14 20	71		15 08	68/64
14·3 Lymington Jnc. (*60)	15 48	64		15 54	65		15 48 sigs	60 50		15 51	73	16½	16 46	
15·2 BROCKENHURST (*60)	16 40	68/75		16 48	70/72		16 55	56/75		16 38	75/80		17 34	74/68
20·0 Beaulieu Road (*75)	20 37	72		20 54	66/69		21 06	70/77		20 18	75/82		21 32	73/65
22·6 Lyndhurst Road	22 54	65/70		23 12 sigs	65 17		23 18	66		22 21	78/83		23 48	72/69
25·5 Totton	—	52		27 30			25 56			24 39	60		26 12	75
26·2 Redbridge (*40)	26 22 sigs	50/53		28 17 sigs	48/51		26 44	44/54		25 20	57		26 53	48/53
28·8 SOUTHAMPTON CENTRAL	31 15		32	33 28		32	30 43		32	29 05		31	30 59	
Estimated net time (mins)	30½			31			30½			29			31	

TABLE 60

BOURNEMOUTH CENTRAL TO SOUTHAMPTON CENTRAL

Detail	A	B	C
Date	3 June 1967	12 June 1965	12 June 1965
Train (ex. Bournemouth Central)	6.33 p.m.	2.40 p.m.	10.10 a.m.
Locomotive no.	34001(R)	73092	34044(R)
Vehicles	13	12	13
Tare load (tons)	398	407	460
Gross load (tons)	430	445	485
Conditions	—	Dry	Dry, lt. wind
Driver	Davis (Wey)	Dean (B'mth)	Bevis (B'mth)
Recorder	P. M. Widgery	DWW	A. Wild

Mls.	Sch.	M. S.	Speed	Sch.	M. S.	Speed	Sch.	M. S.	Speed
0·0 BOURNEMOUTH CENTRAL	0	0 00		0	0 00		0	0 00	
1·2 Boscombe		3 38	36		—			3 51	31
1·7 Pokesdown		4 27	46		4 16	41		4 47	45
3·7 Christchurch (*60)		6 30	63/59		6 13	66/60		6 53	63/60
7·0 Hinton Admiral		9 45	60/55		9 30	62/48		10 04	61/54
9·5 New Milton		12 20	60/65		12 25	51/58		12 43	56/65
12·5 Sway		15 07	67/62		15 32	60/58		15 32	66/64
14·3 Lymington Junction (*60)		16 47	65		17 20	62		17 12	65
15·2 BROCKENHURST (*60)		17 38	68/72		18 18	66/72		18 04	67/71
20·0 Beaulieu Road (*75)		21 44	65/71		22 32	65		22 13	64/70
22·6 Lyndhurst Road		24 02	62/65		25 00	67/70		24 34	68
25·5 Totton		26 59	56		—			27 18	48
26·2 Redbridge (*40)		27 35	52/56		28 38	48	27	28 04	48/51
					sigs			sigs	
28·8 SOUTHAMPTON CENTRAL	37	31 32		32	32 50		32	32 44	

Estimated net time (mins)	31½	32½	32¼

TABLE 61
BOURNEMOUTH CENTRAL TO BROCKENHURST

Detail	A	B	C	D
Date	17 Dec 1966	30 Dec 1966	3 Aug 1964	7 July 1957
Train (ex. Bournemouth Cen.)	10.31 a.m.	6.56 a.m.	9.32 a.m.	6.57 p.m.
Locomotive no.	34040(R)	34044(R)	35011(R)	35017(R)
Vehicles	9	10	11	13
Tare load (tons)	300	337	370	427
Gross load (tons)	320	355	395	470
Conditions	Damp, lt. wind	—	Fine, calm	—
Driver	Budd (Nine Elms)	Skinner (Nine Elms)	—	—
Recorder	A. Wild	P.M. Widgery	A. Wild	P. G. Barlow

Mls.	M. S. Speed	Sch.	M. S. Speed	Sch.	M. S. Speed	Sch.	M. S. Speed
0·0 BOURNEMOUTH CENTRAL	0 00	0	0 00	0	0 00	0	0 00
1·2 Boscombe	3 29 37		4 13 31		3 39 34		3 14 35
1·7 Pokesdown	4 17 51/64		5 06 45/59		4 31 48/62		—
3·7 Christchurch (*60)	6 15 63/59		7 12 56/57		6 34 60/58		6 11 62/54
7·0 Hinton Admiral	9 26 61/56		10 37 61/56		9 44 63/58		9 43 55/50
9·5 New Milton	11 59 62/67		13 08 61/67		12 06 62/69		12 31 56
12·5 Sway	14 40 70/68		15 55 69/61		14 39 70/71		15 20 66/62
14·3 Lymington Junction (*60)	16 15 69		17 31 64	18	16 11 61	19½	17 00 64
15·2 BROCKENHURST	17 43	22	19 13	20	17 35	21	18 42

TABLE 62
BROCKENHURST TO SOUTHAMPTON CENTRAL

Detail	A	B	C	D	E
Date	19 Aug 1966	6 July 1966	30 July 1965	31 Aug 1965	7 July 1957
Train (ex. Brockenhurst)	1.37 p.m.	1.37 p.m.	7.25 a.m.	7.25 a.m.	7.22 p.m.
Locomotive no.	34015	34006	34064	35011(R)	35017(R)
Vehicles	7	9	11	12	13
Tare load (tons)	228 (est.)	257	371	407	427
Gross load (tons)	245	270	380	440	470
Conditions	Very warm	—	—	—	—
Driver	Porter (Nine Elms)	Porter (Nine Elms)	—	Sutton (Nine Elms)	—
Recorder	M. Fraser	P. M. Widgery	K. T. Budden	P. M. Widgery	P. G. Barlow

Mls.	Sch.	M. S. Speed	M. S. Speed	M. S. Speed	M. S. Speed	Sch.	M. S. Speed
0·0 BROCKENHURST	0	0 00	0 00	0 00	0 00	0	0 00
3·3 Woodfidley (*75)		4 10 69/78	4 14 65/72	5 15 54/60	5 17 56/60		4 55 46/61
4·7 Beaulieu Road		5 32 76/86	5 39 69/78	6 56 56/67	7 02 57/67		6 36 56/66
7·4 Lyndhurst Road		7 36 60/69	7 49 59/65	9 27 66	9 30 62/68		9 09 65
8·8 Ashurst		8 53 66	sigs 44	— 69	—		sigs 64

Table 62—Brockenhurst to Southampton Central (contd)

Detail	A			B		C		D		E		
Mls.	Sch.	M. S.	Speed	M. S.	Speed	M. S.	Speed	M. S.	Speed	Sch.	M. S.	Speed
		sigs										
10·3 Totton		11 03	33	10 56	50	12 17	47	12 19	45		—	
10·9 Redbridge (*40)	15½	12 02	44	11 41	50/53	—	—/53	13 12	43	14	12 45	45/50
12·7 Millbrook		14 23	47	13 48		15 06	47	15 17	48		sigs	15
				sigs.								
13·6 SOUTHAMPTON CENTRAL	20½	16 15		16 00		16 50		17 15		19	19 14	
Estimated net time (mins)		15¼		15		16¾		17¼			17	

TABLE 63

BOURNEMOUTH CENTRAL TO SOUTHAMPTON CENTRAL

Detail	A	B	C	D	E
Date	28 July 1951	1 Nov 1965	23 Dec 1963	12 June 1965	18 Aug 1951
Train (ex. Bournemouth Central)	7.50 p.m.	7.23 a.m.	7.30 a.m.	11.0 a.m.	7.30 a.m.
Locomotive no.	34012	35028(R)	35020(R)	34087(R)	34078
Vehicles	9	10	11	11	12
Tare load (tons)	267	330	370	370	393
Gross load (tons)	290	350	400	400	430
Conditions	Fine	Dry	Freezing	Fine	—
Driver	—	Porter (Nine Elms)	—	—	—
Recorder	M. Hedges	C. Bennett	A. Wild	DWW	M. Hedges

Mls.	Sch.	M. S.	Speed	Sch.	M. S.	Speed	M. S.	Speed	M. S.	Speed	Sch.	M. S.	Speed
0·0 BOURNEMOUTH CENTRAL	0	0 00		0	0 00		0 00						
1·2 BOSCOMBE	3	3 15	35		3 22	38	3 56	27					
0·5 POKESDOWN	2	1 45		6½	4 26		2 15						
2·0 CHRISTCHURCH	4	3 25	57	4½	3 36		4 28	39	0 00		0	0 00	
3·3 Hinton Admiral		5 43	47/44		5 45	53	7 02	40/37	5 59	52/48		6 28	44/41
5·8 NEW MILTON	10	8 58	53	10½	8 58		10 57	44	9 28		10	10 04	49
3·0 Sway		4 30	62		4 51	51	5 12	50	5 00	54/56		5 05	54
4·8 Lymington Junction (*60)	7½	6 05	70	8	6 29	68	7 12	58	7 00		7½	6 55	60
5·7 BROCKENHURST	9	7 43		9½	8 23		8 51		8 44		9	8 45	
4·7 Beaulieu Road (*75)		5 51	70/66		6 44	20			6 31	60/68		6 09	64/62
7·4 Lyndhurst Road		8 01	75		10 23	65/74			9 01	68		8 29	70/75
10·3 Totton		10 38			12 59	51			—			11 14	
10·9 Redbridge (*40)	14	11 28	46	15½	13 48	48			12 30			12 00	44/55
12·7 Millbrook		13 28	57		15 51				—			14 04	
13·6 SOUTHAMPTON CENTRAL	19	15 39		20½	17 47				16 49		19	16 09	

TABLE 64
SOUTHAMPTON CENTRAL TO WATERLOO

Detail	A			B			C		D			E	
Date	12 Dec 1966			24 Sept 1965			28 Feb 1967		11 Sept 1957			30 Apr 1964	
Train (ex. Southampton Central)	7.13 p.m.			3.14 p.m.			3.14 p.m.		1.15 p.m.			1.15 p.m.	
Locomotive no.	35028			34001(R)			34044(R)		34041			35029(R)	
Vehicles	11			11			11		12			12	
Tare load (tons)	348			374			370		379			395	
Gross load (tons)	365			400			400		400			425	
Driver	Porter (9E)			Prior (9E)			Hooper (9E)		Hancock(BM)			Rabbetts (BM)	
Recorder	A. Wild			A. Wild			D. J. Maidment		J. G. Webber			J. G. Webber	
Mls.	Sch.	M. S.	Speed	Sch.	M. S.	Speed	M. S.	Speed	Sch.	M. S.	Speed	M. S.	Speed
0·0 SOUTHAMPTON CENTRAL	0	0 00		0	0 00		0 00		0	0 00		0 00	
1·1 Northam Junction (*15)	3	4 14	23	4	3 34	23	3 27	10	3½	3 37	18	3 10	21
2·0 St Denys		5 55	39		5 29	40	5 25	44		—		—	
3·4 Swaythling		7 43	49		7 29	48	—			—		6 47	51
		sigs											
5·7 EASTLEIGH	11	12 58	14	11	10 01	58	9 51	57	10	10 20	40	9 15	60
		sigs											
9·5 Shawford		19 21	50		13 41	64	13 50	60		—		12 55	63
10·2 Shawford Junction		20 21	54		—		—			—		—	
							p.w.s.						
12·7 Winchester City		22 45	59		16 33	67	22 22	15		17 24	61	15 50	65
14·7 Winchester Junction		24 53	60		18 28	66	26 12	48		—		17 51	63/61
17·5 Wallers Ash S.B.		—			20 53	67	—			—		20 30	63/61
18·9 Weston S.B.		28 59	62		22 12	67	27 53	58		—		—	
21·1 Micheldever		31 06	61		24 03	69	29 56	67		25 57	60	23 58	63
23·0 Roundwood S.B.		32 58	63/72		—		—	68		27 52	56	25 44	64
Litchfield Tunnel		—			26 05	65/70							
26·7 Wootton S.B.		36 17	60/58		29 01	61	34 47	75/78		—	73	28 50	78
29·0 Worting Junction (*60)	40½	38 32	64	40½	31 32	20	36 37	65	37	33 12	58	30 56	56
					p.w.s.								
31·4 BASINGSTOKE		40 34	85/95		36 24	49	38 58	72		35 13	77/81	33 29	71/53
												sigs	
37·1 Hook		44 14	91/95		41 16	74	43 10	84		39 33	73	38 31	74
39·4 Winchfield		45 46	98/103		43 09	77	44 46	89		41 24	80	40 17	83/90
42·8 Fleet		47 47	100/94		45 46	75	46 57	95		43 52	80/83	42 35	88
46·0 Farnborough		50 06	78		49 28	33	49 07	94		46 15	80	44 47	88
48·2 Milepost 31		51 57	68		52 36	50/63	—	86		47 58	76	46 23	84
51·3 Brookwood		54 51	73		56 01	19	52 42	84		50 11	85	48 26	94/76
		p.w.s.					sigs						
54·9 WOKING	70½†	59 43	32	69†	60 50	64	56 08	60	58†	52 50	80	50 47	80
57·6 West Byfleet		61 56	81/87		63 03	76/81	—	75		54 48	83	53 02	85
							p.w.s.						
60·1 Weybridge		63 46	86/84		65 00	77	61 35	15		—	81	54 54	79
62·2 Walton-on-Thames		65 10	90/94		66 34	80	66 05	58		58 20	75/80	56 36	68
65·9 Hampton Court Junction		67 37	90		69 28	72	69 38	72		61 17	76	59 37	77
					sigs								
67·2 Surbiton		68 30	86		71 18	30	70 41	74		62 27	63	60 41	70
							sigs			p.w.s.			
69·5 New Malden		70 10	78		74 45	50	72 53	50		65 39	18	62 35	73
72·0 Wimbledon		72 15	63/66		77 34	54/58	75 50	61		69 25	52	64 51	64
75·4 Clapham Junction (*40)	89½	75 53	45/58	88	81 26	34/50	79 28	40	77	72 46	41	68 14	37
		p.w.s.										sigs	
79·2 WATERLOO	96½	83 15		95	87 57		86 08		84	79 45		75 25	
Estimated net time (mins)	74½			75½			72½		77½			73¾	

† At *Woking Junction*

TABLE 65
SOUTHAMPTON CENTRAL TO WATERLOO

Detail	A	B	C	D	E
Date	9 Sept 1959	27 May 1958	9 Apr 1965	3 Apr 1966	15 Sept 1947
Train (ex. Southampton Central)	3.15 p.m.	3.15 p.m.	3.15 p.m.	5.15 p.m.	5.20 p.m.
Locomotive no.	34039(R)	34044	34050(R)	34005(R)	21C14
Vehicles	12	12	12	11	12
Tare load (tons)	400	401	397	428	480
Gross load (tons)	425	430	440	460	505
Driver	Purchase (BM)	—	—	Hendicott (9E)	—
Conditions	Dry	—	Dry	Dry: N. wind	—
Recorder	J. G. Webber	A. J. Baker	R. L. Sewell	M. C. Thompson	J. G. Webber

Mls.	Sch.	M. S.	Speed	M. S.	Speed	M. S.	Speed	M. S.	Speed	Sch.	M. S.	Speed
0·0 SOUTHAMPTON CENTRAL	0	0 00		0 00		0 00		0 00 p.w.s.		0	0 00	
1·1 Northam Junction (*15)	3½	3 15		3 40	22	3 25		3 55	15		3 10	21
2·0 St Denys		—		5 31	43	4 18	40	5 45	40		—	
3·4 Swaythling		7 18	50	7 30	51	7 13	47	7 33	50		6 48	48
5·7 EASTLEIGH	10	9 50	60	10 06	60	9 47	56	10 01 sigs	58	9	9 18	60
9·5 Shawford		—		14 04	58	13 44	58	13 56	63		13 17 sigs	58/47
12·7 Winchester City		16 54	60	17 21	56	17 00	57	16 54	64/63		16 38	51
14·7 Winchester Junction		19 05	58	19 41		19 14	59	18 54	64/65		19 04	52
17·5 Wallers Ash S.B.		—	61	22 42	55	—	55	21 27	62		22 10	53
18·9 Weston S.B.		—		—		—		22 50	63		23 48	54
21·1 Micheldever		25 21	62	26 53		26 02	55	24 49 p.w.s.	61		26 15	55
23·0 Roundwood S.B.		27 11	61	29 00	53	28 04	53	28 08	20		28 37	53/73
26·7 Wootton S.B.		—	73	32 41	73	31 53	66	34 46	56/60		—	
29·0 Worting Junction (*60)	37	32 32	56	34 36	70	34 01	60	37 03	59	36½	34 15	54
31·4 BASINGSTOKE		34 51	71/76	36 37	79/82	36 20	69/72	39 28	68/77		36 33	70/81
37·1 Hook		39 23	73	40 50	76	41 03	69/72	44 00	75/78		40 59	80
39·4 Winchfield		41 17	75/80	42 42		43 07	67	46 48	34		42 48	84
42·8 Fleet		43 50	78/80	45 12	83	45 56	75	50 37	67		45 10	81
46·0 Farnborough		46 24	73	47 40	80	48 37	72	53 22	75		47 33	84
48·2 Milepost 31		48 13	73	49 30	72	50 33	71	—	75/80		49 22	72
51·3 Brookwood		50 32 sig. stop	80/84	51 52 sigs	83	52 54	82	57 25	75/73		51 43 sigs	78/41
54·9 WOKING	58†	55 49		54 56	52	55 38	75	60 19	76	59	55 08	59
57·6 West Byfleet		59 12	62	57 07	84	57 42	78/82	62 19	80		57 38	67
60·1 Weybridge		—		59 08		59 41	77	64 11	78		59 50	71/62
62·2 Walton-on-Thames		63 18	70/75	60 46	71/77	61 22	74	65 45	78		61 43 sigs	64/73
65·9 Hampton Court Junction	67	66 20	75	63 47		64 32 sigs	67	68 40	73		65 03	63
67·2 Surbiton		67 30	67	64 51	72	65 53 sigs	55	69 43 p.w.s.	71		66 24	50
69·5 New Malden		69 33	65	66 43		68 20 sigs	56	72 28	25		69 08	41
72·0 Wimbledon		71 51	67	68 54	73	70 55	63	76 02	57/61		72 14	52/57
75·4 Clapham Junction (*40)	77	75 14	39	72 22 sigs	37	74 26 sigs	30	79 37	41/53	78	76 12	39
79·2 WATERLOO	84	81 35		80 25		83 15		86 20		85	83 50	
Estimated net time (mins)		77½		79		79		76½			77½	

† At *Woking Junction*

TABLE 66
SOUTHAMPTON CENTRAL TO WATERLOO

Detail	A	B	C	D	E
Date	26 July 1960	8 July 1963	4 Aug 1963	4 Apr 1965	2 May 1965
Train (ex. Southampton Central)	3.15 p.m.	1.15 p.m.	5.16 p.m.	5.16 p.m.	5.16 p.m.
Locomotive no.	35027(R)	35021(R)	35016(R)	35012(R)	35011(R)
Vehicles	12	12	12	11	11
Tare load (tons)	399	385	474	429	428
Gross load (tons)	425	410	495	445	445
Driver	Sprague (BM)	Rabbetts (BM)	Pope (9E)	Hooper (9E)	Hendicott (9E)
Conditions	Dry	Fair	Drizzle	Dry: lt. W. wind	Dry: calm
Recorder	DWW	J. G. Webber	D. J. Coomber	A. Wild	A. Wild

Mls.	Sch.	M. S. Speed (A)	Sch.	M. S. Speed (B)	M. S. Speed (C)	M. S. Speed (D)	M. S. Speed (E)
0·0 SOUTHAMPTON CENTRAL	0	0 00	0	0 00	0 00	0 00	0 00
1·1 Northam Junction (*15)	3½	4 05	3½	3 13 21	3 00	3 33 15	3 16 23
2·0 St. Denys		5 44 46			4 33 45	5 26 44	5 03 36
							p.w.s. 21
3·4 Swaythling		7 29 50		6 57 50	6 18 50	7 13 50	8 38
5·7 EASTLEIGH	10	9 48 63	10	9 24 61	8 46 60	9 36 61	12 07 45
9·5 Shawford		13 12 68		—	12 26 64	13 11 64	16 26 60
10·2 Shawford Junction		13 53 68		—	—	— /66	— /64
12·7 Winchester City		15 58 70		16 04 63	15 23 64	16 01 69	19 26 66
14·7 Winchester Junction		17 50 68		18 05 63	17 23 65	17 53 71	21 19 68
17·5 Wallers Ash S.B.		20 10 67		20 40 64	19 55 64	20 11 72	23 43 68
18·9 Weston S.B.		21 35 66		—	—	21 24 72	25 00 68
21·1 Micheldever		23 30 64		24 09 62/59	23 19 63	23 08 75	26 51 71
23·0 Roundwood S.B.		25 14 64		26 00 61	25 06 64	—	—
Litchfield Tunnel		—		—	—	24 59 76	28 46 72
26·7 Wootton S.B.		28 36 58		— 73/77	28 23 70	27 27 82/10 sigs	31 20 78
29·0 Worting Junction (*60)	34	30 57 57/45 sigs	37	31 16 60	30 20 64	31 03 28	33 19 60
31·4 BASINGSTOKE		34 09		33 25 76/92	32 30 78	34 14 62	35 31 72
37·1 Hook		38 44 81		37 27 84/87	36 43 81	38 32 86	39 40 83/85
39·4 Winchfield		40 27 84		39 07 84/90	38 29 82	40 09 89/92	41 22 83/85
42·8 Fleet		42 55 80		41 24 88	40 53 86	42 22 90/91	43 44 82
46·0 Farnborough		45 27 69		43 42 84/86	43 14 83	44 34 89	46 09 83
48·2 Milepost 31		47 17 74		45 18 81/85	44 53 79	46 07 86	47 51 77
51·3 Brookwood		49 32 82/35 sigs		47 46 66/49 sigs	47 12 76/70	48 07 93	50 01 85
54·9 WOKING	54†	53 22 58	58†	51 03† 58	50 10 79	50 36 84/88	52 46 78
57·6 West Byfleet		55 42 76/82		53 46 75/81	52 11 82	52 31 83	54 41 85
60·1 Weybridge		57 36 81		55 42 79/77	54 05 83/79	54 20 81	56 31 81
62·2 Walton-on-Thames		59 05 83		57 15 81	55 39 82	55 48 83/84	58 22 82
65·9 Hampton Court Junction	63½	61 54 76		60 07 74	58 27 79	58 28 83	60 50 77
67·2 Surbiton		63 02 67		61 12 75/70	59 26 77	59 24 85	61 51 75
69·5 New Malden		65 05 58		63 07 73	61 12 78	61 03 80/67	63 43 66
72·0 Wimbledon		67 45 57		65 21 67	63 13 68	63 24 69	66 05 60
75·4 Clapham Junction (*40)	73	71 30 sigs	77	68 51 41	66 40 sigs 20	66 48 40 (2) 15 sigs	69 47 40 sigs 26
79·2 WATERLOO	80	78 37	84	75 36	73 33	74 17	76 47
Estimated net time (mins)		74¾		73	73	70½	73

† At Woking Junction

TABLE 67
WINCHESTER CITY TO WATERLOO

Detail	A	B	C	D
Date	2 July 1967	25 Mar 1967	16 July 1957	30 Dec 1966
Train (ex. Winchester City)	8.38 p.m.	8.49 a.m.	8.47 a.m.	8.08 a.m.
Locomotive no.	34037(R)	35028(R)	34065	34044(R)
Vehicles	9	9	10	10
Tare load (tons)	300	303	337	337
Gross load (tons)	330	325	355	352
Driver	Myles (ELH)	Payne (Nine Elms)	—	Skinner (9E)
Conditions	Dry; SW wind	—	—	—
Recorder	M. D. Barrett	D. W. Tuck	M. Hedges	P. M. Widgery

Mls.	M. S.	Speed	M. S.	Speed	Sch.	M. S.	Speed	M. S.	Speed
0·0 WINCHESTER CITY	0 00		0 00		0	0 00		0 00	
2·1 Winchester Junction	4 54	37	4 21	49	5½	5 06	32	4 19	46
	p.w.s.								
4·8 Wallers Ash S.B.	9 20	50	7 18	59		9 05	48	7 25	58
6·3 Weston S.B.	10 57	58	8 45	61		10 51	51	8 51	63
8·5 Micheldever	13 07	66/65	10 48	63		13 18	52	10 47	69
10·4 Roundwood S.B.	14 56†	68	12 35	64		15 35	46	12 24	71/72
						sigs. sev			
14·1 Wootton S.B.	17 53	75/65	15 55	64		21 08	10	15 33	63/58
			p.w.s.	31					
16·3 Worting Junction (*60)	19 52	66	18 29	36	23	25 55	47	17 47	61
	p.w.s.							sigs	38
18·8 BASINGSTOKE	22 17	67	21 29	64		28 29	67	20 49	47
24·4 Hook	26 28	86	25 44	86		32 58	76/73	26 14	71
26·8 Winchfield	28 11	89	27 20	90/96		34 49	76	28 10	77/80
30·1 Fleet	30 20	94	29 28	94		37 19	82	30 43	75/77
33·4 Farnborough	32 39	76	31 44	77		39 46	80	33 19	74/75
	p.w.s.	62							
35·6 Milepost 31	34 43	63	33 30	76/79		—	81	35 09	70/72
								sigs	
38·6 Brookwood	37 09	83/77	35 51	73		43 39	83	37 44	68
			sigs					sigs	
42·3 WOKING	39 58	82/79	40 57	28	46‡	46 10	89	40 42	66/35
44·9 West Byfleet	41 51	82/84	45 12	50		47 56	90/93	44 08	57
			p.w.s.					sigs	47
47·5 Weybridge	43 40	80	50 15	26		49 39	90	46 53	51
								sigs	47
49·5 Walton-on-Thames	45 18	86	52 59	57		51 03	85	49 14	51
52·2 Esher	47 09	76	55 25	70		52 55	86	52 00	62
53·3 Hampton Court Junction	48 05	71	56 20	69		53 40		53 00	62
						sigs. sev.			
54·6 Surbiton	49 13	72	57 32	66		55 50		54 17	58
56·8 New Malden	51 06	66	59 29	68		59 58		56 35	58
								p.w.s.	12
59·4 Wimbledon	53 30	58	61 51	62		62 29	65	61 54	36
61·0 Earlsfield	55 15	63	63 27	64		64 02	67	64 10	51
			sigs						
62·7 Clapham Junction (*40)	57 01	40/56	65 52	32	65	65 40	39	66 25	39
65·3 Vauxhall	3 sig. stops		sigs			69 05		70 08	
								sig stop	
66·6 WATERLOO	74 55		74 09		72	73 07		77 12	
Estimated net time (mins)	62		62			65½		64¾	

† At Milepost 56   ‡ At Woking Junction

TABLE 68
WINCHESTER CITY TO WATERLOO

Detail		A	B	C	D	E
Date		27 Dec 1963	22 May 1965	24 Aug 1955	12 Feb 1954	21 Aug 1953
Train—*The Royal Wessex*						
Locomotive no.		34001(R)	35026(R)	35030	35012	34107
Vehicles		12	12	12	13	13
Tare load (tons)		397	400	401	441½	442
Gross load (tons)		420	430	425	460	465
Driver		—	Saunders (Nine Elms)	—	—	Hancock
Conditions		Frosty: fog	Fine	Dry	Dull	—
Recorder		A. Wild	M. Smith	M. Hedges	M. Hedges	M. Hedges

Mls.		Sch.	M. S. Speed	M. S. Speed	M. S. Speed	M. S. Speed	M. S. Speed
0·0	WINCHESTER CITY	0	0 00	0 00	0 00	0 00	0 00
2·1	*Winchester Junction*	5½	4 50 38	4 40 46	5 02 38	5 05 40	5 13
4·8	*Wallers Ash S.B.*		8 25 48	7 50 55	8 52 46	8 33 49	9 08 45
6·3	*Weston S.B.*		10 10 51	—	10 46 48	10 08 50	11 03
8·5	Micheldever		12 33 53	11 37 60	13 21 49	12 45 55	13 46 47
10·4	*Roundwood S.B.*		14 58† 56	13 30 57	15 39 49	— 54	— 50
14·1	*Wootton S.B.*		18 03 63	16 52 73	19 35 61	— 69	19 55 62
16·3	*Worting Junction* (*60)	23	20 14 60	18 55 62	21 48 62/60 p.w.s.	20 41 49	22 12 51
18·8	BASINGSTOKE		22 19 73/84	21 03 81/86	24 43 20	23 13 66	24 40 65
24·4	Hook		26 20 81	25 04 84	31 43 —/66	27 42 77	29 01 78/75
26·8	Winchfield		28 05 80	26 43 86	33 45 71	29 30 77	30 52 77
30·1	Fleet		30 27 82	28 59 92	36 23 79	32 00 80	33 25 76 p.w.s.
33·4	Farnborough		32 50 81	31 15 84	38 53 80/79	34 30 74/78	36 43 20
35·6	Milepost 31		34 30 78	32 50 84	40 35 80	— 72	40 20 45
38·6	Brookwood		36 50 75 p.w.s.	35 01 80 sigs	42 49 84	38 43 78/80 p.w.s. 15	43 23 69
42·3	WOKING	46‡	40 40 30	38 00 71	45 23 86	43 10 30	46 18 75
44·9	West Byfleet		44 11 59	40 06 79	47 12 88/90	46 43 61	48 25 76
47·5	Weybridge		46 28 70	42 07 75	48 58	49 03 69	50 28
49·5	Walton-on-Thames		48 09 71	43 46 75	50 23 80/83	50 55 63	52 09 68
52·2	Esher		50 12 78/76	46 00 70	52 48 86 p.w.s.	53 13	54 18 76
53·3	*Hampton Court Jnc.*	55½	51 03	47 00 66	56 21	sig. stop	55 08 sigs
54·6	Surbiton		52 08 67	48 11 66	58 08 46	59 47	56 23 58
56·8	New Malden		54 09 65	50 25 62 p.w.s. 30	60 43 57	62 40 55	58 38 62
59·4	Wimbledon		56 29 64	54 37	63 15 62	65 20 60	60 57
61.0	Earlsfield		58 11 58	57 10 53	64 46 66	67 02 62	62 33
62·7	Clapham Jnc. (*40)	65	60 02 53	59 07 40	66 36 40	69 05 32	64 15
65·3	Vauxhall		63 19 39 sigs	62 55 sigs	69 56 52 sigs	p.w.s.	—
66·6	WATERLOO	72	67 05	69 30	73 39	76 51	71 11
Estimated net time (mins)			63	63	64½	66	67½

† At Litchfield tunnel

‡ At *Woking Junction*

TABLE 69

SOUTHAMPTON CENTRAL TO WINCHESTER CITY

Detail	A	B	C	D	E
Date	7 Nov 1965	28 May 1967	23 Oct 1962	25 Oct 1961	18 Aug 1951
Train (ex. Southampton Central)	8.15 p.m.	6.40 p.m.	8.0 a.m.	8.25 a.m.	8.25 a.m.
Locomotive no.	35030(R)	35013(R)	35005(R)	35014(R)	34078
Vehicles	9	11	11	12	12
Tare load (tons)	300	366	370	399	393
Gross load (tons)	320	390	400	435	430
Driver	Hooper (Nine Elms)	Chapman	—	—	—
Conditions	Rain; strong wind	—	Fine	Fine	—
Recorder	R. M. Grainger	M. Smith	M. H. Cobb	M. H. Cobb	M. Hedges

Mls.		A Sch.	A M. S.	A Speed	B Sch.	B M. S.	B Speed	C Sch.	C M. S.	C Speed	D M. S.	D Speed	E M. S.	E Speed
0·0	SOUTHAMPTON CENTRAL	0	0 00		0	0 00		0	0 00		0 00		0 00	
1·1	*Northam Junction* (★15)	4	3 38	15	4	3 29	23 p.w.s.	3½	3 15		3 25		2 55	
2·0	St. Denys		5 40	39		5 43	36		4 55		5 10		5 05	
3·4	Swaythling		7 25	55		7 36	50		—	55	—	53	6 55	50
5·7	Eastleigh	10½	9 40	64	11	9 55	63	10	9 18	57	9 45	57	9 17	64
6·5	*Allbrook S.B.*		10 28	65		10 43	65		—					
9·5	Shawford		13 06	69/71		13 20	67/68		13 16	58	13 46	55	12 52	61
11·3	*St. Cross S.B.*		—			—			15 11	58	15 47	53	—	
12·7	WINCHESTER CITY	20½	16 32		22	16 49		20	16 45		17 38		16 46	
	Estimated net time (mins)		16¼			16¼			16¾		17¼		16¾	

TABLE 70

WINCHESTER CITY TO BASINGSTOKE

Detail	A	B	C	D	E
Date	28 June 1967	9 Mar 1967	30 June 1967	23 June 1967	6 July 1966
Train (ex. Winchester City)	9.17 p.m.	9.17 p.m.	9.17 p.m.	9.17 p.m.	2.33 p.m.
Locomotive no.	35003(R)	34087(R)	34021(R)	34060(R)	34006
Vehicles	5	6	7	7	9
Tare load (tons)	149	168 (est.)	187½	230	257
Gross load (tons)	160	180	205	250	270
Driver	Burridge (9E)	Anderson (9E)	Burridge (9E)	Hendicott (9E)	Porter (9E)
Conditions	Fine	—	—	Still after rain	—
Recorder	D. W. Tuck	A. C. Rawlings	R. M. Grainger	D. J. Maidment	P. M. Widgery

Mls.		A M. S.	A Speed	B M. S.	B Speed	C M. S.	C Speed	D M. S.	D Speed	E M. S.	E Speed
0·0	WINCHESTER CITY	0 00		0 00		0 00		0 00		0 00	
2·1	*Winchester Junction*	4 36	19 p.w.s.	3 35	56	4 49	19 p.w.s. 17	4 02	54 p.w.s. 15	3 54	54
4·8	*Wallers Ash S.B.*	10 07	54	6 04	72	9 46	55	—	65	6 39	58/60

Table 70—Winchester City to Basingstoke (contd)

Detail	A	B	C	D	E
Mls.	M. S. Speed	M. S. Speed	M. S. Speed	M. S. Speed	M. S. Speed
6·3 Weston S.B.	11 31 66	7 14 77	11 07 65	10 55 72	8 14 51
8·5 Micheldever	13 18 75	8 50 82	12 47 76	12 39 77	10 36 54
10·4 Roundwood S.B.	14 44 78/82	10 14 83/85	14 30† 80/82	— 79 sigs	12 43 51/61
14·1 Wootton S.B.	17 30 81	13 22 64	17 08 74	— 52	16 38 58 p.w.s.
16·3 Worting Junction (*60)	19 26 58 sig.stop	15 52 45 sig.stop	19 06 61 sig.stop	23 34 sig.stop	21 00 34
18·8 BASINGSTOKE	28 17	28 13	27 26	30 07	24 56
Estimated net time (mins)	19	19	18½	20	22

† At *Litchfield Tunnel*

TABLE 71

BASINGSTOKE TO WOKING

Detail	A	B	C	D	E
Date	28 June 1967	5 July 1967	30 June 1967	9 May 1966	14 June 1967
Train (ex. Basingstoke)	9.52 p.m.	7.32 p.m.	9.52 p.m.	7.32 p.m.	7.32 p.m.
Locomotive no.	35003(R)	35008(R)	34021(R)	34006	34102
Vehicles	5	6	7	7	7
Tare load (tons)	—	196	—	212	215
Gross load (tons)	170 (est.)	205	205 (est.)	220	230
Driver	Burridge (9E)	Aynsley (9E)	Burridge (9E)	Parsons (9E)	Gaffney (9E)
Conditions	Fine	Fine	Fine	—	Fine
Recorder	C. Foss	DWW	G. E. Tatton-Brown	R. M. Grainger	M. Smith
Mls.	M. S. Speed	M. S. Speed	M. S. Speed	M. S. Speed	M. S. Speed
0·0 BASINGSTOKE	0 00	0 00	0 00	0 00 p.w.s.	0 00
5·6 Hook	5 47 89	6 00 89	5 50 87	6 34 82	6 30 82
9·0 Winchfield	7 17 98/105	7 37 90/98	7 19 96	8 14 89	8 08 92
11·3 Fleet	9 14 100/102	9 41 98	9 23 95	10 24 94 sigs	10 13 98
14·6 Farnborough	11 18 77 p.w.s.	12 04 76 p.w.s.	11 34 76 p.w.s.	13 27 26 sigs	12 38 62 p.w.s.
16·8 Milepost 31	13 16 66/70 sigs	14 12 58	13 32 69	17 21 48	14 58 60
19·8 Brookwood	16 46 45 sigs	17 11 58 sigs 2	15 46 85	20 00 81/85 sig. stop	17 22 88
23·5 WOKING	22 08	23 07	19 17	28 03	21 37
Estimated net time (mins)	18½	19¼	18¾	19	19¼

TABLE 72
BASINGSTOKE TO WOKING

Detail	A	B	C	D
Date	18 May 1967	19 Feb 1966	17 Dec 1966	29 June 1967
Train (ex. Basingstoke)	7.32 p.m.	2.28 a.m.	7.17 p.m.	†
Locomotive no.	35023(R)	34101(R)	34104(R)	34087(R)
Vehicles	9	10	11	12
Tare load (tons)	295	301	357½	403
Gross load (tons)	315	320	385	430
Driver	Rickman	Porter (9E)	Porter (9E)	Shepherd (ELH)
Conditions	—	—	Drizzle	—
Recorder	DWW	R. M. Grainger	P. M. Widgery	M. Fraser

Mls.	M. S. Speed	M. S. Speed	M. S. Speed	M. S. Speed
0·0 BASINGSTOKE	0 00	0 00	0 00	0 00
5·6 Hook	6 27 75	6 02 82	6 38 75	6 52 75
9·0 Winchfield	8 13 88	7 42 90	8 28 81/87	8 42 82/89
11·3 Fleet	10 25 92	9 59 89	10 47 85/87	11 00 90/92
14·6 Farnborough	12 40 80	12 15 82	13 05 82	13 17 80 p.w.s.
16·8 *Milepost 31*	14 19 82	13 54 80	14 45 77	15 10
19·8 Brookwood	16 23 95 sigs	16 02 85 sigs	16 58 81	17 48 74
23·5 WOKING	21 42	21 16	20 36	21 32
Estimated net time (mins)	19½	19½	20½	21

† 4.0 p.m. ex. Weymouth Quay

TABLE 73
WOKING TO WATERLOO

Detail	A	B	C	D	E
Date	10 Dec 1966	4 July 1966	19 Dec 1966	21 Dec 1966	6 June 1967
Train	7.5 a.m. ex. Basingstoke	6.35 p.m. ex Salisbury	6.35 p.m. ex. Salisbury	6.35 p.m. ex. Salisbury	6.38 p.m. ex. Salisbury
Locomotive no.	34077(R)	34015	34100(R)	34057	34023
Vehicles	4	7	8	8	9
Tare load (tons)	132	204½	214 (est.)	223 (est.)	284
Gross load (tons)	145	215	225	235	300
Driver	Gale (Nine Elms)	—	Evans (Nine Elms)	Evans (Nine Elms)	Dente
Recorder	D. A. Foale	P. M. Widgery	A. C. Rawlings	A. C. Rawlings	M. Smith

Mls.	M. S. Speed	M. S. Speed	M. S. Speed	M. S. Speed	M. S. Speed
0·0 WOKING	0 00	0 00	0 00	0 00	0 00
2·7 West Byfleet	3 30 74	3 27 74†	3 45 68	3 57 69/56†	3 56 68
3·9 Byfleet	—	4 28 76	4 46 77	5 10 59	4 58 77
5·2 Weybridge	5 19 87	6 10 44†	5 46 81/78	6 22 66	5 58 81

Table 73—Woking to Waterloo (contd)

Detail	A		B		C		D		E	
Mls.	M. S.	Speed	M. S.	Speed	M. S.	Speed	M. S.	Speed	M. S.	Speed
7·3 Walton-on-Thames	6 41	92	8 26	65	7 17	83/86	8 05	76	7 27	87/91
9·9 Esher	8 34	86	10 40	78	9 11	81	10 05	84	9 17	85
11·0 *Hampton Court Junction*	9 19	78	11 28	77	10 00	76	10 54	76	10 03	79†
12·3 Surbiton	10 20	77	12 28	78/83	11 02	77	11 57	73	11 05	75
14·6 New Malden	12 04	80	14 16	69	12 45	79	13 45	79	12 50	79
17·1 Wimbledon	14 14	62	16 30	65/69	14 50	70	15 49	68	14 55	70
18·8 Earlsfield	15 51	60	17 58	67	16 15	72	17 15	70	16 22	69
20·4 Clapham Junction (*40)	18 10		19 50	37†	18 08	43/65	19 02	41/63	18 01	46
	pws									
23·0 Vauxhall	22 27		23 11	39/42	21 03	40	21 55	46	21 02	42
24·3 WATERLOO	25 49		26 02		24 00		24 28		24 10	
Estimated net time (mins)	25		24½		24		23¾		24	

† Signal check

TABLE 74
WOKING TO WATERLOO

Detail	A		B		C		D	
Date	4 Mar 1966		30 Dec 1966		17 Dec 1966		Dec 1957	
Train	11.6 a.m. ex.		7.5 a.m. ex.		5.11 p.m. ex.		6.45 a.m. ex.	
	B'mth Cen.		Basingstoke		B'mouth Cen.		Salisbury	
Locomotive no.	35027(R)		34019		34104(R)		35004	
Vehicles	10		11		11		11	
Tare load (tons)	340		358		357½		362	
Gross load (tons)	365		385		385		390	
Driver	—		—		Porter			
					(Nine Elms)			
Conditions	—		Drizzle		Drizzle		Fine	
Recorder	P. M. Widgery		D. J. Maidment		P. M. Widgery		D. J. Maidment	
Mls.	M. S.	Speed	M. S.	Speed	M. S.	Speed	M. S.	Speed
0·0 WOKING	0 00		0 00		0 00		0 00	
2·7 West Byfleet	3 52	69	4 13	73	4 12	68	3 59	70
3·9 Byfleet	4 53	77	—		5 15	74	—	
5·2 Weybridge	5 52	79	6 28	71	6 18	73	6 02	78
7·3 Walton-on-Thames	7 19	88/90	8 12	77	7 55	79/82	7 33	83
9·9 Esher	9 09	85/86	10 16	82	9 54	81	9 23	88
11·0 *Hampton Court Junction*	9 52	85	11 05	80	10 40	78	—	86
12·3 Surbiton	10 47	81	12 15	62†	11 41	77	11 00	78
14·6 New Malden	12 36	61	14 40	55†	13 37	64	12 36	75
17·1 Wimbledon	14 55	66/64	19 58	15	16 09	49†	14 46	73
				p.w.s.				
18·8 Earlsfield	16 26	66	22 06	59	18 21	36†	sigs	66
20·4 Clapham Junction (*40)	18 18	38/60	24 08	40/57	20 49	42/59	18 44	40
23·0 Vauxhall	21 33	†	27 28	5†	24 13	24†	23 41	10†
24·3 WATERLOO	24 56		32 05		27 11		26 56	
Estimated net time (mins)	24½		26½		25¾		24	

† Signal check

TABLE 75

BOURNEMOUTH CENTRAL TO DORCHESTER SOUTH

Detail		A	B	C	D	E
Date		14 Jan 1966	22 Jan 1966	24 Aug 1966	25 Aug 1966	20 Oct 1956
Train (ex. Waterloo)		10.30 a.m.	10.30 a.m.	10.30 a.m.	8.30 a.m.	12.35 p.m.
Locomotive no.		35026(R)	35022(R)	34098(R)	34066	34010
Vehicles		3	4	5	5	5
Tare load (tons)		100	135	165	168½	166
Gross load (tons)		107	142	175	175	175
Driver		Parker	Watts	Dore	Watts	—
		(Weymouth)	(Weymouth)	(B'mouth)	(Weymouth)	—
Conditions		Sunny;	Misty;	Fine;	Damp;	Cloudy
		NE wind	calm	calm	NE wind	
Recorder		A. Wild	A. Wild	A. Wild	A. Wild	M. Hedges
Mls.	Sch.	M. S. Speed	M. S. Speed	M. S. Speed	M. S. Speed	M. S. Speed
0·0 BOURNEMOUTH CENTRAL	0	0 00	0 00	0 00	0 00	0 00
2·2 Gas Works Junction (*50)		3 54 51/46	4 39 50/46	4 50 42	4 58 46	4 12 52
2·6 Branksome (*30)		4 30 37	5 12 39	5 28 34	5 33 38	4 43
3·9 Parkstone		6 17 53	6 45 63/67	7 07 59/64	7 06 61/64	6 06 63/65
5·8 POOLE	10	9 31	9 10	9 43	9 30	8 23
0·6 Holes Bay Junction (*30)		1 30 39/50	2 04 32	1 43 36/48	1 44 34/35	1 28 —/55
2·2 Hamworthy Junction (*35)		3 43 39	4 29 45	3 58 44	4 07 40	3 32 42
5·0 Holton Heath		6 27 74	7 09 74/76	6 49 66/68	7 10 65/67	6 22 71/73
7·1 WAREHAM	10	8 45	9 39	9 17	9 32	8 28
1·1 Worgret Junction (*45)	3	2 07 51/69	2 23 47	2 34 44	2 30 44	2 35 36
5·0 Wool		5 29 72/81	5 46 77/81	6 14 72	6 21 68/70	6 13 74/72
9·4 Moreton		8 57 75/67	9 10 80	9 58 70/73	10 13 70	10 20 32†
11·1 Woodsford		10 20 75/83	10 24 81/82	11 21 72/77	11 36 73/80	— 64/71
15·0 DORCHESTER SOUTH	18	14 06	14 14	15 03	15 13	16 14

† Signals

TABLE 76

BOURNEMOUTH CENTRAL TO DORCHESTER SOUTH

Detail	A	B	C	D	E
Date	20 Feb 1965	18 June 1966	10 June 1967	17 Aug 1963	2 July 1967
Train	10.40 a.m.	8.30 a.m.	8.30 a.m.	12.35 p.m.	9.55 a.m.
	ex. B'mth	ex. W'loo	ex. W'loo	ex. W'loo	ex. W'loo
Locomotive no.	34024(R)	34002	35008(R)	34028(R)	35008(R)
Vehicles	7	10	11	11	11
Tare load (tons)	235	336	374	376	370½
Gross load (tons)	245	360	405	400	380
Recorder	A. Wild	D. A. Foale	D. J.	D. A. Foale	R. O.
			Coomber		Havery
Mls.	M. S. Speed	M. S. Speed	M. S. Speed	M. S. Speed	M. S. Speed
0·0 BOURNEMOUTH CENTRAL	0 00	0 00			
2·2 Gas Works Junction (*50)	5 19 45	5 21 45			
2·6 Branksome (*30)	5 53 40	6 01 35			
3·9 Parkstone	7 37 55/63	7 46 55/63			

Table 76—*Bournemouth Central to Dorchester South* (contd)

Detail	A			B			C			D			E		
Mls.	M.	S.	Speed	M.	S.	Speed	M.	S.	Speed	M.	S.	Speed	M.	S.	Speed
5·8 POOLE	10	08		10	30		0	00		0	00		0	00	
0·6 *Holes Bay Junction* (*30)	1	54	30	—		—/44	sig.stop			—		—/43	—		
2·2 *Hamworthy Junction* (*35)	4	30	42/39	4	46	37	8	03	36	4	33	41	4	42	40
5·0 Holton Heath	7	40	62	7	57	61	—		62	7	33	66	7	47	62
7·1 WAREHAM	10	05		10	39		13	43		10	27		9	43	65
										sigs					
1·1 *Worgret Junction* (*45)	3	00	35	3	40	30/61	3	04	38	3	12	38	11	02	50
5·0 Wool	7	20	62/67	8	30		7	20	61/65	7	07	69/58	14	51	65/63
9·4 Moreton	11	31	66	7	33	49/55	11	35	62/65	11	17	62/64	18	53	—/71
11·1 *Woodsford*	—		67	—		62/67	—		70	—		61/66	—		
15·0 DORCHESTER SOUTH	17	12		13	33		17	23		17	19		24	31	pass

TABLE 77

DORCHESTER SOUTH TO BOURNEMOUTH CENTRAL

Detail		A			B				C			D			E		
Date		21 Dec 1963			30 July 1966				18 Sept 1960			26 Aug 1961			6 Aug 1955		
Train (ex. Weymouth)		5.35 p.m.			5.35 p.m.				5.50 p.m.			11.25 a.m.			5.35 p m.		
Locomotive no.		35014(R)			34044(R)				35016(R)			35021(R)			34006		
Vehicles		4			9				9			10			11		
Tare load (tons)		130			296				302			331½			373		
Gross load (tons)		135			330				315			355			400		
Conditions		Freezing; NW wind			Fine				Fine			—			—		
Recorder		A. Wild			D. Mothersole				M. Hedges			D. A. Foale			M. Hedges		
Mls.	Sch.	M.	S.	Speed	M.	S.	Speed	Sch.	M.	S.	Speed	M.	S.	Speed	M.	S.	Speed
0·0 DORCHESTER SOUTH	0	0	00		0	00		0	0	00		0	00		0	00	
5·6 Moreton		5	58	81/75	6	10	75		6	39	70	6	46	70/78	7	02	55/82
10·0 WOOL	12	10	19		10	24			10	06	81	10	58		11	10	
3·9 *Worgret Junction* (*45)	5	5	03	60/45	5	34	54/46	15	13	24	43	7	09		5	51	58/—
												sigs					
5·0 WAREHAM	7½	7	07		7	29		18	15	37		9	34		7	33	
2·1 Holton Heath		3	18	65	3	40	65		3	55	62	4	07	57/64	4	10	52
4·9 Hamworthy Junction (*35)		6	33	38/47	6	39	40/48		7	05	31	7	08	40/53	7	22	56/40
6·5 *Holes Bay Junction* (*30)		8	56	36	—				9	25		—			9	15	51/—
7·1 POOLE	10	10	45		10	16		10	11	11		10	19		10	39	
1·9 Parkstone		3	16	45/42	3	50	41/34		4	21	37	4	04	37/33	3	15	45/52
3·1 Branksome (*30)		5	06	48/34	6	02	39		6	50	27	6	15	37	4	53	46
3·6 *Gas Works Junction* (*50)		5	41	50	—		—/53		7	39		6	50	44/53	5	23	45/62
5·8 BOURNEMOUTH CENTRAL	10	9	54		9	56		10	11	52		10	06		8	27	

Note: Last stage of detail E relates to No. 35027 with 4 vehicles (132/145 tons), recorded by D. A. Foale.

TABLE 78

WEYMOUTH TO POOLE

Detail		A	B	C
Date		16 May 1966	27 May 1967	7 June 1965
Train†				
Locomotive no.		34018(R)	34093(R)	35023(R)
Vehicles		11	12	12
Tare load (tons)		368½	400	401½
Gross load (tons)		395	425	430
Driver (Weymouth shed)		—	Allen	—
Conditions		—	Fine; SW wind	—
Recorder		DWW	A. Wild	DWW

Mls.	Sch.	M. S.	Speed	M. S.	Speed	M. S.	Speed
0·0 *WEYMOUTH S.B.*	0	0 00		0 00		0 00	
2·0 Upwey and Broadwey		5 31	32	4 59	32	5 48	30/22
4·0 *Bincombe S.B.*		9 59	24/51	9 32	24/44	10 34	23/48
6·3 *Dorchester Junction* (*15)	13	13 24		13 29	17	14 03	
6·6 DORCHESTER SOUTH							
(*20)		14 04		14 17	21	14 57	—/74
12·2 Moreton		20 24	70/85	21 09	64/70	21 28	69/72
16·6 Wool		24 00	78	25 12	67	25 24	70
20·5 *Worgret Junction* (*45)		27 32		28 53	48	29 02	45
21·6 WAREHAM		29 01	56	30 15	56	30 23	56
		p.w.s.					
23·7 Holton Heath		31 32	45	32 29	60/62	32 34	62/64
26·5 Hamworthy Jnc. (*35)		35 19	45/50	35 25	40/46	35 22	
28·1 *Holes Bay Junction* (*30)		37 24		37 45	37	—	
28·7 POOLE	36	38 47		39 32		39 03	
Banker Weymouth S.B. to							
Bincombe S.B.		73083		D6506		73020	

| Estimated net time (mins) | | 37¼ | | 39½ | | 39 | |

† Channel Islands Boat—4.23 p.m. ex. Weymouth Signal Box

TABLE 79

DORCHESTER JUNCTION TO POOLE

Date	8 Aug 1964		
Train	9.10 a.m. ex. Llanelly†		
Locomotive no.	34064 (fitted with Giesl ejector)		
Vehicles	10		
Tare load (tons)	318		
Gross load (tons)	345		
Conditions	Fine		
Recorder	D. J. Maidment		

Mls.		Sch.	M. S.	Speed
0·0	*DORCHESTER JUNCTION*	0	0 00	
0·3	DORCHESTER SOUTH (*20)		2 40	
4·2	*Woodsford*		7 22	71
5·9	Moreton		8 50	70/77
10·3	Wool		12 35	75/72
14·2	*Worgret Junction* (*45)		16 00	60
15·3	WAREHAM	17	17 04	65/69
17·4	Holton Heath		19 00	68
20·2	Hamworthy Junction (*35)		21 46	35/48
22·4	POOLE	28	25 14	

† 3.16 p.m. ex. Dorchester Junction

TABLE 80
HAVANT TO GUILDFORD

Detail	A			B		
Date	2 Apr 1966			21 Jan 1961		
Train	6.19 p.m. ex. Fareham			1.25 p.m. ex. Weymouth		
Locomotive no.	34032(R)			34039(R)		
Vehicles	9			11		
Tare load (tons)	301			373		
Gross load (tons)	310			400		
Conditions	Fine			Fair		
Recorder	DWW			S. C. Nash		
Mls.	Sch.	M. S.	Speed	Sch.	M. S.	Speed
0·0 HAVANT (*30)	0†	0 00†	22	0	0 00†	15
		sigs				
3·2 Rowlands Castle (*50)		6 27	42		5 25	50
5·3 Idsworth Crossing		9 05	52		7 47	55
8·2 Milepost 58¼ (*45)		—	38		11 44	37
8·5 Milepost 58 (*45)		13 17	42		—	
9·2 Buriton Siding		14 17	60/68		13 04	57
		sigs				
11·6 PETERSFIELD	15	17 24	22	18	15 34	62/70
					p.w.s.	
15·0 Liss		21 57	61		18 55	33
		sig. stop	(3 min.)			
19·6 Liphook		33 05	50/64		25 54	51/63
23·5 HASLEMERE	29	37 00	60/80	33	30 05	51
28·0 Witley		41 03	51		34 38	66/52
30·2 Milford		43 22	62		36 55	65
		sigs				
32·0 Godalming		46 12	30		38 50	55
		sigs				
32·9 Farncombe (*60)		48 32	25		39 58	50
34·4 Peasmarsh Junction		50 39	50		41 44	57
36·1 GUILDFORD	43†	54 04		48	44 52	
Estimated net time (mins)	42			43		

† Passing timing

TABLE 81
PETERBOROUGH NORTH TO GRANTHAM

Date	25 May 1948
Train	1.10 p.m. ex. King's Cross
Locomotive no.	35017
Vehicles	15
Tare load (tons)	503
Gross load (tons)	535
Driver (SR)	G. James
Recorder	R. N. Clements

Mls.	Sch.	M. S.	Speed
0·0 PETERBOROUGH NORTH	0	0 00	
3·1 *Werrington Junction* (*60)		6 40	55
8·5 Tallington		11 52	64
12·3 Essendine		15 29	61
15·9 Little Bytham		18 53	53/47
20·8 Corby Glen		25 00	55
23·8 *Stoke S.B.*		28 26	50/64
29·1 GRANTHAM	38	34 56	

TABLE 82
RETFORD TO GRANTHAM

Date	18 May 1948
Train	7.50 a.m. ex. Leeds
Locomotive no.	35019
Vehicles	14
Tare load (tons)	450
Gross load (tons)	485
Conditions	Fine; very warm
Recorder	J. F. Clay

Mls.	Sch.	M. S.	Speed
0·0 RETFORD	0	0 00	
6·7 Tuxford North		9 52	45
12·2 Carlton-on-Trent		14 28	—/75
18·5 Newark	22	20 36	58
23·2 Claypole		25 27	61
27·1 Hougham		29 23	53
28·9 Barkston	37	31 22	50/47
		sig. stop	
33·1 GRANTHAM	44	38 10	

TABLE 83

YORK–NEWCASTLE–YORK

Date		22 Oct. 1966				22 Oct 1966		
Train		11.43 a.m. ex. York				1. 45 p.m. ex. Newcastle		
Locomotive no.		35026(R)				35026(R)		
Vehicles		9				9		
Tare load (tons)		304				304		
Gross load (tons)		325				325		
Conditions		Fine				Fine		
Recorder		D. J. Maidment				D. J. Maidment		

	Mls.	Sch.	M. S.	Speed	Mls.	Sch.	M. S.	Speed
YORK	0·0	0	0 00		80·6	87	83 31	
Skelton Junction	1·6		4 53		79·0		79 04	
Beningborough	5·5		9 23	54/61	75·1		75 35	77
Tollerton	9·7		13 17	68/70	70·9		72 14	80
Pilmoor	16·1		18 46	71	64·5		67 30	84
Sessay	18·0		20 18	70	62·6		66 17	85
Thirsk	22·2	23	23 48	75/80	58·4	65	63 21	90
Otterington	26·5		27 05	77	54·1		60 28	82/85
NORTHALLERTON	29·9	30	29 40	79/84	50·6	58	57 49	80
Cowton	37·2		34 58	75	43·4		52 16	74/78
Eryholme Junction	38·9		36 21	72	41·7		50 41	71
Croft Spa	41·5		38 22	76	39·1		48 20	60/65
			sigs					
DARLINGTON	44·1	48	44 33	15†	36·5	46	45 14	25†
Aycliffe	49·6		53 25	*60/70	31·0		38 17	76/63*
Ferryhill	57·0	61	60 02	73	23·6	30	31 13	66/73
Relly Mill Junction	65·1		68 08	30*	15·5		23 05	*32/72
DURHAM	66·2	71	70 03	20*	14·4	19	20 33	25*
Chester-le-Street	71·9		76 38	70/74	8·7		13 01	56/46
Birtley	74·7		78 58	76	5·9		10 00	53
King Edward Bridge Junction	—		—	20*	1·0		4 08	38/58
Gateshead West	—		—		0·6		2 28	20*
NEWCASTLE	80·2	91	87 28		0·0	0	0 00	
Estimated net time (mins)		83½				80½		

† P. W. Slack

DETAIL FROM MILEPOST 25 TO 20

Milepost	Mins	Secs (from passing Darlington)	Speed
25	16	10	90
24	16	50	90
23	17	30	90
22	18	10	90
21	18	50	90
20	19	31	85

Recorded separately (from full log) by DWW

TABLE 84

CARNFORTH TO PENRITH

Date	13 June 1964
Train	10.56 a.m. ex. Carnforth
Locomotive no.	35012(R)
Vehicles	9
Tare load (tons)	302½
Gross load (tons)	320
Driver/Fireman (SR)	A. Hooker/K. Seabey(Nine Elms)
Conditions	Fine
Recorder	A. G. S. Davies

Mls.	Sch.	M. S.	Speed
0·0 CARNFORTH	0	0 00	
3·3 Milepost 9½		6 13	
7·3 Milnthorpe (*80)		10 15	66
9·2 Hincaster Junction		11 59	63
12·8 Oxenholme (*70)	15	15 25	60
15·7 Milepost 22 (*70)		18 24	55
17·7 Milepost 24		20 35	54
19·9 Grayrigg S.B. (*60)		23 06	52
21·7 Low Gill S.B.		24 49	70/78
23·7 Milepost 30 (*80)		26 22	80
25·9 TEBAY	30	27 58	82
27·7 Milepost 34		29 26	66
28·8 Scout Green		30 31	57
30·2 Shap Wells I.B.S.		33 04	sig. stop
		34 30	restart
		sigs	
30·7 Milepost 37 (*60)		38 00	
31·3 Shap Summit S.B.	39	41 35	
		p.w.s.	20
33·5 Shap (*80)		46 18	22/73
44·7 Penrith No. 1 S.B.	52	58 55	
44·9 Penrith No. 2 S.B.	53	60 10	

TABLE 85

CARLISLE TO HELLIFIELD

Date	13 June 1964
Train	7.25 p.m. ex. Carlisle
Locomotive no.	35012(R)
Vehicles	9
Tare load (tons)	302½
Gross load (tons)	320
Driver/Fireman (SR)	A. Hooker/K. Seabey (Nine Elms)
Conditions	Fine
Recorder	A. G. S. Davies

Mls.		Sch.	M. S.	Speed
0·0	CARLISLE	0	0 00	
0·9	*Petteril Bridge Junction*	3	3 19	
2·5	*Milepost 305½*		6 45	34
3·9	*Cumwhinton*		8 49	40
8·0	*Milepost 300*		13 35	57/72
10·0	Armathwaite		15 16	71/45
15·5	Lazonby	25	21 02	75/68
19·8	Langwathby		24 43	71/75
			sigs	
23·4	Culgaith		29 57	20
			p.w.s.	30
27·9	Long Marton		38 15	44
30·8	APPLEBY WEST		42 02	60
33·0	*Milepost 275*		44 11	73
36·1	*Griseburn S.B.*		47 07	57
38·4	*Crosby Garrett S.B.*		49 10	68
41·5	Kirby Stephen West		52 18	61/52
44·9	*Mallerstang S.B.*		55 49	57/53
48·4	*Aisgill S.B.*	75	59 48	50/65
51·4	Garsdale		62 42	57
54·7	Dent		65 47	68
59·6	*Blea Moor S.B.*	88	70 45	54
65·6	Horton-in-Ribblesdale		75 54	80/64
69·9	*Stainforth Sidings*		79 34	72
73·6	*Settle Junction*	101	83 10	sig. stop 1¾ m.
75·6	Long Preston		93 00	
76·8	HELLIFIELD	105	97 11	

TABLE 86
OXFORD TO READING WEST

Detail		A		B	
Date		9 June 1964		27 July 1963	
Train—*Pines Express*					
Locomotive no.		34103		35002(R)	
Vehicles		12		12	
Tare load (tons)		423		414	
Gross load (tons)		450		445	
Driver (Bournemouth)		G. Dean		—	
Fireman (Bournemouth)		T. Upshall		—	
Recorder		D. W. Tuck		C. M. Napper	

Mls.	Sch.	M. S.	Speed	M. S.	Speed
0·0 OXFORD	0	0 00		0 00	
2·4 *Kennington Junction*		5 20	43	—	
5·1 Radley		8 38	56	9 11	59
7·3 Culham		10 51	60/64	11 29	57
9·6 *Didcot North Junction*	15	13 30	48	13 55	54
10·7 *Didcot East Junction*	16½	14 38	40	14 59	41
15·0 Cholsey and Moulsford		19 30	64	20 02	60
18·8 Goring and Streatley		22 46	71	23 38	62
22·0 Pangbourne (*80)		25 24	76	26 39	64
24·9 Tilehurst (*80)		27 49	66	29 18	65
		sigs	13	sig. stop	
26·5 *Reading West Junction* (*20)	37	31 02	15	33 05	
(*15)		sig. stop			
27·1 READING WEST	39	35 35		35 08	
Estimated net time (mins)		32		33¾	

TABLE 87

SALISBURY TO WESTBURY

Detail	A	B
Date	15 Oct 1966	9 May 1964
Train (ex. Salisbury)	10.40 a.m.	3.0 p.m.
Locomotive no.	35023(R)	34038
Vehicles	8	12
Tare load (tons)	260	375
Gross load (tons)	270	400
Conditions	Fine	Fine
Recorder	DWW	A. G. S. Davies

Mls.	Sch.	M. S.	Speed	M. S.	Speed
0·0 SALISBURY	0	0 00		0 00	
2·5 Wilton North		5 14	58/68	6 12	50
5·0 Wishford (*35)		7 50		9 35	38
		p.w.s.	20		
9·8 Wylye		13 46	—/72	15 34	51/55
13·6 Codford		17 13	70	20 06	53
15·9 Heytesbury		19 13	72/74	22 49	57
19·7 Warminster (*35)		22 52	35/72	27 27	40/62
23·1 Dilton Marsh Halt	28	26 32	eased	—	
24·4 WESTBURY	33	29 35		35 22	

TABLE 88

CHIPPENHAM TO WOOTTON BASSETT

Date	9 May 1964
Train	3.39 p.m. ex. Westbury
Locomotive no.	34038
Vehicles	12
Tare load (tons)	375
Gross load (tons)	400
Conditions	Fine
Recorder	A. G. S. Davies

Mls.	M. S.	Speed
0·0 CHIPPENHAM	0 00 pass	60
4·1 Christian Malford Halt	3 49	73/69
6·3 Dauntsey	5 44	72
8·0 Milepost 86	7 15	60/57
11·1 Wootton Bassett	10 25 pass	60

TABLE 89
WESTBURY TO EXETER ST DAVID'S

Detail	A	B
Date	13 Nov 1966	15 Oct 1966
Train (Specials ex. Westbury)	2.10 p.m.	11.20 a.m.
Locomotive no.	34019	35026(R)
Vehicles	7	8
Tare load (tons)	236	260
Gross load (tons)	255	278
Driver (Salisbury, SR)	Parsons	Parsons
Recorder	S. C. Nash	S. C. Nash

Mls.	Sch.	M. S.	Speed	Sch.	M. S.	Speed
0·0 WESTBURY	0	0 00		0	0 00	
1·4 Fairwood Junction (*40)	3	4 34		3	3 58	
4·7 Clink Road Junction		9 38	40 (*50)	8	8 33	52 (*80)
5·8 Frome (*30)	9	11 32	30		avoiding line†	
6·8 Blatchbridge Junction	11	13 21	42 (*50)	12	10 34	64
11·0 Witham (*70)		17 55	56		14 24	63
12·8 Brewham S.B. (*70)		19 56	53		16 08	60
16·3 Bruton (*70)		23 26	64/68		19 14	72
19·8 Castle Cary (*60)	25	26 38	60	26	22 24	58
24·6 Keinton Mandeville (*80)		31 02	71		26 44	73
26·8 Charlton Mackerell (*80)		33 10	64/71		28 37	70/78
30·1 Somerton (*80)		36 05	65		31 16	68
35·4 Curry Rivell Junction (*80)		40 39	75		35 48	75
39·4 Athelney (*80)		44 03	78		39 00	
42·6 Cogload Junction (*80)		46 36	72		41 46	69
44·9 Creech Junction (*80)		48 38	69		43 44	72
47·3 TAUNTON (*80)	51	50 58	57	53	45 47	71/68
49·3 Norton Fitzwarren		53 08	61		47 33	69
		sig. stop (1½ min.)				
54·5 Wellington		62 04	20		52 13	65
		p.w.s.				
55·2 Milepost 171		63 46	29		52 54	65
56·2 Milepost 172		65 46	31		53 53	60
57·2 Milepost 173		67 39	33		54 55	57
		p.w.s.				
58·2 Whiteball S.B.	67	69 59	5	68	55 59	55/72
		p.w.s.				p.w.s.
61·5 Sampford Peverell		74 55	62/40		59 12	38
63·3 Tiverton Junction (*80)		77 11	50		61 27	50
					p.w.s.	
65·5 Cullumpton (*80)		79 33	64		65 14	29
71·0 Silverton (*65)		84 40	68		71 34	68
74·7 Stoke Canon (*80)		88 11	70		74 52	70
76·9 Cowley Bridge Junction (*50)	86	90 45		88	77 04	
					sig. stop (1¼ min.)	
78·1 EXETER ST DAVID'S	89	94 30		91	83 29	
Estimated net time (mins)		84			75	

† Distances via avoiding line at Frome 0·2 mls. less from Blatchbridge Junction

TABLE 90

EXETER ST DAVID'S TO WESTBURY

Detail	A			B		
Date	26 June 1966			20 Sept 1958		
Locomotive no.	35023(R)			35023(R)		
Vehicles	9			9		
Tare load (tons)	306½			318		
Gross load (tons)	330			334		
Recorder	M. B. Warburton			J. M. B. Edwards		
Mls.	Sch.	M. S.	Speed	Sch.	M. S.	Speed
0·0 EXETER ST DAVID'S	0	0 00		0	0 00	
1·2 Cowley Bridge Junction (*50)		3 43	41	3	3 36	28
3·8 Stoke Canon		6 29	54		6 40	47
7·1 Silverton (*65)		10 36	55		10 51	57
8·4 Hele and Bradninch		11 54	57		12 11	59
12·6 Cullompton		16 10	56		16 17	63
14·8 Tiverton Junction		20 56	10		18 33	59/63
		sig. stop (½ min.)				
16·6 Sampford Peverell		27 19			20 16	61
19·9 Whiteball S.B.		32 17	45		24 00	46/62
					p.w.s.	
23·6 Wellington (*80)		35 35	77/72		29 35	24
28·8 Norton Fitzwarren (*80)		39 45	69		35 27	71
30·8 TAUNTON (*80)	37	41 38	62	37	37 21	61
33·1 Creech Junction (*80)		43 43	72		39 41	64
35·5 Cogload Junction (*80)		45 36	71		—	
38·7 Athelney (*80)		48 18	71/72		44 46	66
42·7 Curry Rivell (*80)		51 40	71		48 32	60
48·0 Somerton (*80)		56 28	63		53 57	62/68
51·3 Charlton Mackerell (*80)		59 13	74		57 02	63
53·5 Keinton Mandeville		60 55	80/84		59 04	67/72
58·3 Castle Cary (*60)		64 48	60/64	65	63 46	53/58
61·8 Bruton (*65)		68 09	60/63		67 25	53
65·3 Brewham S.B. (*65)		71 43	56		71 34	48
67·1 Witham (*65)		73 18	73/78		73 25	68
71·3 Blatchbridge Junction (*50)		77 26	36/38	81	77 27	60
72·3 Frome (*30)	79	79 29	30	via avoiding line†		
73·4 Clink Road Junction (*50)		81 16	39/68	84	79 27	58
76·7 Fairwood Junction (*40)		85 00	41	88	83 02	64
78·1 WESTBURY	88	89 10		90	87 22	
Estimated net time (mins)	81			83¼		

† Distances via avoiding line at Frome 0·2 mls. less from Clink Road Junction

TABLE 91

PLYMOUTH NORTH ROAD TO EXETER ST DAVID'S

Date	20 Sept. 1958
Locomotive no.	35023(R)
Vehicles	9
Tare load (tons)	318
Gross load (tons)	334
Driver	Gidley (Exmouth Junction, SR)
Recorder	Wing Commander
	J. M. B. Edwards

Mls.		Sch.	M. S.	Speed
0·0	PLYMOUTH NORTH ROAD	0	0 00	
4·0	Plympton (*60)		7 08	56
5·5	Milepost 240½		—	14
6·5	Milepost 239½		—	20
6·7	Hemerdon siding (*50)	15	14 02	20
8·4	Cornwood (*50)		16 41	40
10·8	Ivybridge (*50)		20 07	43/48
13·0	Bittaford (*50)		22 53	47
14·1	Wrangton		24 16	47
16·3	Brent (*50)	28	26 30	66
18·6	Rattery		28 51	54
23·1	TOTNES	37	33 30	56/52
28·0	Dainton (*40)		40 25	18
30·8	Aller Junction (*45)	50	44 14	58/41
31·9	NEWTON ABBOT (*35)	52	45 57	26
37·1	Teignmouth (*45)		55 04	37/28
39·8	Dawlish (*40)		60 04	36
43·5	Starcross (*45)		64 51	56
47·3	Exminster (*60)		69 23	46
			sigs	
52·1	EXETER ST DAVID'S	82	77 20	

TABLE 92
PLYMPTON TO CORNWOOD

Detail				A			B	
Date				26 July 1957			24 July 1957	
Train				4.32 p.m. ex. Plymouth			4.32 p.m. ex. Plymouth	
				North Road			North Road	
Locomotive no.				34061			34023	
Vehicles				6			9	
Tare load (tons)				195			291	
Gross load (tons)				225			330	
Driver (Exmouth Junction, SR)				Gidley			Gidley	
Recorder				S. C. Nash			S. C. Nash	
Mls.	Sch.	M.	S.	Speed		M.	S.	Speed
0·0 PLYMPTON	0	0	00			0	00	
0·9 Milepost 241		2	45	26		2	36	28
1·9 Milepost 240		5	06	25		5	10	23
2·7 Hemerdon siding		7	00	25/38		7	12	22/38
4·3 CORNWOOD	11	9	42			9	55	

TABLE 93
TOTNES TO NEWTON ABBOT

Date			24 July 1957	
Train			4.32 p.m. ex. Plymouth	
			North Road	
Locomotive no.			34023	
Vehicles			9	
Tare load (tons)			291	
Gross load (tons)			330	
Driver (Exmouth Junction, SR)			Gidley	
Recorder			S. C. Nash	
Mls.	Sch.		M. S.	Speed
0·0 TOTNES	0		0 00	
			p.w.s.	
1·8 Milepost 221			3 49	50
2·8 Milepost 220			4 58	52
3·8 Milepost 219			6 11	48
4·8 Dainton (*40)	9		8 13	22/60
7·6 Aller Junction (*45)	14		12 01	41
8·7 NEWTON ABBOT	16		14 07	
Estimated net time (mins)			13½	

TABLE 94

WATERLOO TO FAREHAM

Date	8 Jan. 1966
Train	9.20 a.m. ex. Waterloo
Locomotive no.	34001(R)
Vehicles	9
Tare load (tons)	297
Gross load (tons)	320
Driver/Fireman	Edwards/Hewson (Guildford)
Conditions	Fine
Recorder	DWW

Mls.		Sch.	M.	S.	Speed	Cut-off %	S'chest lb/sq. in	Boiler lb/sq. in
0·0	WATERLOO	0	0	00				
3·9	Clapham Junction (*40)	7	8	09	40	25	170	225
7·2	Wimbledon		12	22	58	20	180	230
13·3	*Hampton Court Junction*	17	18	28	64	20	150	220
21·7	West Byfleet		25	41	78	20	170	210
			sigs					
24·3	WOKING		28	20	30	20	0	240
24·8	*Woking Junction* (*20)	28	29	14	30	35	100	245
26·8	Worplesdon		32	42	59/62	20	220	230
30·3	GUILDFORD (*30)	36	36	53	25	20	100	245
33·6	Farncombe (*60)		41	37	56	20	200	245
34·5	Godalming		42	38	61	20	200	245
36·3	Milford		44	27	60/58	30/25	220	240
38·5	Witley		46	39	62/70/40	25	220	240
43·0	HASLEMERE	53	51	42	45	20	150	220
46·9	Liphook		55	18	72/60	15	125	220
51·5	Liss		59	31	76	20	145	240
54·9	PETERSFIELD	64	62	41	62/67	20	160	240
			sigs. sev. 15			35	200	240
58·0	*Milepost 58* (*45)		67	43	25	—	—	—
63·3	Rowlands Castle (*50)		73	48	50/64	25	0	245
66·5	HAVANT (*30)	76	77	36	35/56	30	180	220
			sigs					
69·5	*Farlington Junction* (*20)	79½	81	27	30	25	0	250
			sigs					
70·5	Cosham	82	83	20	40	25	220	240
73·2	Portchester		86	28	60/62	25	210	220
			sigs					
76·3	FAREHAM	90	91	00				

TABLE 95
SIDMOUTH JUNCTION TO SALISBURY

Date	2 Apr 1966
Train	4 p.m. ex. Sidmouth Junction
Locomotive no.	34006
Vehicles	9
Tare lead (tons)	300
Gross load (tons)	315
Driver	Moore (Salisbury)
Recorder	DWW

Mls.		Sch.	M. S.	Speed	S'chest lb/sq. in.	Boiler lb/sq. in.
0·0	SIDMOUTH JUNCTION	0	0 00			
1·3	*Milepost 158*			50	120	230
4·6	Honiton		7 44	41	160	230
5·8	*Milepost 153½*		9 29	41	160	240
6·8	*Milepost 152½*		10 53	52	0	230
11·5	*Seaton Junction* (*60)	14½	15 35	61/72	0	240
			sigs. sev.			
14·8	Axminster	17	19 27	30	160	220
19·9	*Chard Junction*		25 53	58/60	125	230
28·0	Crewkerne	29	34 02	80/85	40	220
34·5	*Sutton Bingham*		39 32	68	0	240
36·8	YEOVIL JUNCTION	36	41 27	70	120	220
41·3	Sherborne	39½	45 30	68/50	120	220
45·0	*Milborne Port*		49 15	58	120	220
47·4	*Templecombe*	45	51 33	70/82	100	220
52·0	*Milepost 107½*		55 17	58	80	220
54·3	Gillingham		57 20	74	120	220
58·3	*Semley*		61 12	58	120	220
63·3	Tisbury (*75)		65 40	70	60	240
67·6	*Dinton*		69 17	75	40	240
73·4	*Wilton South* (*40)	70	74 35	40	0	190
75·9	SALISBURY	75	78 52			

Estimated net time (mins)	75¼

TABLE 96
CANNON STREET TO TONBRIDGE

Train	6.21 p.m. (ex. Cannon Street)
Locomotive no.	34025(R)
Vehicles	11
Tare load (tons)	364
Gross load (tons)	395
Driver/Fireman (Bricklayers Arms)	Hobday/Dente
Recorder	A. F. Mercer

Mls.		Sch.	M. S.	Speed	Cut-off %	S'chest lb/sq. in.	Boiler lb/sq. in.
0·0	CANNON STREET	0	0 00		70	190	250
0·7	LONDON BRIDGE (*20)	2½	2 18	26	30	220	240
3·7	New Cross	7	6 11	57		0	230
4·4	St John's (*45)		6 59	53	30	195	225
6·0	Hither Green	10	8 53	50	28	155	210
7·8	Grove Park		11 10	44	40	185	205
9·1	Elmstead Woods		12 57	44	28	160	210
10·1	Chislehurst	17	14 15	45	32	100	205
11·1	*Petts Wood Junction*		15 32	43	38	185	205
12·7	Orpington	20	17 42	53	28	195	220
14·2	Chelsfield		19 24	49	28	190	215
15·4	Knockholt		20 58	46	32	185	210
19·4	Dunton Green		24 48	78		0	195
21·0	SEVENOAKS	31	26 25				230
0·0	SEVENOAKS	0	0 00		70	230	245
0·6	*Sevenoaks Tunnel North*		2 31	28	32	220	240
3·0	*Weald S.B.*		5 23	69	20	200	220
4·9	Hildenborough (*75)		6 56	79/82		0	
7·4	TONBRIDGE	10	9 46				

TABLE 97

WATERLOO TO SALISBURY

Date	15 Oct 1966
Train	9.10 a.m. ex. Waterloo
Locomotive no.	35023(R)
Vehicles	8
Tare load (tons)	260
Gross load (tons)	275
Driver/Fireman (Nine Elms)	Hooker/Dedman
Conditions	Fine
Recorder	DWW

Mls.	Sch.	M. S.	Speed	Cut-off %	S'chest lb/sq. in.	Boiler lb/sq. in.
0·0 WATERLOO	0	0 00				
1·3 Vauxhall		4 10	37/55	30	100	230
3·9 Clapham Junction (*40)	7	7 35	40	25	120	210
5·6 Earlsfield		9 48	54	20	110	200
7·2 Wimbledon		11 38	58	20	105	200
9·8 New Malden		14 06	66	20	105	200
12·0 Surbiton		16 05	70	20	105	200
13·3 *Hampton Court Junction*	17	17 09	76	20	105	200
17·1 Walton		20 05	79	20	120	220
19·1 Weybridge		21 38	82/85	20	120	220
21·7 West Byfleet		24 00	12	—	0	240
		p.w.s.				
24·3 WOKING		30 40	55	30	140	250
24·8 *Woking Junction*	28	31 06	—	—	—	—
28·0 Brookwood		34 08	70	25	140	230
31·0 *Milepost 31*		36 41	74	25	160	230
33·2 Farnborough		38 26	80	25	120	230
36·5 Fleet		40 52	84/86	25	130	230
39·8 Winchfield		43 13	85	25	130	225
		p.w.s.				
42·2 Hook		45 36	18/70	50	130	240
47·8 BASINGSTOKE (*65)		52 05	65	25	190	240
50·3 *Worting Junction*	50	54 18	71	25	200	240
52·4 *Oakley*		56 02	79	25	200	240
55·6 Overton		58 20	88	25	160	240
59·2 Whitchurch North		60 45	92	25	120	240
61·1 *Hurstbourne*		62 02	95/102	25	140	240
66·4 Andover		65 20	101	25	150	230
67·8 *Red Post Junction*		66 10	96	25	150	230
72·7 Grateley		69 32	83	25	170	220
75·6 *Allington*		71 38	88	25	120	230
78·2 Porton		73 24	95/98	20	110	200
82·6 *Tunnel Junction* (*50)	75½	76 32				
83·7 SALISBURY	78	79 41				

Estimated net time (mins)	71¼

25. Although never permitted over the Ilfracombe route the rebuilt light Pacifics were eventually permitted to operate to Plymouth. Here No. 34062 *17 Squadron* approaches Brentor with an up Eastleigh train in a spring evening of 1961.

26. *Westward Ho*, shorn of its nameplates (although retaining the support framework for the purpose) and smokebox numberplate 34036, heads the up Channel Island boat express past Holes Bay Junction on 29 May 1967.

27. Also bereft of nameplates No. 34023 pilots rebuilt No. 34108 towards Dorchester on an up railtour train on 18 June 1967.

28. Nos. 35013 and 35030, neither sporting nameplates, power an up special from Weymouth at Upwey on 11 June 1967.

29. Last of the *Merchant Navy* class, No. 35030—without nameplates— very fittingly hauls the last steam-operated ordinary passenger train (14.11 ex Weymouth) on the Southern Region past Micheldever towards Waterloo on 9 July 1967.

30

31

30. *Merchant Navy* type as mounted on rebuilt engine. 31. *West Country* type on the original design. Note the class scroll has been lowered to accommodate the shield which, in this case, was a later addition. 32. *Battle of Britain* class plate with plaque displaying Squadron badge, as mounted for the rebuilt engines.

32

Appendix 1

MERCHANT NAVY CLASS RECORDS

Dates of renumbering, cab modification and tender modification may vary by one month when compared with other published reports: so far as possible the month quoted is that in which the alteration took place (e.g. a locomotive reported as leaving works during week ending 1 June would have any alterations noted as occurring in May).

MERCHANT NAVY CLASS RECORDS

Number and Name	Date to Traffic	Naming Ceremony Date	Date Re-numbered	Date of Cab Modification	Date Acquired Modified Tender	Rebuilding Date	Withdrawal Date
21C1/35001 CHANNEL PACKET	June 1941	10 March 1941	September 1949	December 1950	June 1956	August 1959	November 1964
21C2/35002 UNION CASTLE	June 1941	4 July 1941	January 1950	January 1954	(1)	May 1958	February 1964
21C3/35003 ROYAL MAIL	September 1941	24 October 1941	May 1948	May 1950	(1)	August 1959	July 1967
21C4/35004 CUNARD WHITE STAR	October 1941	1 January 1942	April 1948	October 1950	(1)	June 1958	October 1965
21C5/s21C5/35005 CANADIAN PACIFIC	January 1942	27 March 1942	April 1948	February 1950	(1)	May 1959	October 1965
21C6/35006 PENINSULAR & ORIENTAL S.N. CO.	January 1942	4 June 1942	1948 (2)	March 1951	(1)	October 1959	August 1964
21C7/35007 ABERDEEN COMMONWEALTH	June 1942	30 July 1942	December 1948	March 1950	September 1956	May 1958	July 1967
21C8/35008 ORIENT LINE	June 1942	2 November 1942	July 1949	August 1947	(1)	May 1957	July 1967
21C9/35009 SHAW SAVILL	June 1942	30 July 1942	August 1949	February 1953	(1)	March 1957	September 1964
21C10/35010 BLUE STAR	July 1942	18 December 1942	December 1948	November 1949	(1)	January 1957	September 1966
21C11/35011 GENERAL STEAM NAVIGATION	December 1944	20 February 1945	November 1948	September 1950	August 1957	July 1959	February 1966

21C12/35012	UNITED STATES LINES	10 April 1945	March 1949	March 1949	July 1952	February 1957	April 1967
21C13/35013	BLUE FUNNEL CERTUM PETE FINEM (3)	17 April 1945 (3)	July 1948	December 1952	December 1952	May 1956	July 1967
21C14/35014	NEDERLAND LINE	27 November 1945	May 1949	May 1949	November 1952	July 1956	March 1967
21C15/35015	ROTTERDAM LLOYD	27 November 1945	June 1949	June 1949	July 1956	June 1958	February 1964
21C16/35016	ELDERS FYFFES	5 July 1945	October 1948	June 1949	(1)	April 1957	August 1965
21C17/35017	BELGIAN MARINE	22 October 1945	April 1948	April 1948	(1)	March 1957	July 1966
21C18/35018	BRITISH INDIA LINE	13 December 1945	May 1948	May 1948	July 1952 (4)	February 1957	August 1964
21C19/s21C19/35019	French Line C.G.T.	22 September 1945	April 1948 (2)	April 1948	(1)	May 1956	September 1965
21C20/35020	BIBBY LINE	18 October 1945	May 1948	May 1948	June 1953 (5)	May 1959	February 1965
35021	NEW ZEALAND LINE	24 November 1948	—	—	February 1952	June 1959	May 1965
35022	HOLLAND AMERICA LINE	24 January 1949	—	—	(1)	June 1956	June 1966
35023	HOLLAND-AFRIKA LINE	24 January 1949	—	—	(1)	February 1957	July 1967
35024	EAST ASIATIC COMPANY	5 May 1949	—	—	May 1958	April 1959	January 1965
35025	BROCKLEBANK LINE	20 September 1949	—	—	(1)	December 1956	September 1964

Number and Name	Date to Traffic	Naming Ceremony Date	Date Re-numbered	Date of Cab Modification	Date Acquired Modified Tender	Rebuilding Date	Withdrawal Date
35026 LAMPORT & HOLT LINE	December 1948	15 January 1951	—	—	(1)	January 1957	March 1967
35027 PORT LINE	December 1948	24 April 1950	—	—	(1)	May 1957	September 1966
35028 CLAN LINE	December 1948	15 January 1951	—	—	(1)	October 1959	July 1967 (6)
35029 ELLERMAN LINES	February 1949	1 March 1951	—	—	(1)	September 1959	September 1966
35030 ELDER-DEMPSTER LINES	April 1949	5 June 1950	—	—	(1)	April 1958	July 1967

Notes

(1) Acquired modified tender at time of rebuilding
(2) s prefix acquired March 1948
(3) Named BLUE FUNNEL LINE on 17 April 1945. Nameplates altered later
(4) Fitted with original type tender November 1952 and then acquired modified tender at time of rebuilding
(5) Fitted with unmodified tender for short period in May 1956
(6) Preserved in working order by Merchant Navy Preservation Society

In addition to No. 35028 (preserved) the following locomotives were still extant in September 1972, although all ten were in Messrs. Woodham's scrapyard at Barry: Nos. 35005/6/9/10/1/8/22/5/7/9. Since then No. 35005 has been purchased (in April 1973) by Steamtown Railway Museum, Carnforth, No.35009 reserved for possible purchase for restoration and No. 35029 earmarked for inclusion in York Railway Museum.

Appendix 2

WEST COUNTRY AND BATTLE OF BRITAIN CLASS RECORDS

Dates of renumbering, cab modification and tender modification may vary by one month when compared with other published reports: so far as possible the month quoted is that in which the the alteration took place (e.g. a locomotive reported as leaving works during week ending 1 June would have any alterations noted as occurring in May).

WEST COUNTRY and BATTLE OF BRITAIN CLASS RECORDS

Number and Name	Date to Traffic	Naming Ceremony Date	Date Re-numbered	Date of Cab Modification	Date Acquired Modified Tender	Rebuilding Date	Withdrawal Date
21C101/34001 EXETER†	June 1945	10 July 1945	March 1949	January 1955	(1)	November 1957	July 1967
21C102/34002 SALISBURY†	June 1945	9 July 1945	October 1948	June 1951	April 1962	—	April 1967
21C103/34003 PLYMOUTH†	June 1945	11 July 1945	April 1948	September 1953	(1)	September 1957	September 1964
21C104/34004 YEOVIL†	June 1945	2 November 1945	May 1948	May 1948	(1)	February 1958	July 1967
21C105/s21C105/34005 BARNSTAPLE†	July 1945	30 August 1946	May 1948 (2)	May 1948	(1)	June 1957	October 1966
21C106/s21C106/34006 BUDE†	August 1945	1 November 1946	May 1948 (3)	May 1948	July 1961	—	March 1967
21C107/s21C107/34007 WADEBRIDGE†	September 1945	31 October 1945	March 1949 (2)	May 1951	November 1962	—	October 1965
21C108/s21C108/34008 PADSTOW†	September 1945	31 October 1945	March 1949	June 1950	(1)	June 1960	June 1967
21C109/s21C109/34009 LYME REGIS†	September 1945	27 August 1946	April 1949 (2)	November 1950	(1)	January 1961	October 1966
21C110/s21C110/34010 SIDMOUTH†	September 1945	27 June 1946	January 1950 (3)	January 1955	(1)	January 1959	March 1965
21C111/34011 TAVISTOCK†	October 1945	13 June 1947	May 1948	September 1952	September 1952	—	November 1963
21C112/s21C112/34012 LAUNCESTON†	October 1945	1 November 1945	June 1948 (4)	January 1951	(1)	January 1958	December 1966

21C113/34013 OKEHAMPTON†	October 1945	12 June 1947	June 1948	May 1954	(1)	October 1957	July 1967
21C114/34014 BUDLEIGH SALTERTON†	November 1945	26 June 1946	October 1949	November 1954	(1)	March 1958	March 1965
21C115/34015 EXMOUTH†	November 1945	26 June 1946	April 1948	March 1957	November 1961	—	April 1967
21C116/s21C116/34016 BODMIN†	November 1945	28 August 1946	July 1948 (4)	May 1953	(1)	April 1958	June 1964 (5)
21C117/34017 ILFRACOMBE†	December 1945	29 August 1946	May 1948	December 1953	(1)	November 1957	October 1966
21C118/34018 AXMINSTER†	December 1945	25 June 1946	June 1948	October 1950	(1)	September 1958	July 1967
21C119/34019 BIDEFORD†	December 1945	29 August 1946	April 1948	December 1955	September 1961	—	March 1967
21C120/34020 SEATON†	December 1945	25 June 1946	April 1948	July 1950	May 1961	—	September 1964
21C121/s21C121/34021 DARTMOOR†	January 1946	—	July 1948	July 1953	(1)	December 1957	July 1967
21C122/34022 EXMOOR	January 1946	—	June 1948 (4)	April 1953	(1)	December 1957	April 1965
21C123/34023 BLACKMORE VALE (6)	February 1946	—	April 1948	October 1954	February 1962	—	July 1967 (7)
21C124/34024 TAMAR VALLEY	February 1946	—	June 1948	February 1955	(1)	February 1961	July 1967
21C125/34025 WHIMPLE (8)	March 1946	—	September 1948	September 1954	(1)	October 1957	July 1967
21C126/34026 YES TOR	April 1946	—	May 1949	May 1949	(1)	February 1958	September 1966
21C127/34027 TAW VALLEY	April 1946	—	July 1948	June 1953	(1)	September 1957	August 1964

Number and Name	Date to Traffic	Naming Ceremony Date	Date Re-numbered	Date of Cab Modification	Date Acquired Modified Tender	Rebuilding Date	Withdrawal Date
21C128/34028 EDDYSTONE	May 1946	—	December 1948	February 1954	(1)	August 1958	May 1964
21C129/s21C129/34029 LUNDY	May 1946	—	February 1949 (3)	January 1955	(1)	December 1958	September 1964
21C130/34030 WATERSMEET	May 1946	—	November 1948	January 1952	September 1961	—	September 1964
21C131/s21C131/34031 TORRINGTON†	June 1946	24 November 1949	January 1949 (2)	May 1949	(1)	November 1958	February 1965
21C132/34032 CAMELFORD	June 1946	—	April 1948	January 1951	March 1959	October 1960	October 1966
21C133/34033 CHARD	June 1946	—	December 1948	June 1949	November 1958	—	December 1965
21C134/34034 HONITON†	July 1946	—	July 1948	March 1949	(1)	August 1960	July 1967
21C135/34035 SHAFTESBURY	July 1946	—	January 1949	February 1955	October 1959	—	June 1963
21C136/s21C136/34036 WESTWARD HO	July 1946	—	May 1948 (2)	February 1952	(1)	August 1960	July 1967
21C137/34037 CLOVELLY	August 1946	—	March 1949	March 1949	(1)	March 1958	July 1967
21C138/34038 LYNTON	September 1946	—	February 1949	April 1955	July 1961	—	June 1966
21C139/34039 BOSCASTLE	September 1946	—	June 1948	November 1952	(1)	January 1959	May 1965
21C140/34040 CREWKERNE†	September 1946	20 October 1948	October 1948	March 1954	(1)	October 1960	July 1967

21C141/34041 WILTON	October 1946	—	January 1949	February 1952	June 1959	—	January 1966
21C142/s21C142/34042 DORCHESTER†	October 1946	29 September 1948	May 1948 (3)	April 1949	(1)	January 1959	October 1965
21C143/34043 COMBE MARTIN	October 1946	—	September 1948	June 1952	June 1952	—	June 1963
21C144/34044 WOOLACOMBE	October 1946	—	December 1948	March 1954	(1)	May 1960	May 1967
21C145/34045 OTTERY ST. MARY	October 1946	—	January 1949	October 1951	(1)	October 1958	June 1964
21C146/s21C146/34046 BRAUNTON	November 1946	—	January 1949 (3)	January 1954	(1)	February 1959	October 1965
21C147/34047 CALLINGTON	November 1946	—	January 1949	February 1954	(1)	November 1958	June 1967
21C148/s21C148/34048 CREDITON†	November 1946	4 March 1948	August 1948 (2)	May 1949	(1)	March 1959	March 1966
21C149/s21C149/34049 ANTI-AIRCRAFT COMMAND†	December 1946	28 April 1948	April 1949 (4)	March 1948	November 1959	—	December 1963
21C150/s21C150/34050 ROYAL OBSERVER CORPS†	December 1946	—(9)	January 1949 (2)	February 1948	(1)	August 1958	August 1965
21C151/34051 WINSTON CHURCHILL†	December 1946	11 September 1947	November 1948	August 1947	January 1960	—	September 1965 (10)
21C152/34052 LORD DOWDING†	December 1946	11 September 1947	February 1949	August 1947	(1)	September 1958	July 1967
21C153/34053 SIR KEITH PARK†	January 1947	19 September 1947	June 1949	August 1947	(1)	November 1958	October 1965
21C154/34054 LORD BEAVERBROOK†	January 1947	16 September 1947	March 1949	August 1947	February 1963	—	September 1964 (11)
21C155/34055 FIGHTER PILOT†	February 1947	19 September 1947	July 1949	August 1947	September 1961	—	June 1963

Number and Name	Date to Traffic	Naming Ceremony Date	Date Re-numbered	Date of Cab Modification	Date Acquired Modified Tender	Rebuilding Date	Withdrawal Date
21C156/34056 CROYDON†	February 1947	—	May 1948	November 1947	(1)	December 1960	May 1967
21C157/s21C157/34057 BIGGIN HILL†	March 1947	24 February 1948	June 1949 (2)	November 1947	November 1961	—	May 1967
21C158/s21C158/34058 SIR FREDERICK PILE†	April 1947	28 April 1948	December 1948 (3)	January 1948	(1)	November 1960	October 1964
21C159/s21C159/34059 SIR ARCHIBALD SINCLAIR†	April 1947	24 February 1948	March 1949 (2)	December 1947	(1)	March 1960	May 1966
21C160/34060 25 SQUADRON†	April 1947	—	September 1948	September 1948	June 1959	November 1960	July 1967
21C161/34061 73 SQUADRON†	April 1947	—	January 1949	January 1949	November 1962	—	August 1964
21C162/34062 17 SQUADRON†	May 1947	—	January 1949	January 1949	(1)	March 1959	July 1964
21C163/34063 229 SQUADRON†	May 1947	—	January 1949	January 1949	July 1958	—	August 1965
21C164/34064 FIGHTER COMMAND†	July 1947	11 September 1947	June 1948	Altered in works before entering traffic	April 1962	—	May 1966
21C165/34065 HURRICANE†	July 1947	16 September 1947	June 1948	—	November 1952	—	April 1964
21C166/34066 SPITFIRE†	September 1947	16 September 1947	February 1949	—	February 1958	—	September 1966
21C167/s21C167/34067 TANGMERE† (12)	September 1947	19 September 1947	July 1949 (4)	—	April 1958	—	November 1963
21C168/34068 KENLEY†	October 1947	—	October 1948	—	December 1958	—	December 1963

21C169/34069	HAWKINGE†	October 1947	28 June 1948	June 1948	—	—	—	November 1963
21C170/s21C170/34070	MANSTON†	November 1947	9 March 1948	March 1949 (4)	—	February 1963 (1)	—	August 1964
34071	601 SQUADRON† (13)	April 1948	16 September 1948	—	—	—	May 1960	April 1967
34072	257 SQUADRON†	April 1948	—	—	—	August 1958	—	October 1964
34073	249 SQUADRON†	May 1948	—	—	—	—	—	June 1964
34074	46 SQUADRON†	May 1948	—	—	—	April 1964 (14)	—	June 1963
34075	264 SQUADRON†	June 1948	—	—	—	August 1959 (1)	—	April 1964
34076	41 SQUADRON†	June 1948	—	—	—	—	July 1960	January 1966
34077	603 SQUADRON†	July 1948	—	—	—	—	—	March 1967
34078	222 SQUADRON†	July 1948	—	—	—	May 1959	—	September 1964
34079	141 SQUADRON†	July 1948	—	—	—	June 1959 (15)	—	February 1966
34080	74 SQUADRON†	August 1948	—	—	—	July 1959 (1)	—	September 1964
34081	92 SQUADRON†	September 1948	—	—	—	—	April 1960	August 1964
34082	615 SQUADRON†	September 1948	8 October 1948	—	—	November 1958	—	April 1966
34083	605 SQUADRON†	October 1948	—	—	—	—	—	July 1964

Number and Name	Date to Traffic	Naming Ceremony Date	Date Re-numbered	Date of Cab Modification	Date Acquired Modified Tender	Rebuilding Date	Withdrawal Date
34084 253 SQUADRON†	November 1948	—	—	—	May 1960	—	October 1965
34085 501 SQUADRON†	November 1948	—	—	—	(1)	June 1960	September 1965
34086 219 SQUADRON†	December 1948	—	—	—	January 1960	—	June 1966
34087 145 SQUADRON†	December 1948	—	—	—	(1)	December 1960	July 1967
34088 213 SQUADRON†	December 1948	—	—	—	(1)	April 1960	March 1967
34089 602 SQUADRON†	December 1948	—	—	—	(1)	November 1960	July 1967
34090 SIR EUSTACE MISSENDEN SOUTHERN RAILWAY†	February 1949	15 February 1949	—	—	(1)	August 1960	July 1967
34091 WEYMOUTH†	September 1949	29 December 1949	—	—	August 1961	—	September 1964
34092 CITY OF WELLS†(16)	September 1949	25 November 1949	—	—	September 1962	—	November 1964 (5)
34093 SAUNTON	October 1949	—	—	—	(1)	May 1960	July 1967
34094 MORTEHOE	October 1949	—	—	—	January 1962	—	August 1964
34095 BRENTOR	October 1949	—	—	—	(1)	January 1961	July 1967
34096 TREVONE	November 1949	—	—	—	(1)	April 1961	September 1964

APPENDIX 2

Number / Name	Built					Withdrawn
34097 HOLSWORTHY	November 1949	—	—	(1)	February 1961	April 1966
34098 TEMPLECOMBE	December 1949	—	—	December 1959	February 1961	June 1967
34099 LYNMOUTH	December 1949	—	—	October 1961	—	November 1964
34100 APPLEDORE	December 1949	—	—	November 1958	September 1960	July 1967
34101 HARTLAND	February 1950	—	—	(1)	September 1960	July 1966
34102 LAPFORD	March 1950	—	—	June 1961	—	July 1967
34103 CALSTOCK	February 1950	—	—	October 1958	—	September 1965
34104 BERE ALSTON	April 1950	—	—	(1)	May 1961	June 1967
34105 SWANAGE	February 1950	—	—	August 1958	—	October 1964 (16)
34106 LYDFORD	March 1950	—	—	June 1961	—	September 1964
34107 BLANDFORD FORUM†(17)	April 1950	—	—	April 1961	—	September 1964
34108 WINCANTON	April 1950	—	—	May 1959	April 1961	June 1967
34109 SIR TRAFFORD LEIGH MALLORY†	May 1950	—	—	(1)	March 1961	September 1964
34110 66 SQUADRON	January 1951	—	—	July 1958	—	November 1963

Notes overleaf

Notes

(1) Acquired modified tender at time of rebuilding
(2) s prefix acquired February 1948
(3) s prefix acquired January 1948
(4) s prefix acquired March 1948
(5) Acquired for restoration
(6) Name altered from BLACKMOOR VALE in 1950
(7) Acquired by Bulleid Pacific Preservation Society
(8) Named ROUGH TOR for a few days in 1948
(9) Long service medal unveiled 2 July 1961
(10) Awaiting restoration
(11) Worked in traffic after this date
(12) Acquired badge and motto shield additionally in 1955
(13) Carried name 615 SQUADRON from April to August 1948
(14) Damaged tender ex. 34080 attached upon withdrawal
(15) Unmodified tender attached April 1964
(16) Named WELLS on 25 November 1949. Nameplates altered in March 1950
(17) Name altered from BLANDFORD in October 1952

† Fitted with shield or plaque.

In addition to Nos. 34016/23/51/92 saved for preservation, the following sixteen engines were still extant in September 1972 in Messrs. Woodham's scrapyard at Barry: Nos. 34007/10/27/8/39/46/53/8/9/67/70/2/3/81/101/5. Since then No. 34039 has been purchased (in January 1973) by the Main Line Steam Trust and Nos. 34081/101/5 reserved for possible purchase by other preservation societies.

Appendix 3

INDEX TO PERFORMANCE RECORDS OF BULLEID PACIFICS APPEARING IN *THE RAILWAY MAGAZINE*

(M) = *Merchant Navy* Class
(W) = *West Country/Battle of Britain* Class

(MR) = Rebuilt *Merchant Navy* Class
(WR) = Rebuilt *West Country/Battle of Britain* Class

Route (including parts thereof)	*Month(s) of appearance*
Waterloo–Salisbury	November 1941(M); November/December 1943(M); March/April 1944(M); November/December 1948(M); April 1950(W); August 1951(W); February 1953(M); May 1953(M); October 1953(W); October 1954(M); May 1956(M)(W); December 1956(MR); June 1958(MR); December 1958(MR); February 1960(M) (MR) August 1960(MR); March 1962(MR); November 1962(MR); June 1963(MR); August 1964(MR)(W); November 1964(MR); April 1968(MR)
Salisbury–Exeter Central	November 1941(M); November/December 1942(M); November/December 1943(M); September/October 1944(M); March/April 1945(M); March/April 1946(M); September/October 1946(M); January/February 1947(M); March/April 1948(M); March/April 1949(M); May 1951(M); August 1951(M); February 1952(M)(W); February 1953(M); May 1953(M); October 1954(W); October 1956(M) (W); December 1956(MR); December 1958(MR); February 1960(M) (MR); August 1960(MR); March 1962(MR); November 1962(MR)(WR); June 1963(MR); August 1964(MR) (W); November 1964(MR)

Route (including parts thereof)	Month(s) of appearance
Exeter (St Davids)– Tavistock	March/April 1947(W); November/December 1948(W); December 1955(W)
Braunton– Ilfracombe	November/December 1945(W)
Waterloo– Southampton Central	January/February 1947(M); March/April 1948(M); April 1950(M); December 1955(M) (W); May 1956(M); October 1957(M) (MR) (W); June 1958(MR); June 1959 (M) (MR) (W); February 1960(MR) (WR); August 1960(MR); June 1963(W); June 1965(MR); February 1966(MR); April 1968(MR) (W) (WR); June 1968(MR)
Southampton Central– Bournemouth Central	January/February 1947(M); March/April 1948(M); December 1955(M) (W); October 1957(M) (MR) (W); June 1958(MR); June 1963(W); February 1966(WR)
Bournemouth Central– Weymouth	August 1955(W)
Havant– Guildford	August 1964(W) (WR)
Redhill– Brighton	June 1963(WR); August 1964(W) (WR)
Victoria– Dover Marine	January/February 1947(W); October 1959(MR); February 1966(M)
Waterloo (Eastern)– Folkestone Central	August 1950(W); November 1951(W); October 1953(W); October 1955(W); April 1961(WR)
Bromley South– Chatham	November 1951(M) (W); April 1955(W); June 1955(W)
Carnforth– Penrith	October 1964(MR)
Carlisle– Hellifield	August 1962(M); October 1964(MR)
Perth General– Inverness	January/February 1949(W)

Bibliography

Allen, Cecil J, *British Pacific Locomotives* (Ian Allan, 1962).
Allen, Cecil J, *The Locomotive Exchanges 1870–1948*, 2nd edn (Ian Allan, 1950).
Allen, Cecil J. and Townroe, S.C, *The Bulleid Pacifics of the Southern Region* (Ian Allan, 1951).
British Transport Commission. *Locomotive Performance and Efficiency Test Bulletins: No.10 MERCHANT NAVY Class.* 1955. *No. 20 Modified MERCHANT NAVY Class.* 1960.
Day-Lewis, Sean, *Bulleid Last Giant of Steam* (George Allen & Unwin, 1964).
Evans, Martin, *Pacific Steam. The British Pacific Locomotive* (Percival Marshall, 1961).
Railway Executive. *Report of The Locomotive Testing Committee on The Locomotive Interchange Trials 1948.* British Railways, 1949.

PERIODICALS
British Railways Southern Region Magazine
Modern Railways
Modern Transport
Railway Gazette
Railway Magazine
Railway Observer
Railway Pictorial
Railway World
Railways
Southern Railway Magazine
Trains Illustrated

INDEX